International's Series in

ECONOMICS

The Economic and
Financial System

The Economic and Financial System

RICHARD A. WARD

University of Southern California

INTERNATIONAL TEXTBOOK COMPANY
Scranton, Pennsylvania

Preface

The economic system is one interdependent whole. To the initiated this complex mechanism offers something of a seductive challenge. To the student and his teacher it asks a frustrating question: where can we start when it cannot all be mastered at once? The attempt at divisibility has led to a certain compartmentalization of subject matter, within courses and between courses, that sometimes obscures the system as a whole.

The approach in this macroeconomic survey is first to view the system as a whole with a limited number of parts, and then gradually to expand the complications. Essential to this approach is the parallel development of the financial and the real sectors of the economy. To expedite integration a simplified flow of funds concept provides the basic foundation. In this way each expansion of the system does not appear as a digression. Each type of financial asset falls in place as an intermediary claim or a direct claim matching a deficit on current account by the debtor. The government and foreign sectors assume their places as different types of product demand and different sources of net claim creation or destruction. Stocks of assets and flows of income are linked, and the effects of each are considered in the great economic equations, such as the consumption function and the liquidity-preference theory.

The development of the financial and real system as a whole precludes digressions in discussion of any one sector of the economy. If for example, we considered all the problems of monetary policy in the presentation of the financial sector, the student might lose his grip on the system as a whole. It is this consideration that leads to the two-part presentation, "analytical" and "applied" economics. The difficulties of policy implementation appear only after the system as a whole is presented.

The descriptive section presents more concretely the working of the analytical methodology. For example, whereas the analytical section develops the concept of claim creation and its origin in deficit finance, the descriptive part explains the practice of flow of funds accounting. Again, the analytical section explains the income-output identity, while the descriptive chapter develops the final expenditure, factor cost, and value-added methods of computing national product.

Each chapter is a relatively self-contained unit when read by someone who has a grasp of the system as a whole. One reason for this style is that it facilitates review after the student has read the entire book; he does not have to review all chapters to review a particular subject. Another reason is that as the book progresses there is a minimum necessity to refer to preceding chapters. This calls for some repetition of material between chapters, but the gains in comprehensibility outweigh this minor degree of duplication. Finally, self-contained chapters enable the instructor to vary the sequence of assignments, depending on the backgrounds of the students and his format for the course. The theoretical and applied sections can be integrated by assigning chapters in the following sequence: 1-2, 13-14, 3-6, 16, 7-10, 15, 17, 18, 11, 19, 20, 12.

The book throughout is written for the student who is interested in the world-wide application of economics rather than in the economics of one country. The descriptive chapters, for example, explain the United Nations system of national accounts and the International Monetary Fund balance-of-payments accounting rather than the procedures of any one country. The money and banking discussion works with the general attributes of monetary systems around the world. Fiscal problems in a variety of countries are examined. The orientation is largely to market-type economies, though some aspects of the Communist alternative are presented in considering the nature of economic systems.

The book is intended primarily as a text for a second course in undergraduate macroeconomics. It pays somewhat more attention to money and banking and to public finance than do similar books, and is concerned more with welfare criteria. I have devoted less space to analytical tools, such as the multiplier and accelerator, on the assumption that these are well covered in the principles course—and have somewhat less relevance in the world today.

I am grateful to my colleague, Henry Schloss, for many helpful suggestions; to Professor Melville Eggers, Syracuse University, for comments on an earlier draft; and to staff members of International Textbook Company, especially David Gabriel, for their support.

RICHARD WARD

West Hollywood, California
September, 1969

Contents

PART I
ANALYTICAL ECONOMICS

1   Fundamental Economic Systems.   3
2   Money.   14
3   Aggregate Demand.   24
4   Consumption and Saving.   35
5   Investment and Rates of Return   53
6   The Theory of Interest   65
7   Asset Differentiation   85
8   Prices   99
9   Dynamic Equilibrium   112
10 Fiscal Economics.   126
11 International Economic Relations.   143
12 Welfare Economics.   157

PART II
DESCRIPTIVE ECONOMICS

13 Social Accounting: National Output   177
14 Social Accounting: Financial Flows.   189
15 The Economy and the State.   202
16 Government Financial Policy   215
17 Fiscal Policy   238
18 The Social Distribution of Income.   254
19 International Monetary Policy   271
20 Underdeveloped Economies.   285
    Index   299

PART I

ANALYTICAL ECONOMICS

1

Fundamental Economic Systems

Contemporary societies are essentially economic societies. The widely used description, "socioeconomic class," is really one system; a man's financial standing is the same as his social standing. No less than freedom itself is dependent upon economic opportunity lest obedience to a job replace obedience to the state.

The early twentieth-century American and economist and sociologist Thorstein Veblen wrote:

> The accountancy to which all phenomena of modern economic life are amenable is an accountancy in terms of price; and by the current convention there is no other recognized scheme of accountancy, no other rating, either in law or in fact, to which the facts of modern life are held amenable. Indeed, so great and pervading a force has this habit (institution) of pecuniary accountancy become that it extends, often as a matter of course, to many facts which properly have no pecuniary bearing and no pecuniary magnitude, as, *e.g.*, works of art, science, scholarship, and religion.[1]

As a social study, economics attempts to stand back from the hum of machinery and the monotony of toil and ask, How did it all get this way? Where is it all going? It is behavioristic in nature, making assumptions about man's conduct, from which are formed theories about the performance of his economic creations.

To the practical man such theories sometimes seem dry, unrealistic, unrewarding, unimportant. But they cannot be, for they are concerned about the successes and failures of society itself. The great political philosophies that dominate the world are in large part contrasting economic systems. It is over economics that revolutions flourish, wars are waged, crimes are committed, and science is nour-

[1] *The Place of Science in Modern Civilization* (New York: B. W. Huebsch, 1919), p. 245. Copyright 1919 by B. W. Huebsch; copyright renewed 1947 by Ann B. Sims and Becky Meyers.

ished. The industrial society is as dominant under communism as under capitalism. The ancient reindeer tribes of Northern Russia were no less organized for economic purposes than is the corporate society.

Why this overpowering influence of economic pursuit? It seems to be a combination of man's acquisitive instinct and the niggardliness of nature. An economic system consists of the means which a society employs to determine the amount of goods and services which it produces and the means of distribution of this output. The need for such a system derives from the scarcity of resources. When an economy reaches a relatively abundant level of output, the fact of scarcity becomes less evident, but it is nevertheless present. In one way or another the desire of man for goods relative to his ability and desire to produce them has necessitated some type of economic system. We can assume that this necessity has been present since man evolved from a hunting to a producing animal.

Anthropological studies indicate that primitive tribal societies organized distribution along collectivist lines. The produce of the tribe belonged to the tribe as a whole, rather than to individual producers. The distribution of production was on some basis other than the contribution of the individuals making it. There were, for example, the Inca of Peru, whose rulers exacted large tribute from their subjects and in turn regulated the distribution of the goods so obtained. With collective tribal distribution there is no need for a market, i.e., a system in which producers of goods exchange with each other to increase the amount and variety of goods available to each. The collective system undoubtedly allows for some subjective notion of the worth of individual goods, but there is no valuation process as is necessary in a market economy.

With the institution of private property—as opposed to collective distribution—the goods available to each individual become more closely associated to the amount which he produces. The capacity to produce, rather than the need for consumption, becomes the determining factor in the economy's distribution of its product.

Contemporary systems have elements of both of these economic extremes, and it is probable that this has always been so. According to the late Melville Herskovitz, an anthropologist, in all social groups studied there have been elements of both individualism and subordination of the individual to the group.[2] Nevertheless, there is some value in classifying economic systems on the basis of predominant characteristics. Those economies which stress the collectivist nature

[2] Melville Herskovitz, *Economic Anthropology* (New York: Knopf, 1952).

of output come under the broad heading of socialism. In these systems the state assumes the principal role in the determination of output, and appropriates for distribution under its own terms a relatively large share of that output. When the major determination of production and distribution is largely with private individuals and their organizations, the system is "capitalistic" in nature.[3]

The major interest in the present book is in capitalism. This does not mean that socialist systems are unimportant or that the two systems do not have much in common. The major problems facing the two systems differ in relative importance, however, and on these practical grounds it is possible to limit ourselves to capitalism without implying it is the only system worthy of attention.

THE FACTORS OF PRODUCTION

Behind the fundamental fact of scarcity of goods is scarcity of the means of producing goods. Man starts with two fundamental means for creating things that satisfy his needs and desires. These are man himself and his capability of laboring with the raw elements of the earth. These are two of the fundamental factors of production—labor and land. Man cannot increase the amount of available land, although he can devise ways of using it more effectively. Society as a whole cannot increase the available labor supply except by increasing the population. But each additional worker is also an additional user of goods, and thus beyond a certain optimum population, it is no longer possible to increase product per capita by increasing population. (This is in fact one definition of "optimum" population from an economic point of view.)

Under these pressures man has devised ways to make labor more productive, of increasing his work efficiency by producing goods which in turn make his work more productive. These goods fall under the broad heading of *capital*. In this context capital can be defined as man-made goods whose sole use is in the production of other goods which will satisfy his needs and wants. A capital good is not an item which man will use directly. Its purpose is to increase the output of those things which will satisfy desires. Through capital goods, production becomes "roundabout." This presents man with something of a dilemma—one that is more apparent under collectivist decision-making but no less real under private systems. For the maximum satisfaction of present desires, a society would use up all of its

---

[3] Allen G. Gruchy employs these definitions in *Comparative Economic Systems* (Boston: Houghton Mifflin, 1966).

productive facility for goods which it can immediately use directly, called *consumption.* Alternatively, in order to increase future satisfaction it can produce capital goods, but to the extent that it is producing capital goods it must forgo consumption goods. Which then does the society wish to maximize—future or present consumption? In a purely private economy the decisions of many individuals together will arrive at some distribution between capital goods and consumption goods. In a collectivist economy this is one of the more important choices which the state must make.

The existence of roundabout methods of production gives us a third factor of production—capital. Unlike the other two, it is a man-made factor. In any one time period society can take as a given factor its past accumulation of capital, but over time society can increase the amount of capital relative to the population.

VARIABLE PROPORTIONS

Any production of capital is necessarily at the expense of goods which the society can consume immediately and directly. This cost, in terms of forgone consumption, is a limiting factor in the accumulation of capital. A second limitation on society's willingness to accumulate capital lies in the decreasing usefulness of capital as its amount increases. The reason for this decreasing usefulness is that production must use land and labor in conjunction with capital. As capital accumulates, land and labor do not increase proportionately, and the productive ability of capital tends to diminish.

Let us illustrate with an individual example and assume that the same tendencies would prevail in the aggregate economy. A man can haul, say, twenty stones a distance of one mile in one hour by pulling them in a cart. The man-hour output (labor productivity) is 20 stone-miles; the cart output (capital productivity) is also 20 stone-miles. Now let us equip the man with a second cart which he is able to attach to the first. Because of limitations in his physical ability he cannot fill both carts, and he pulls the carts more slowly. The two carts allow him to haul 30 stone-miles per hour. His productivity has increased but it has not doubled. The productivity of a cart is now 15 stone-miles (30 stone-miles divided by 2 carts). The productivity of capital, the variable factor, has diminished because additional labor did not accompany the additional cart.

The illustration is an application of the law of variable proportions, which holds that if one factor of production is increased, while the other factors remain constant, returns to the variable factor will diminish. This tendency is also known as the *principle of diminishing returns.*

This "law" is not inviolable, in that under some circumstances it might be possible to increase output proportionately with an increase in one factor. The princeple merely means that if one factor continues to increase without increases in the other, diminishing returns will eventually tend to set in.

OUTPUT AND INCOME

In analyzing an economy we need a procedure for organizing its performance and assessing its size. We have begun such a procedure in classifying goods into two categories—consumption and capital. Consumption goods are those which society uses immediately after their production. Capital goods are intermediate goods used to produce other goods.[4] Even the most simplified economy—a one-man producing and consuming unit—is susceptible to this treatment. A man growing a crop can dig with his hands and eat all of the proceeds, of his labor. Alternatively he can devote a portion of his time to making a hoe. He is then producing consumption goods (food) and capital goods (hoe). If he performs satisfying work which results in no tangible product, such as cutting hair, we still consider he is producing an economic good.

Let us now expand the economy to a number of producer-consumers, each of whom exchanges some of his output with other producers to maximize his consumption and production. The society is still turning out two types of goods, but the individual as a consumer is no longer the same as the individual as a producer. He makes one kind of good but consumes another. In this case we can employ separate terminology for the total goods produced and the total goods available to the society. Goods produced we call output. Goods received in exchange, as well as goods one produces for himself, we call income. In both instances we are looking at the same goods, and thus the total of output and income must be equal. In a more complex economy the distinction between output and income will be more useful, but even in this simplified economy each participant does look separately upon the goods which he produces and the goods available for his use, even though for society as a whole the two are the same.

The total output, or income, of this economy is the total of all goods produced. If we want to be precise, however, we must recognize that some capital goods passed out of existence during the time

[4] Consumption goods which are held over, rather than used, are available to satisfy future wants, and thus have characteristics of both consumption and capital goods. Such refinements are not important at this juncture, but later we shall classify these carried-over stocks as capital goods, regardless of their nature.

period observed. By this we mean that they wore out or became unusable. For the true output of goods during this period we would need to subtract the loss of goods through their use in the production process. We call this loss "depreciation." If an economy produces 100 plows, for instance, but if the equivalent of 10 became unusable during the period, then its net output of plows is 90. If we treat the total of output in this way, then our measure is net product (gross product less depreciation). This treatment does not destroy the equality between income and product, since the owner of capital subtracts its depreciation in looking at the total goods becoming available to him during the period. Gross product and gross income are equal, and net product and net income are equal.

THE VALUATION PROBLEM

We have thought of the output of a society as the total of individual goods and services produced. Though this is conceptually sound, we get an unmanageable total when considering a society with many products. To solve this problem we need some system of valuation so that we can assign the importance to society of each product with some common measuring unit. No society today has conceived a perfectly satisfactory solution to this problem, since each good has a different subjective value to each man. Capitalistic societies today use as an approximation the value of the good on the market place, but even then there is difficulty in finding a common unit of expression.

In our simplified economy, where all goods are exchanged on the basis of barter (individual exchange of one good for another) the only way we can affix a common unit of value is to single out one good as a standard. We can express all goods in terms of this unit of value even if the goods do not directly exchange with the unit of value. As long as the unit of value does exchange somewhere in the market place, we can relate any good to the unit of value until we follow a series of exchanges and reach the unit of value. This procedure will be more meaningful, however, if the unit of value good is one which itself is an important component of market transactions.

Suppose that we choose a healthy cow as the standard—a standard which in fact found widespread acceptance at many times and in many places around the world. If plows exchange for rice and rice for cows, we can derive the cow value of plows even though cows and plows do not actually exchange. Now we can express the whole of output and income in terms of cows. If we say that the society had a thousand-cow output, we mean that the total of output in a given time period had a market exchange equivalent of 1,000 cows. This example shows, by the way, that we are not interested in "things exchanging on the market place" as our measure of economic activity. Many things exchange on the market place which society produced in prior periods or, as in the case of land, never produced at all.

Our cow standard of value accepts the market place as the final arbiter of the value to society of the goods produced. The individuals who actually produced and consumed goods may have gotten more or less than a cow's satisfaction, which is called the "utility" of the goods.

Another problem with our cow standard is that it is useful only as cow value has some meaning to the observer. If we are viewing this society some years after the event, it becomes increasingly difficult to visualize the significance of cow value. Also, if we want to compare output over time, we do not know whether total cow values have changed because of a change in actual output or because of change in the ratio at which cows exchange for goods on the market place. Contemporary economic observers have methods for dealing with this problem, though they do not entirely solve it, and our exercise is far from academic.

SAVING

So far we have presumed that each participant in the economy acquires during a period goods whose cow values are exactly equal to the value of goods he produces. Each person's acquisition of consumer and capital goods may bear no relation to the type of goods he produces, but for society as a whole, production and acquisition of these goods is identical. The individual who acquires capital goods has used a part of the total proceeds of his income for this purpose, and we say that he has engaged in an act of *investment*. Investment for the society as a whole is its increase in capital goods over the time in question. If we allow for losses through depreciation, then the measure is net investment.

The individual who makes the investment is acting to increase the amount of total goods available to him over his lifetime. The acquisition of the capital good increases his productivity and thereby the amount of product available to him in future time periods.

Another way to describe the behavior of the person who has accumulated capital is to say that he has engaged in an act of *saving*. Here we are emphasizing the fact that he has produced more goods than he has consumed. The amount of his saving is measured by the excess of his production over his consumption. One definition emphasizes the motivation for capital accumulation—to increases output. The other definition emphasized the motive for saving—to defer consumption. Quantitatively the two are the same, since the economy as a whole can save only by accumulating capital. As we introduce more complexities into the economy, we shall see that those who do the investing may not be the same persons as those who do the saving. The distinction between the two will then become somewhat more meaningful, but it will still be true that the total of saving and the total of investing will remain equal. This is because the only source of saving is production in excess of consumption, and the only production in excess of consumption is necessarily capital goods.

DEFERRED CLAIMS

The next complexity we introduce in the economic system is *deferred claims*, meaning an obligation to make payment in a specified form at some date in the future. A producer who wishes eventually to separate his production from his acquisition of goods can offer his goods for payment in the form of a promise to complete the exchange at a later date. He is thereby extending credit. According to Herskovitz, "The institution of credit is widely spread in nonliterate societies, accompanies all types of exchange, and is found in cultures of all degrees of economic complexity."[5]

The manner of designating the claim is a part of the barter process. The lender is charging interest if he requires that upon repayment he receives more in exchange than he would if the parties completed the exchange immediately. In a later chapter we consider ways of computing interest, but its fundamental nature is the exchange of higher value in the future for lower value in the present.

The parties to the credit arrangement cannot calculate with exactitude the true terms of the contract because, by its very nature, credit concerns the uncertain future. Suppose for example that one of two parties to a barter asserts that he will offer his goods now, while the other party promises to complete the transaction at a later date. It is possible that at the later date conditions are such that the two goods exchange in the market at a different ratio, and the debtor fulfills his obligation with a good that is worth relatively less to society than when he entered the agreement. In this case the debtor has gained from the transaction, but the results could just as well have been the reverse.

[5] Herskovitz, *op. cit.*, pp. 225-226.

If some good becomes a widely used standard of valuation, it is likely that it also will be the standard for credit arrangements. This still does not avoid the uncertainty in credit arrangements, because it is possible that the standard of value itself can become more or less valuable to the community relative to all other goods. Repayment in the standard of value itself, or its present equivalent in some other good, may then be more or less burdensome than at the time when the parties made the loan agreement. Contemporary economies have complex arrangements for loan contracts, but they still do not avoid the valuation problem endemic in contracts involving time.

The existence of credit arrangements allows some producing units in the economy to produce in excess of their acquisition of goods. They take the differential in the form of claims on future output. Other members of the economy may acquire goods in excess of their current production. In total the economy can acquire no more goods than it produces; income equals output. Indivudual economic units are not bound by this restriction. Those who produce more than they acquire take a portion of their income in the form of claims on others, and we call them the *surplus units*. Those who acquire obligations are the *deficit units*.

It is now apparent that there are two ways by which members of the economy may save—or produce in excess of their consumption: they may acquire capital goods, or they may acquire claims on others as the means by which they take their surplus over consumption. There are likewise two ways of investing (accumulating capital): by producing in excess of consumption, or by borrowing. It is through this device that saving may take place among some participants in the economy while the investing takes place among others. This spatial separation of saving and investing does not give rise to temporal separation. The total of saving and investment over any given period of time is always constant.

In a credit using economy the creation of claims and the creation of product are closely associated. Production gives rise to goods for lending and is therefore the source of claims. Production may also be the source of claim destruction. If we start with an existing stock of claims, then surplus producers may use their surpluses to pay off obligations previously incurred. The payment from current production cancels the claim. Claims and production are intimately associated, but there are no rules specifying the exact relation between the two. The relationship is dependent upon institutions of the economy in developing surplus and deficit units. The greater this tendency, the greater will be the claim creation associated with a given product creation. At this stage it is probably more useful to think of production as the causal force and claim creation and destruction as passive, though in theoretical analysis we shall have to move to mutual interrelationships.

Although claims arise from production, claims outstanding at any one time are not necessarily claims on any particular product existing at that time. The deficit unit may consume the products acquired from the surplus unit, and the product is no longer in existence. If the deficit unit acquires capital, for a time there is a product fortifying the claim, but as the capital depreciates it drops below the value of the claim. Consequently we must consider a claim as the right to future output rather than present product. Present product is the basis of the loan; future product is the basis of repayment.

SUMMARY

Economic systems arise from the necessity of man to devise ways of distributing the output of limited resources. Under capitalism the major form of this distribution is through private production and exchange. Under socialism the society determines collectively, through the state, the distribution of the major portion of product.

Scarcity of product arises from the scarcity of land and labor. Capital goods are intermediate goods which man produces to increase the output of land and labor. As capital goods increase relative to land and labor, the ratio of output to capital employed tends to fall. This tendency is the law of variable proportions, or the law of diminishing returns.

All goods and services which an economy produces over a time period are its product. The goods and services accruing to members of the economy are their income. For the economy as a whole, total output and total income are equal. The net product and net income subtract from the total product the loss of previously produced capital in the production process. Income can arise only from output. The market place determines relative values of goods exchanged on the basis of the ratios at which they exchange. A common unit of value expresses values of all goods in terms of the ratio at which each good exchanges for the good used as the unit of value. This system accepts market determination as the true value to society of the goods produced.

The exchange process normally gives rise to deferred claims, by which producers may take income in the form of claims to future product. This production in excess of current consumption is saving. The producer may also save by acquiring capital goods, another form of income in excess of consumption. Investment is another term referring to acquisition of capital goods. For the economy as a whole saving and investment are two ways of looking at the same process, since all income in excess of consumption goods is necessarily capital goods. An agreement for deferred claims may set the terms so that the borrower pays back more than he receives, and this excess is interest. The value of what he pays back depends on market values at the expiration of the agreement, and thus it is impossible to determine the market value of the terms of the agreement at the time of its origination.

SELECTED REFERENCES

Eggers, Melville, and A. D. Tussing, *The Level of Economic Activity.* New York: Holt, 1965.

Heilbroner, Robert, *The Making of Economic Society,* 2d ed. Englewood Cliffs, N.J.: Prentice-Hall, 1968.

Herskovitz, Melville, *Economic Anthropology,* paperback ed. New York: Norton, 1952.

DISCUSSION QUESTIONS

1. What are the social considerations involved in the allocation of output between capital and consumption?

2. Why does the law of variable proportions assume diminishing, rather than increasing, returns to the variable factor?

3. Should capital goods be classed as a part of output? Should they be classed as a part of income? State the case both for and against.

4. If a single commodity were used as a unit for expressing all market values today, what would be the most appropriate commodity? Why?

5. If an economy consumes more than it produces, the economy is engaging in "dissaving." Explain how dissaving can occur.

6. If someone takes saving in the form of a deferred claim, why is it still true that the total of an economy's saving is equal to its capital formation?

2

Money

Specialization in production and variety in consumption characterize economies as they move from the primitive state. Specialization increases output, and variety in consumption increases the utility of economic goods. These developments inevitably separate production and consumption, leading to exchange. The process of exchange is facilitated if the producer offering goods on the market can take payment in the form of a claim rather than actual goods and exercise the claim at a more propitious time and place. Such a claim, regardless of its physical nature, is *money*. The money claim may be a promissory obligation or it may be a tangible good accepted not for its own sake but because it serves as a continuing claim on other goods. Milton Friedman, a contemporary American economist, has expressed this concept of money as follows:

> The economic function of "money" in this sense is to permit exchange without barter, to enable an individual to exchange the goods or services he owns for other goods or services he wishes to consume or to hold without having to match up each transaction. Instead he can sell at one time to one set of individuals for generalized purchasing power and buy at a different time from other individuals by drawing on his stock of generalized purchasing power. Money in this sense consists of anything that serves the function of providing a temporary abode for general purchasing power.[1]

This definition is perilously close to the concept used earlier with regard to general claims, and to differentiate them it is necessary to place great emphasis on the word "temporary" in the Freidman definition. Indeed, the separation of money claims from nonmoney claims rests on somewhat arbitrary delineations as to what is "temporary" and what is not.

If a thing serves the payments function, it obviously must acquire some value in terms of the goods for which it serves as payment; or

[1] "The Demand for Money," *Proceedings of the American Philosophical Society* (Philadelphia), June 1961, p. 259. Reprinted in Richard Ward (ed.), *Monetary Theory and Policy* (Scranton, Pa.: International Textbook, 1966).

to put it another way, goods must have a money value. This means that we use money as the standard of valuation, just as we used cows as the standard in the barter economy, which did not use cows as the means of effecting payment. It also follows that money becomes the likely standard for the designation of claims.

But what in fact is so important that it can serve such a function in the economy—the value reference for all goods and the one thing that everyone will be willing to exchange for all goods? Oddly enough, the thing that serves that function in contemporary economies has no value itself; it is only a particular form of one of those claims to future production. Claims to future production serve as the basis of exchange of the fruits of present production. We can best understand this system by examining how it got that way, but let us first conjecture how it might have come about. The purpose of this exercise is to attempt to develop the logic of money in the system.

As the barter economy develops surplus and deficit units, some individuals hold claims on others as the means by which they have realized value from their surpluses. If the claim is of value to one individual, there is no reason that he could not transfer the claim, if executed in proper form, to another individual. If so, he can offer the claim in exchange for goods rather than offering goods. It was, after all, through such an exchange that he acquired the claim in the first place, so why not reoffer it if he wishes to exercise the claim prior to its stated maturity? If the economy has evolved some standard of value, such as the cow, designation of claims by this standard will facilitate the reoffer of the claim in exchange.

If we assume a society in which debt is sacred and default is unimaginable, we could think of all debt as being money. But if all debt is money, then everyone could buy things by paying for it with his debt. But surely this won't work, since no one has the incentive to produce goods. We are still confronted with the fundamental scarcity of goods, and money is not goods. Perhaps it would be better to envision that sellers will accept only certain types of debt. Let us say that the sovereign ruler is the only one who is well enough known and sufficiently trusted that sellers will accept his debt. If the ruler wishes to acquire more goods than he collects in tribute from the people, he acquires the goods by issuing a claim on himself. Whoever acquires the claim can in turn acquire goods by passing on the claim, which is stated in terms of cow equivalent value. The ruler never creates claims except by the purchase of goods, and because of the claims' general usability, he never has to redeem them, though he can destroy them by requiring that they be paid in taxes. He has created something that the economy needs because of the awkward problems involved in barter. The economy is willing to buy this claim with goods because the claim serves a function.

We now have all goods in the economy trading in terms of cow values, and all debt denominated in cow values. We can classify debt according to money debt and individual debt, but both are denominated in the same form, cow-value equivalents, even though no cow ever passes as a medium of exchange. The medium of exchange is claims on the sovereign. No individual creates his own debt except as he is able to negotiate terms with an individual lender. The ruler can always create debt, and he pays no interest, since the holder of the ruler's debt has the equivalent of a claim on present production. The principal distinction between money debt and nonmoney debt is the ready usability of money in exchange. An alternative way of differentiating them is that one bears interest and the other does not.

Although the above development is apocryphal, its essential features are applicable to contemporary capitalist economies. They apply also to a lesser extent to collectivist economies, but money plays a smaller role in these societies because of the lesser importance of the market mechanism.

Actually money did not originally develop out of claims. It started as tangible commodities, and eventually claims substituted for these commodities. According to Quiggin, money originated in the custom of payments to the family of a bride. So formalized were such gifts that definite scales of values for brides in terms of cattle or wooden bowls or other payment media became established. From this developed money as a medium of exchange. "The objects that came to be used as money are mainly nonlocal, or if local are the product of a special area or special class; and they have prestige or essential virtue, religious or magical."[2]

But Quiggin emphasized that it was such ceremonial uses, rather than trade, that led to money. "The evidence suggests that barter—in its usual sense of exchange of commodities—was not the main factor in the evolution of money. The objects commonly exchanged in barter do not develop naturally into money and the more important objects used as money seldom appear in ordinary everyday barter. Moreover, the inconveniences of barter do not disturb simple societies."[3]

After ritualistic practices developed the money concept, its uses spread to more mundane exchanges, and articles easily transferred came to predominate as money. Certain metals such as bronze, cop-

[2] A. Hingston Quiggin, *A Survey of Primitive Money* (London: Methuen, 1949), p. 322.
[3] *Ibid.*, p. 321.

per, and silver serve the money function well because they are easily divisible, uniform in quality, and durable.

In their first use as money metals simply passed by weight. There were no special features to distinguish the commodity as money as distinct from its use for other purposes. Nevertheless a money commodity occupies a rather unique place in the economic order. People become willing to accept the commodity in exchange not because they want it but because they can use it to acquire goods they do want. In a sense the money commodity is a claim on future output, and is more akin to an intangible claim than to a commodity. Employment of a commodity in the money function tends to increase its relative worth in the community. If, for instance, gold is money and tobacco is not, it is doubtful that gold and tobacco would exchange in the market at the same ratio as they would if neither was money. The money function bestows upon gold a higher tobacco value than it would otherwise have.

Private merchants were the first to make impressions upon pieces of the money commodity, attesting to the weight and fineness of the metal so stamped. Thus was born the coin, apparently around the Eastern Mediterranean about 700 B.C. Coinage facilitates money transactions by making it unnecessary to weigh and assay the metal each time it passes in exchange. Coinage does not change the essential commodity nature of money, as famed Spanish "pieces of eight" exemplify. The Spanish crown issued these silver coins during the era of American explorations. It was not unusual to break the large coin into "bits" and use them separately, since the coin was essentially a known quantity of silver.

Not all coins were "pure," however, in that some governments issued coins containing alloys other than the money commodity. In this way it was possible for the monarch to acquire goods in excess of what it acquired through required tribute to the crown. This practice, known as debasement, is a rather important step in money development, for it is an early instance of "creating" money in excess of the availability of the money commodity. As long as the economy accepts the new coinage, it serves its function just as well as the money commodity.

Aside from the obvious advantage to the crown, there is a strong society-wide incentive to minimize the use of the money commodity. This is because the production of any commodity requires the factors of production. Production of a commodity which serves only as a claim function deprives the community of factors of production for making goods that will directly satisfy public wants. If an alloy requires less real resources than gold, the economy effectively adds to its available goods by switching to the alloy. Noting that commodity money requires real resources, Milton Friedman has observed, "The use of so large a volume of resources for this purpose establishes a strong social incentive in a growing economy to provide cheaper ways to provide a medium of exchange."[4]

Another way in which governments have economized on use of the money commodity is through the issuance of paper substitutes for coin. The paper substitutes are "promises to pay," but if the community accepts the promise, it is as good as commodity payment itself. With the existence of these money substitutes, it becomes necessary to specify when an economy is and is not on a commodity standard, i.e., using a commodity as its essential form of money. In order for a government to be on a commodity standard, all forms of money which it issues must be either the money commodity itself or some medium which is redeemable on demand for the money commodity at a fixed ratio. As far as the holder is concerned, one form of money is a perfect substitute for the other. By the issuance of substitutes it is possible for the economy to have more money than it has money commodity. The government must keep some of the money commodity on hand to meet possible needs for redeemability, but it need not have an amount equal to the total of its monetary issue.

In modern times the most common commodity standard has been the gold standard. When this system prevailed, governments held gold equal to only a portion of their monetary issues. At times the governments' supplies of gold became inadequate because of gold's use for foreign purchases or because the public made large redemptions as a result of financial uncertainty. It then became necessary for the government to suspend specie payments (redeemability), in which case it was no longer meeting the conditions of the gold standard. The last such suspensions occurred in the mid 1930's, and no government has since restored the commodity standard in the full meaning of the term. As later chapters will detail, gold still plays some role in the monetary system, but it is no longer a medium of exchange.

Governments have not been the only means of stretching the money commodity. Private agencies too have issued substitutes for the money commodity, and in time we have come to regard these substitutes on an equal footing with money itself. These substitutes have arisen in the course of money lending, first in Italy in the thirteenth century and then in England. In these early operations

[4] *A Program for Monetary Stability* (New York: Fordham U. P., 1960), p. 5.

Italian merchants and English goldsmiths accepted coin money from persons who had surplus money, and these borrowers agreed to repay the coins on demand. In England these "depositors" of money received receipts which were made to bearer, rather than the individual depositor, and the holder of the receipt could use it to effect payment. This avoided the inconvenience of carrying bulky coins. In Italy depositors received interest on their deposited coin, but in order to use the deposits to effect payment it was first necessary to make a withdrawal, though the depositor could do so on demand. In these early deposit arrangements in both countries the merchants and goldsmiths who took in deposits in turn lent the money at interest. They found that they could do this because all depositors did not demand withdrawal at the same time. It was necessary to keep some money "reserve," but they could lend the rest.

Such a lending operation effectively increases the amount of money in the economy if the definition of money includes the deposit or the receipt for it. The person who borrows money from the goldsmith has money to use, and surely this is a part of the total money in the economy. The person who maintains the deposit can also use the receipt in the same way as money, so that the deposit too is really a part of the money stock. The characteristic that makes the receipt money is the community's willingness to accept it, which is really the same test that makes the money commodity distinct from other commodities.

The successors to these early deposit institutions became known as banks, and the deposit receipts became known as bank notes. As the acceptability of bank dept increased, banks were able to increase their operations by making loans with bank notes rather than coin. In this way it was not necessary to wait for depositors to enlarge the amount of bank debt. Bank owners used their own coin to serve as reserve needs, and with this as a base, expanded their loans and paid for them by issuing bank notes. This reversal in procedure transforms the bank into a somewhat more active creator of money (bank notes) than it would be as a passive creator of notes in return for deposited coin.

Another modification came in the nineteenth century when banks began making loans with deposits as bookkeeping entries rather than bearer notes. The usability of such claims increased as facilities developed for deposit holders to transfer their deposit claim to another party by writing an order to the bank to do so (a check). This meant that deposits became the equivalent of money and it was then possible to pay for loans with deposits. In the twentieth century, deposits have largely replaced bank notes.

In the steps described, then, two things have evolved as money. One of these is claims issued by government. Since the 1930's these claims have had no specific redemption value in any commodity. The second money is deposit claims on banks subject to transfer by check. The units of denomination of both of these claims evolved from the commodity origin of money. In the United Kingdom they are in pound sterling, because the British money unit was a pound of sterling silver. In the United States they are in dollars, because the American coinage took its name from the Spanish silver dollar, "pieces of eight."

The money of today, as a type of claim, no longer requires real resources for its production. A simple way, in fact, of creating money is to substitute money claims for nonmoney claims. The government, for instance, can do this by buying nonmoney claims (loan contracts previously made) and paying for them with money claims. The economic significance of such a move will depend upon the extent of the difference between the money and the nonmoney claim, but this matter will have to await closer scrutiny in later chapters. Suffice it to say at this point that governments do maintain some control over money creation, both the money liabilities of the government and of banks. By controlling their own monetary issues, governments limit the amount available to banks as reserve.

The introduction of money now allows us to use money equivalents as the standard of value. In a sense this is less useful than cow values, because now we use an abstract name such as pounds or dollars. But then any single-value measure is abstract when we try to apply it to a conglomeration of quantities and varieties of products. Perhaps it is better that the value unit has an abstract name, for it is only in a relative sense that values are important. To each producer value is still the amount of goods which he can get for the amount which he produces. The existence of money values does not destroy the fact that products have a subjective value to their user and that we are able to measure only relative values.

CLAIMS AND PRODUCT

Now that we are dealing with a money economy, claim creation becomes a bit more complicated. Money is a claim which by definition is transferred around among holders in the course of market transactions. Just as the emergence of deficit and surplus units in the economy creates claims, the same phenomenon creates money claims. Let us assume now that the government receives some goods by mandatory transfer from the private sector (taxes) and that it creates a money claim on itself to acquire goods in excess of taxes. For this to happen it was necessary for some producers in the private sector to be surplus units. They take their surplus in the form of a claim on the government. In a real sense of the word, this is how the economy accommodates the deficit acquisition by government. (Some would call this a problem of "financing," but a financing problem is really a resource problem. The resulting claim may be financial—denominated in money—but this claim is the result of the producers's surplus, not its cause.)

Those who acquire money claims on government may not wish to retain money. If they choose to acquire goods, then in some future time period they run a deficit: the value of purchases exceeds production. They accommodate the deficit by a transfer of money claims to the surplus producers. In this case surplus and deficit positions do not create claims—they transfer claims. Rather than acquiring obligations, the deficit units surrender claims.

If the surplus producers in the original example choose to convert their money claims to interest-bearing claims, then they lend their newly acquired money claims to others. In the first instance this is merely an exchange of claims, but the borrowers will then likely convert their money claims to goods by exchanging them with some other surplus producer in a subsequent time period. In this second step again the economy has accommodated surplus and deficit positions by an exchange of claims.

The banks, like the government, can create money claims on themselves. They do so, however, by making loans in the first instance rather than by running a deficit-goods position. When a bank makes a loan, the borrower and bank are exchanging claims. The borrower creates a nonmoney claim (a loan), and the bank creates a money claim on itself. The bank's claims are readily usable in exchange, while the borrowers's claims are not. In this first instance the exchange of claims is actually claim creation outside of production. The borrower, however, makes the loan for the purpose of running a deficit position, and he transfers the money to surplus producers. In the end the surplus producer holds a money claim on the bank and the bank holds a nonmoney claim on the deficit unit. The bank has served as an intermediary by providing the surplus and deficit units each with the type of accommodation to its position which it desires. It is possible that in the absence of this intermediation the surplus producer would have been unwilling to provide the surplus for the deficit unit. It is in this sense that claim creation becomes an active force in determining the amount of surplus production, and ultimately the amount of production itself. There are, however, many other institutions that serve in such an intermediary capacity, and these will come up later in discussions of claim differentiation.

SUMMARY

Money is anything which an economy widely uses as a medium for effecting exchanges and a common standard of value for the exchanges. In contemporary economies, claims on specific debtors serve this function, but money originated as particular commodities used to make ritualistic compensation, as in bride purchase. As the money practice spread, metals came to be the predominant money commodity; in this usage the commodity can be regarded as similar to a claim. Coinage, begun about 700 B.C., circulated the money commodity in units of uniform weight and appearance.

Societies economized on the use of the money commodity—which requires real resources for its production—by the use of money substitutes. Governments issued coins with diminishing amounts of the money commodity, and in addition they issued claims to the commodity. An official commodity "standard" still existed, however, as long as the holder of a money substitute had the right to exchange it at a fixed rate for the money commodity. The private sector of the economy began issuing money commodity substitutes as early as the thirteenth century. These substitutes were in the form of deposit receipts to persons who left money with others on condition they could reclaim it at any time. The receiver of the deposited money lent it to others at interest. The use of the deposit claim itself as money served to increase the amount of money in existence. Later these deposit institutions became known as banks and began lending claims on themselves—bank notes and deposits—without the necessity of first receiving the money commodity in deposit. These commodity money substitutes became so acceptable that today money consists of claims on banks and governments which are not convertible to a commodity. Society values its goods in money units, and any given amount of money claim has value only to the extent that it will exchange for goods.

Money introduces some complications in the relationship between claims and income. Participants in the economy normally hold some money to facilitate purchases. In the first instance they acquire or give up money as the means of settling surplus or deficits among themselves, and thus in a money economy such imbalances do not necessarily lead to claim creation or destruction. Loans made with money are an exchange of claims rather than a result of income and product imbalances.

Product deficits and surpluses create money. The government can issue money claims to purchase product in excess of that it acquires through taxation. Banks issue money claims for loans, and the borrower runs product deficits by transferring these claims. In this way the bank serves as an intermediary between the surplus producer and the borrower who acquires the surplus.

SELECTED REFERENCES

Einzig, Paul, *Primitive Money.* New York: Pergamon, 1966.

Haines, Walter W., *Money, Prices and Policy,* 2d ed. New York: McGraw-Hill, 1966.

Pigou, A.C., *The Veil of Money.* London: Macmillan, 1949.

Quiggin, A. Hingston, *A Survey of Primitive Money.* London: Metheun, 1949.

DISCUSSION QUESTIONS

1. Why is it difficult to distinguish between claims and money?

2. What are the advantages of using debt, rather than commodities, as money?

3. In what sense can a commodity, when used as money, be looked upon as a claim?

4. Trace the steps by which credit becomes substituted for commodities as the society's money.

5. Why does the text state that a financing problem is really a resource problem? Is this statement true for both the society and the individual?

6. What is meant by the terms "deficit units" and "surplus units" in the economy? Cite some examples.

3

Aggregate Demand

In a capitalistic economy the science of economics concentrates most of its attention on analysis of demand for products. Demand refers to offers to purchase. Aggregate demand concerns the whole economy's desires and ability to make purchases, while product demand refers to markets for particular goods or services.

Potential aggregate supply in an economy is the total of goods which the economy could produce with its existing factors of production. Over time there can be some alteration in these factors through capital accumulation and growth in the labor force, but in the short run the economy takes its factors as being fixed. In any period observed, aggregate demand is the amount of purchases that actually take place in the period at the prices that prevailed. If actual output is less than the economy is capable of producing, the cause is a deficiency of aggregate demand. In an economy which employs roundabout production, most workers depend upon the owners of capital to provide them with productive employment. If demand is deficient, capitalists do not need all labor available, with the result that there is unemployment of some labor and underemployment of others. Unemployment of capital expresses itself in "excess capacity" of the producing firm.

Contemporary analysis of deficiency of aggregate demand owes most to John Maynard Keynes (1883-1946), who provided a theoretical basis for what he called "involuntary unemployment." Lord Keynes wrote his major work, *The General Theory of Employment, Interest and Money*, in 1936, at a time of widespread unemployment.[1] Much of contemporary economic theory incorporates his analysis, and thus his theories will appear often in the present book without explicit reference to their creator.

The problem of deficiency of demand seems to be a product of

[1] For a useful analysis of this work, see Dudley Dillard, *The Economics of John Maynard Keynes* (Englewood Cliffs, N.J.: Prentice-Hall, 1948).

the complexity of economic organization. In a subsistence economy it does not exist, since the producer is also his own consumer and presumably knows his own demand. As soon as producers specialize in production and depend upon trade to dispose of their surplus, they are faced with uncertainty about the demand of others for their surplus production. In a barter economy without credit, however, supply and demand tend to be equivalent, although there can be special problems with particular products. The reason for this equivalence is that no man produces except that he either uses the product himself or offers it in exchange. Thus every product is both demand and supply, and in the aggregate there is no surplus of either. This doctrine is known as Say's law, after its originator, J. B. Say, a nineteenth-century French economist.

Say's law is purely theoretical, however, because credit seems to arise in all economies, barter included. The possibility of lending and borrowing can create a divergence between supply and demand. The producer may wish to defer acquisition of products until the indefinite future. He will then seek to produce more than he acquires, and his desired surplus production represents an excess of supply over demand. At the same time others may wish to acquire more than they produce. Unless intended surpluses match intended deficits, demand is not equal to supply.

In a money economy it is quite possible that the surplus producers may wish to take their surplus in the form of money, but this is only one of many types of claims which they could acquire. Even in a barter economy, if there is a desire to exchange a surplus for claims, rather than goods, there is a possibility for inequality between supply and demand.

In considering the possibility of inequality of supply and demand, we are now thinking in terms of intentions, or desired purchases and sales. This is an *ex ante*, or before the fact, type of analysis. After the fact (*ex post*) actual supply and demand become equal, since the economy in some way disposes of all goods which it produces. We can assume, however, that economic conditions had to change in some way to bring supply and demand into equality. A listing of some of these possibilities follows, and later chapters will treat these in more detail.

One possibility is that there will be unexpected changes in producers stocks of goods held for sale. If demand for currently produced goods exceeded supply, producers may have met the demand by drawing down on their stocks. Likewise, if they overproduced and were unable to dispose of all the intended surplus, they may have had involuntary inventory accumulations. In either case it was impossible to clear the market without a disturbance to equilibrium.

An economy is in equilibrium when there are no forces within the economic system leading to further change. Involuntary inventory changes are a clear example of a type of disequilibrium force. By definition it follows that inventories are either deficient or in excess of the intentions of those who hold them. In the following period producers will take into account their inventories in deciding production levels. The unintended inventory changes have cleared the market, but they set up forces leading to change. If there was an unintended rise in inventories, producers will reduce output in subsequent periods. Eventually, then, the fall in demand causes output to fall.

The next possibility for clearing the market is even more involved than inventory changes. It may be that supply and demand came into equality as a result of changes in the valuation of products. Here the reference is largely to revaluations which are widespread throughout the economy. Particular markets clear through revaluations, but that is not necessarily a measure of aggregate disequilibrium. A market revaluation in one direction may offset a revaluation in the oppposite direction, as when demand shifts from one product to another.

For the aggregate analysis, let us take the case where demand was less than supplies. One way of expressing aggregate revaluations is that large numbers of producers must strike bargains in the market process which were below their expectations. In a monetary economy this takes the form of lower money receipts than expected. Although goods sold are worth less in terms of money, money is worth more in the purchase of goods. This is necessarily so if the revaluations in terms of money are widespread throughout the economy, it is thus not clear that revaluations in terms of money necessarily set up forces leading to further change.

It is quite possible, however, that producers (including laborers) do not consider the changing goods value of money and thus view the lower money receipts as a loss of real income. This phenomenon is known as *money illusion*, and if it exists it is possible that the lower money receipts will lead to a fall in production in subsequent periods. The changing value of money also alters the real value of existing money holdings and assets and liabilities expressed in terms of money. Again, this is a complex matter which we shall have to consider later in a more elaborate treatment of changes in money values.

The purpose of raising these problems at the present time is to contrast supply and demand in the *ex ante* sense, before changes in market valuations, and in the *ex post* sense in which total demand must necessarily equal supplies, since someone in the economy must hold all goods.

A central problem in a capitalistic economy is maintaining demand at the level that would equal supplies forthcoming when the economy is using its available factors of production. Let us look once again at the economy's maximum production when it employs all of its labor and capital. We call this the *full-employment economy*. The full-employment economy yields a given amount of income for each person in the economy. All income recipients will not, however, wish to take the whole of their income in the form of goods. Some will prefer to receive deferred claims. To this extent, demand would not equal supply at the full-employment level, unless others wished to acquire goods in excess of their income. If, viewed in the *ex ante* sense, these deficit desires are less than the surplus desires elsewhere in the economy at the full employment, there exists what is called a *deflationary gap*. As a result of this deficiency of demand, output will fall. It will continue to fall until it reaches a level at which desired surpluses and deficits are equal. The fall in output reduces the surpluses and increases the deficits at the same time. As incomes get lower, the amount of surpluses will tend to diminish as it becomes necessary to consume a larger proportion of output in order to maintain living standards. At the same time, some who would be surplus units at the larger level of employment become deficit units at the lower level, again in an attempt to maintain living standards.

We can summarize the above analysis by saying that full employment will not come about if desired surpluses at full employment exceed desired deficits. *Ex post* deficits and surpluses must always be equal, but it is the change in output (and income) which brings the equality. Starting from any position of output, a rise in desired claims will cause a fall in output. Even if it initially resulted in an increase in production by those wanting claims, rather than a fall in demand, the rise in output would be short-lived, since there is no increase in demand to absorb it. Likewise, a rise in desired deficits is the same as an increase in demand.

The condition for an increase in output is an *ex ante* excess of desired deficits over desired surplus. Such an excess may come about in two ways. (1) Some producing units may increase the proportion of their production (income receipts) which they wish to take in present goods (spending on current output) rather than deferred claims. (2) Some members of the economy may increase the excess of spending over their incomes. Either of these contingencies represents an increase in demand. The condition for a decrease in output is an excess of *ex ante* desired surpluses over desired deficits. This too may come about by an increase in the desired proportion of income taken in the form of claims or by a decrease in desired borrowing.

SAVING AND INVESTING

A treatment analogous though not identical to the above looks at the relation between saving and investing. For this analysis we must devide the economy into two distinct sectors: the consuming sector and the investing sector. The consuming sector reqresents all persons in their role as users of the economy's output for the direct satisfaction it yields. By definition they purchase consumer goods. The investing sector represents *units* in the economy who acquire capital goods. These units may be individuals in their capacity as self-employed producers, or businesses, various legal organizations of persons acting as a producing unit. Although ultimately persons are the owners of both capital and consumer goods, this form of economic analysis separates individuals in their two roles as producers and consumers. In contemporary capitalistic systems this is by no means an artificial distinction, though it would have had less meaning in the handicraft period prior to the industrial revolution. Government transactions and trade with foreigners provide a basis for two other sectors, but we defer their consideration until a later stage of the analysis.

In the two-sector system described individuals demand only consumer goods. Saving is the excess of their income from production over their spending for consumer goods. At the full-employment income (output) we assume that the amount which persons wish to consume is less than their total income. Consumption demand is less than total supply. Total demand will equal total supply only if investment demand is adequate to take up the slack. If investment demand at the full-employment level is less than saving desires, then total demand is less than full-employment supply. In the short run there may be some unintended inventory accumulation as a result of the deficiency of demand. This is itself a form of investment, but the excessive stocks will lead to a fall in output in later periods. Thus ultimately the excess of desired saving over investment demand leads to a fall in income.

Starting from any position, the condition for a fall in demand is an excess of intended saving over investment demand. This excess may result from an increase in savings desired (a reduction in consumer demand) or a decrease in investment demand. The condition for a rise in demand is an excess of investment demand over intended saving, which may arise from a reduction in saving desires or an increase in investment demand.

In the *ex post* sense saving and investment are always equal. This is because income can only arise from production, and there are only two kinds of production—consumption goods and investment goods. Saving is the excess of income over consumption, but investment is also the excess of output over the output of consumption goods. Saving and investment are necessarily equal as long as all goods are classed as either consumption or investment and saving is the excess of output over consumption.

Despite their equality, the saving and investment decisions come from separate sources, and in large measure the saver and investor hold different assets. Let us look first at the saver, who has essentially two ways in which he takes his saving. He may acquire real capital goods, or he may improve his claim position. The farmer who trades part of his crop for a plow is a saver, even though he has in fact used all of his output to purchase goods. His saving is a plow. Alternatively he might trade a portion of his crop for a claim. In this case he takes his saving in the form of a claim to future product. Finally, he may use a portion of his crop to pay off a claim which others hold on him. Either of the latter two cases improves his claim position.

The investor holds only one kind of asset representing his investment—capital goods. The saver who takes his saving in capital goods is at the same time an investor. If there are investors who acquire capital goods in excess of saving, then they must do so by creating claims on themselves or by using past claims held on others. To the extent that saving and investing are done by different groups, changes in claims will necessarily accommodate the difference between the investing groups' saving and investing. Equality between saving and investment remains, even though the acts are separate.

If we separate all persons into two groups as producers and consumers, then changes in claims will accompany all investment. This is because we consider that a person buying capital goods is at one and the same time a saver and investor. As consumer he holds a fictitious "claim" on himself as producer. This treatment is somewhat artificial, but is justifiable in an economy in which most investing is the act of business firms, rather than individuals, and does give rise to actual claim changes. The fictitious portion is then necessary only as a matter of completeness.

The equality between saving and investing is sometimes hard to visualize in a complex economy where the acts are so widely spread. Let us consider a few cases that might offer problems. Suppose that a business firm steps up its production on a particular day and accumulates inventory. How does saving immediately match this inventory investment if the two are always equal? Saving, remember, is the difference between income and consumption, and one or both of these must change if saving is to rise. In this example, income rises on the particular day without a change in consumption. In the instant of product creation, those who create it also have income. The firm may postpone the actual payment of income to, for example, the laborers involved, but nevertheless laborers immediately have income in the form of a claim on the firm. Thus this is the way that they have, for this brief period of time, taken their saving, which matches the inventory accumulation of the firm.

Another problem that sometimes arises is the case in which "saving is not invested." As stated, this is an impossibility. If there is saving out of income, then there necessarily was output in excess of consumption, which means there was investment. The only way the statement can have any meaning is with reference to two different time periods. The investment of one time period may in fact be less than the saving of a previous time period. But this means that saving also falls, because of the fall in output.

METHODS COMPARED

Let us now compare the two approaches to demand analysis: the surplus and deficit relationship and the saving and investment relationship. Under the following conditions, the two approaches would be identical (still ignoring the foreign and government sectors):

(a) Business firms make all investment; consumers make all saving decisions.

(b) Every act of investment in the business sector gives rise to an equal amount of claim improvement in the consumer sector.

(c) There are no surplus and deficits with respect to consumption goods—that is, no consumer borrowing. Only business units run deficits, and these are for the acquisition of capital goods.

Under these assumptions, the desire to save is the same thing as the desire to run surpluses. The desire to invest is the same thing as the desire to run deficits, since business firms have no income out of which they can invest. All business income passes to individuals. If we examine an *ex ante* excess of saving over investment, we are at the same time examining an excess of desired surpluses over desired deficits.

All of the above assumptions are not true in contemporary economies, and we must make certain adjustments in order to reconcile the two approaches. For one thing, in contemporary economies some deficits are for the purpose of consumption. If we are to reconcile the two approaches under consideration, it will be necessary to aggregate persons as consumers into one sector and consider their net surplus as a whole. This approach washes out deficits and surpluses of considerable quantitative importance, and this is one of the limitations of the saving-investment approach.

Another serious problem concerns business saving. In an economy in which business firms are functioning economic units, a considerable portion of the income from output accrues first to business firms who then pass it along to their owners. But they do not pass it all along, and the firm retains control itself over some income. A firm may, for instance, take a portion of its income in the form of capital goods. To this extent, income received by individuals is not equal to output of the economy as a whole. Income and output are always equal as a whole, but some income has accrued to firms. Business has engaged in a form of saving without individuals as income receivers making the saving decision. In this case the *ex ante* desire to invest is not the same as the *ex ante* desire to run deficits. Actually this is similar to the problem in which individuals may also be investors: the saving and investment decision is a single act. In the present case, however, it is the firm, rather than individuals, who make the simultaneous decision. We can reconcile this problem by considering that all income of the firm gives rise to an equal claim by individual owners of the firm. In this case a firm which is building capital through retained income is at the same time increasing claims held on it. When we think of desired claim creation, we must think of it from the standpoint of both individuals and firms. In some way individuals make this decision, either themselves or through the firms they hold. They consider as income the goods and claims their firms acquire as well as the goods and claims which they acquire.

Each of the two approaches to disequilibrium analysis has its advantages. The deficit-surplus method has the advantage that it looks at all desired inequality between supply and demand. This includes deficits for both consumption and investment purposes. The saving-investment approach must net out desired borrowing and lending within the consumer sector. The deficit-surplus approach looks only at imbalances which the economy must match for equilibrium to prevail. The saving-investment approach considers total saving as a reduction in demand, when in fact some saving is the act of purchase or capital goods, in which case saving and investing occur simultaneously.

The saving-investment approach has the advantage that it focuses on a specific item of demand—investment. This is somewhat easier to grapple with than "desired deficits." *Ex post*, it is simpler to measure saving and investment. Investment is the same as output of investment goods plus inventory changes, and saving is the excess of output over all consumption goods. Deficits and surpluses involve both claim destruction and claim creation, and these are difficult to measure where wide varieties of claims are involved.

In the past, analysts have used the saving-investment approach more widely than the alternative, and for this reason the saving-investment approach will receive more attention in this book. In recent years more information on claims has become available, and this type of analysis is gradually beginning to supplement the saving-investment analysis.

With proper adjustment, as noted above, there is a close link between saving-investment and claim creation. It is incorrect to regard either as passively following the other. It is true that investment tends to cause claim creation, since claims are the predominant way in which savers take their excess income. But the willingness of savers to acquire claims is what allows the investment to take place. If savers were willing to hold only claims on government, the investment could not take place, and consequently the income and saving could never arise. Measures which facilitate claim creation facilitate demand, and thereby income, and thereby saving.

An important reason for the study of economics is the development of governmental policy to stabilize economic activity. Government can directly affect demand by absorbing part of output, but it would be a mistake to neglect its indirect role through measures it takes to encourage or discourage claim creation. How it does this is a topic for later discussion, but it is important to realize at this juncture the close link between claim creation and output. Comparison of the deficit-surplus and saving-investment approaches to analysis is one means of studying this link.

SUMMARY

Aggregate demand determines the extent to which an economy utilizes its available factors of production. Supply and demand are equal in a theoretical noncredit economy, but a tendency to imbalance can exist if some producers wish to take their income in deferred claims. In any one period actual supply and demand are necessarily equal, but the changes necessary to bring the equality may cause movements in demand or supply in subsequent periods. One such change may be inventories, as producers experience unexpected changes in their stocks relative to sales. Widespread price changes may affect future real demand, but the effects of such price adjustment are ambiguous.

Will demand be adequate to absorb the output of a fully employed economy? It will be adequate only if the desire to run deficits—acquire goods in excess of production—by some sectors of the economy is enough to offset the surpluses which other sectors would desire at the full-employment level of income. Income (demand) necessarily adjusts until it reaches a level at which deficits and surpluses are equal. A similar analytical approach divides the economy into two sectors, consuming units and producing units, and classifies all goods as consumer or capital goods. If consuming units desire less consumption than their income, they wish to save by acquiring claims on producing units. Producing units invest (acquire capital goods) by borrowing from the consumer sector. Demand is equal to supply at the full-employment level only if desired saving at that level is equal to investment. Investment demand must match saving, which is nondemand. Actual saving and investment are equal *ex post* because both measure the excess of production over consumer goods. Desired saving and investment are not necessarily equal, and it is changes in demand (income) which make them equal. The two methods of analysis are similar if consuming units do not engage in investment and if all business units' saving (undistributed income) is treated as saving of the individual owners. The saving-investment approach also does not consider deficits for consumer goods purchases, since it treats the consumer sector on an aggregate basis.

SELECTED REFERENCES

Dillard, Dudley, *The Economics of John Maynard Keynes.* Englewood Cliffs, N. J.: Prentice-Hall, 1948.
Hansen, Alvin, *Fiscal Policy and Business Cycles.* New York: Norton, 1941.
Harris, Seymour (ed.), *The New Economics.* New York: Knopf, 1948.
Kurihara, Kenneth (ed.), *Post-Keynesian Economics.* New Brunswick, N. J.: Rutgers U.P., 1954.
Lekachman, Robert (ed.), *Keynes and the Classics.* Boston: Heath, 1964.

DISCUSSION QUESTIONS

1. Define "aggregate demand."
2. Explain Say's law and the conditions under which it is applicable.
3. Why can actual demand, *ex post*, not differ from actual supply?
4. Explain how price declines affect a person's real income if his money income remains unchanged.

5. Suppose that at a given income level the public decides to reduce the amount of income taken in deferred claims. How does this action affect aggregate demand?

6. Using the saving-investment approach, state the conditions necessary for aggregate demand to equal full-employment supply.

7. Compare the saving-investment and deficit-surplus approaches to aggregate demand analysis.

8. Suppose that business units retain income but in the same time period do not make an equivalent investment. Is it still true that saving equals investment for the economy as a whole?

4

Consumption and Saving

Man's desire for economic goods seems to have no limit, and yet the effective demand for output is not always equal to that which the economy is capable of producing. Why does the economy not always produce at capacity and exchange output in the market place until consumer satisfaction is maximized? The theory of *consumption demand* attempts to explain the possibility of a gap between aggregate output and demand for that output.

Demand for goods takes the form of offers to exchange money for such goods. From the standpoint of the buyer the ability to purchase goods is dependent upon his money income, the possession of claims which he can offer for current goods, and the ability to acquire goods by incurring liabilities to repay in the future. This is the framework in which we shall analyze factors influencing the demand for consumption goods.

John Maynard Keynes (Chapter 3) believed that consumption demand was directly dependent upon income, and this theory is widely followed today. In a sense it is somewhat paradoxical to state that consumption depends upon income, since consumption output is a type of income. What this theory attempts to do is to isolate the independent forces that may lead to changes in demand. If it is true that consumption reacts passively to changes in income, then consumption itself will not be an independent cause of changes in income.

Consumption is usually the largest component of output, and if it is possible to exclude consumption demand as an independent force in changes in total demand, then it becomes possible to explain changes in the total on the basis of much smaller components. This approach is useful only if the public's desired amount of consumption out of any income level is relatively stable and not significantly influenced by other factors, as Keynesian theory holds. It is important to note that this theory does not take income as a given factor, as did pre-Keynesian prevailing doctrine, which assumed the economy produced at a level that maintained full employment. The problem was in determining the relative allocations of income between consumption and saving, and the interest rate was assigned this role. The higher the interest rate, the greater the incentive to save. Keynesian theory denies that the interest rate affects saving directly, believing that saving is a function of income.

Although consumption is taken as dependent upon income, that does not mean that it plays no role in income determination, since consumption is the major type of output which gives rise to income. In Keynesian theory the public's desire to consume out of income interacts with other components of demand to determine the income level, in a manner explained below.

Consumption demand can change, but it changes only in response to changes in other components of demand, called *autonomous factors*. These are essentially the demand for government goods, for capital goods, and for exports. For simplicity we shall consider an economy consisting only of capital goods and consumer goods. These and other simplifying assumptions will help bring out the important economic decisions which influence total demand and hence output. We assume that all money income arises from the sale of consumption and capital goods. Saving takes the form of claims on business enterprises, which acquire their capital goods through such borrowing. The public's saving is the excess of money income over consumption, which is necessarily equal to income from investment goods. Dissaving, the excess of consumption over income, is possible for some groups in the economy, but an equal amount of saving necessarily takes place among other groups. The public's saving is the net of saving over dissaving.

Output Y consists of consumption C and investment I. If the demand for consumption goods is not independently determined, we can then express it as a function of income, which is always equal to output. This function f is merely the proportion of income which the public would devote to consumption. To simplify an equation showing income determination, we can then substitute in the equation, $Y = C + I$, the following: $Y = fY + I$. By algebraic manipulation,

$$Y (1 - f) = I$$

and

$$Y = \frac{I}{(1 - f)}$$

We now have an expression stating that the demand for output is determined by the demand for investment goods and the desired ratio of consumption to income. This does not mean to say that these relationships will always be fulfilled. If investment demand were to

> *Example of Income Determination*
>
> Consumption = $^3/_4$ income
>
> $$\text{Multiplier} = \frac{1}{1 - ^3/_4} = 4$$
>
> Investment = 20   Investment = 30
>
> $$Y = \frac{20}{1 - ^3/_4} \qquad Y = \frac{30}{1 - ^3/_4}$$
>
> $$= 80 \qquad\qquad = 120$$
>
> Change in investment: 10
>
> Change in income: 40
>
> Multiplier effect: 4

fall suddenly in some period, people would not automatically reduce their consumption in the same period so that the desired relationship is maintained. They would, however, find themselves consuming a larger proportion of their income than desired. As a result they would reduce consumption demand until in some subsequent period the desired relationship were restored. In any period observed consumption is a component of income, but this does not mean that over the long run it is an active force determining demand. The theory is that consumption is a passive factor in income determination.

Another way of stating the desired relationship is in terms of saving. We can say that out of any income level the public wishes to save a portion of income. In our simplified economy any income which is not consumed is saved. Therefore, the desired saving function is the complement of the desired consumption function. In one stage of our previous equation we arrived at the formulation:

$$Y - fY = I$$

But $Y - fY$ is the same thing as the desired saving ratio, for the proportion of income which is not consumed is saved. Therefore at this stage we could substitute sY where s is the desired ratio of saving to income. If $sY = I$, then $Y = I/s$, another way of stating the equilibrium income level.

Again, the above relationship would not always have to prevail. If investment falls, saving may temporarily drop below the desired relationship to income. Consumption will then fall until the desired relationship is restored in a subsequent period. But note what hap-

pens to effect equilibrium. As consumption is reduced, income falls
until equilibrium is restored. Saving does not change—it is equal to
investment—but income does change. Graphically we can depict the
relationships as in Fig. 4-1, which assumes a saving function equal to

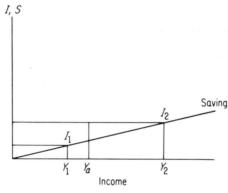

Fig. 4-1

$1/4$ of income. Investment demand then determines aggregate demand.
If investment rises from I_1 to I_2, income will rise from Y_1 to Y_2.
Temporarily income will rise to Y_a, but now the public's saving
(equal to investment) is higher than desired in relation to income.

Any change in investment leads to a change in total demand
larger than the change in investment. This is because the change in
investment induces further changes in consumption demand. The size
of this "multiplier" effect can be determined from the previous
equation:

$$Y = \frac{I}{1-f}$$

To see the relationship of income to any level of investment, we can
take I out of the fraction to get

$$Y = I \times \frac{1}{1-f}$$

The multiplier is then $\frac{1}{1-f}$.

If the desire for consumption goods is unlimited, why is there
not demand for all the output the economy can produce? Consumption theory hypothesizes that people will always wish to delay some
of their consumption. As long as they are producing more than a

subsistence level, they can attempt to save some portion of their output by taking a claim to future output. In our simplified economy the source of such claims is investment demand. *Total demand will be equal to the economy's maximum output only if investment demand is equal to the saving that the public desires at that output level.*

The consumption function which we have employed is greatly oversimplified in that it assumes the public would desire the same ratio of consumption to income (or saving to income) regardless what the level of income is. For one thing we could never visualize zero consumption even if there were zero demand. This can be taken care of by assuming some constant level of consumption that would always prevail regardless of the level of income. The function then becomes a bit more complicated, appearing $Y = k + fY$, where k is the consumption constant.[1] The saving function would then be saving $= -k + sY$, and s remains as 1 - the consumption function. The saving function would be plotted as in Fig. 4-2. There is no need to

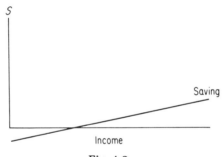

Fig. 4-2

dwell on the significance of a "negative" figure for saving. It will not occur any more than there will actually be positive consumption and zero income. These functions are ways of stating how the total of the

[1] This is the slope intercept form of an equation. The simple fY form assumed that a geometric expression of the equation would pass through the origin. The $k + fY$ form does not change the slope of the line (3 on the Y-axis and 4 on the X-axis). It changes the curve's position so that it does not pass through the origin but intercepts the Y-axis at k rather than zero.

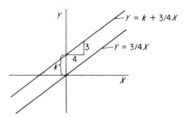

public views the matter at all possible levels of income. The level of investment will determine the actual level of income that prevails.

The revised functions do not destroy our concept of the multiplier, but we must now employ it specifically for changes in income rather than as a way of looking at total income. We cannot use it for total income because the desired ratio of consumption to income now differs at different levels of income. The amount by which consumption will change in response to any change in income remains the same, however, so we can still use the multiplier as

$$\text{Change in demand} = \text{Change in investment} \times \frac{1}{1 - f}$$

A more realistic form of the consumption function would, however, assume that the proportion of income saved would change at different income levels. It is probable that the larger the income the greater the proportion that would be saved, yielding a saving function as in Fig. 4-3. In this case the saving-income ratio used in the multi-

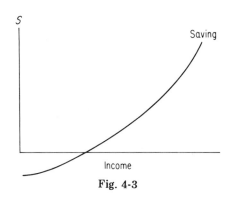

Fig. 4-3

plier will depend upon where along the curve the change occurs. Higher mathematics is applicable in dealing with these more refined equations, but it is not necessary in understanding the economics of the matter. The essential point of the theory of the consumption function is that consumption is dependent upon income. Active determination of demand must arise from other sources. Even though autonomous expenditures are the smaller component, they determine total income.

PERMANENT INCOME

One modification of the rigid consumption-income relationship suggests that the public attempts to maintain a relation between consumption and its "permanent" income, rather than the actual income of any period. Permanent income is the public's expectations about normal income. It is assumed that expected permanent income will change in the same direction, but by a lesser magnitude, than actual income. If there is a sharp rise in income, for example, the public might consider that only a portion of this is permanent, the remainder being "transitory" income. In this theory the public may be in equilibrium with its long-run, permanent income, even though there are fluctuations in the observed consumption-income ratio that might give the appearance of an unstable-consumption function. We can formalize the relationship in the following way:

$$\frac{\text{Desired consumption}}{\text{Income}} = \frac{\text{Desired consumption}}{\text{Permanent income}} \times \frac{\text{Permanent income}}{\text{Actual income}}$$

Thus a constant relationship to permanent income does not imply a constant relationship to actual income. If permanent income rises less than actual income, the public will desire to consume a smaller proportion of its actual income.

The permanent-income hypothesis has implications for the theory of the multiplier. If investment causes an increase in income, the public may consider this increase as transitory and save a large portion of the incremental income. The multiplier is smaller than it would be if the consumption-income relationship remained rigid. This would indicate that changes in autonomous elements of demand must be sustained if they are to generate multiplied changes in total demand.

Example of Permanent Income

Desired consumption C is $3/4$ of permanent income

Public's assumed permanent income Y_p rises by $1/4$ the increase in actual income Y_a.

In the beginning period, permanent and actual income are equal at 400:

$$\text{Desired } \frac{C}{Y_a} = \text{desired } \frac{C}{Y_p} \times \frac{Y_p}{Y_a}$$

$$\text{Desired } \frac{C}{Y_a} = 3/4 \times \frac{400}{400} = 3/4 = 75\%$$

Income rises to 500:

$$\text{Desired } \frac{C}{Y_a} = 3/4 \times \frac{425}{500} = 63\%$$

One way to consider this permanent-income effect in our graphical analysis is with respect to the temporary income position, Y_a in Fig. 4-1. The permanent-income approach would indicate that this position may not be so temporary. Y_a was the income position resulting from a rise in investment before there was time for an induced rise in consumption. If the incremental income is considered transitory, the public is content with the higher ratio of saving to income and will not bring income to the saving function line until the original increase in income is considered permanent.

Though many attempts have been made to test the consumption function emperically, there is no sure way to prove or disprove its validity. We can look at data *ex post* and determine the ratio of consumption to income, but that does not tell us in what way this level of income came about, and it is the process of income determination that the theory attempts to explain. Even if we accept the theory as being correct, we still cannot be certain that past data will yield an accurate consumption function. Each period in the past shows us only one ratio, the consumption that did take place at the income level that prevailed. To know the function we need to know what would have taken place at other levels of income. We could attempt to solve that problem by taking many periods and thus getting a range of income and consumption relations. The difficulty with that approach is that we are not looking at the same function in observing different periods. We do not know whether changes in the ratio between years take place because of the change in income or whether in fact the whole consumption function has shifted.

The consumption function is a theoretical formulation of the way that desired consumption-income relationships at all levels of income enter into the actual determination of demand. The theory can incorporate a function of any shape, but the most usual assumption holds that as income rises the proportion of desired consumption falls. One way of testing this proposition indirectly is to measure the ratio of consumption to income at any one time for various income earners according to size of income. Such tests show that the larger the income size, the greater the proportion saved. If this is an accurate description of the way the total public consumption function is formed, then it implies that changes in the distribution of income will change the aggregate consumption function. Distribution refers to the differences in size of income among income earners. If a large proportion of income goes to a relatively small group, the propensity to save will be high because of the saving of these high-income earners. A redistribution of income in the direction of decreasing these income differentials would tend to decrease the saving function. More income goes into the hands of those inclined to use it for consumption.

Systematic redistribution is one way in which the average propensity to consume may change with fluctuations in national income.
As income rises, wages tend to rise at a slower rate than the return to
capital. Owners of capital tend to be in higher income categories, since
capital accumulation is the result of their higher incomes. As the
proportion of income going to higher-income classes rises, the desire
to consume relative to total income tends to fall. This effect is
especially true if income recipients behave according to the permanent-income hypothesis. If returns to capital fluctuate more than
labor income, owners of capital will tend to regard fluctuations in
income as transitory rather than permanent and will not respond
proportinately with changes in consumption.

ASSETS

Changes in permanent income can alternatively be treated as
changes in the value of wealth. In this broad concept of the term,
wealth is anything existing at a point in time which will yield income
in the future. The value of wealth is determined by the value of
expected income from it. The present value is less than the future
value because society places a greater value on a product in the present
than the same product in the future. (Chapter 5 develops this concept
in more detail.) The value of existing capital is the present value of
the expected output of capital during its life. In the same manner,
the value of an individual in an economic sense is determined by the
expected value of his lifetime earnings. Any individual's wealth at any
time is derived from the expected income from his own labor and
from his assets. By this broad definition of wealth, to include human
wealth, changes in expected income and changes in wealth are
mathematically linked, and are alternative ways of treating the same
phenomenon.

Whether or not this concept of wealth is useful in explaining
consumption demand depends upon human behavior. Consumers may
react more to current than to expected income, in which case
perceived changes in wealth will be more limited, but they still may
exert some influence on consumption decisions.

When an individual consumes out of income, he is exchanging
his own current production for the output of others. An alternative
means of acquiring current production is to exchange for it some
previously acquired asset. If an individual uses an existing asset to
acquire new consumer goods in excess of his income, he is dissaving.
Whoever in the economy takes the asset is saving, since he has taken
a portion of his output as a claim. The possession of assets which can

be exchanged for goods provides the individual with a ready means of augmenting his consumption beyond his income.

Let us divide assets into three broad categories. *Real wealth* will be defined to consist of tangible economic goods acquired from the past, thus excluding human wealth. Such wealth is essentially capital and land, though for this purpose we must use a very broad definition of capital to include all goods which last beyond the period in which they are produced. *Internal assets* consist of claims which one sector of the private economy holds on another sector of the economy. For every asset in the economy there is a matching liability. Loans are clearly in this category, for the debtor has an explicit contractual obligation to the creditor. Corporate shares we think of as claims to real wealth, and thus categorize them with real wealth rather than internal assets. Corporate debt, expressing a fixed obligation in the future, is an internal type of asset. *External assets* consist of claims held by the private economy which do not have a matching liability in the private economy. The claims involved are claims held on the government and claims held on foreigners. The reason for making this distinction is that influences on external assets will not be offset by the same influences on liabilities, since these are held outside the economy.

Since assets are a source of purchasing power for the consumer, we assume that the larger the stock of assets, the larger is consumption demand. But what is the source of a rise in claims? Claims are closely tied to output and to the tendency to sectoral imbalances in the economy. The larger the output, the larger the growth in claims. Except for real wealth and external claims, however, there is an equal rise in liabilities for every rise in claims. If liabilities depress demand by the same amount that assets raise demand, the only net effect on demand will come from real wealth and external assets. There is no certainty that in all cases matched assets and liabilities are neutral in their effects on demand, but certainly the effects of liabilities are sufficiently strong to justify treating internal claims separately. If real wealth and external claims rise along with output, we are merely saying that the economy has been able to engage in saving. If a rise in asset wealth tends to increase consumption, then we are saying that the saving of one period tends to decrease the propensity to save in future periods. This is indeed a difficult question: what does the accumulation of saving do to the future incentive to save? George Katona, a leading student of consumer behavior, believes that the desire to save is self-reinforcing:

> Psychological theory postulates that aspirations rise with accomplishment and that concrete and attainable rewards exert a positive stimulus

on action. In view of these considerations it is not necessarily true that the larger the assets, the less will consumers save (and therefore the more they will spend). Empirical studies, conducted for the purpose of testing derivations from both economic and psychological hypotheses, showed that consumers with large initial liquid assets both saved more and dissaved more than consumers with small initial assets, and that those with private pension rights saved more than those without such rights (when income, age, etc., were held constant). When families who look forward to substantial retirement benefits save more than families who look forward to small retirement benefits, they do not act "irrationally" but in accordance with specific behavioral principles: People exert a greater effort when they are close to their goal than when their goal appears hardly attainable.[2]

Although Katona's viewpoint is a defensible hypothesis regarding behavior, it would be difficult to reconcile with the general body of economic theory. Income is, in the first instance, an addition to assets. It would be rather difficult to say that a rise in income increases consumption demand while a rise in assets decreases it. Thus, despite the strength of the counterargument, the tendency still is to treat increases in assets as exercising a positive stimulus on consumer demand. Wealth enables its holder at times to be a dissaver, reducing society's net saving. As in the case of the retired, wealth enables its holders to become perpetual dissavers. Although some may be saving more for retirement because their goal is within reach, those who have retired will be spending. In the aggregate it does not seem unreasonable to attribute to wealth a positive influence on consumption.

We have looked at the growth of claims through saving—the result of the economy's accumulating capital and of its lending a part of current production to the government and to foreigners. The second way by which the growth of assets may come about is through a revaluation of existing claims in terms of their command over current production. Claims are expressed in money terms, and thus a change in their value can occur through either a change in their money value or a change in the goods value of money. If prices of goods rise in terms of money, then the goods value of a given amount of money will fall. We must thus look at both the price level and the money value of the asset to determine its real value in terms of present goods. A rise in the price level reduces the real value of claims but not of real wealth, and thus the rise affects only the internal and external claims in our classification of assets. Again we can assume that the asset and liability effects of internal claims are offsetting, but the fall

[2] "On the Function of Behavioral Theory and Behavioral Research in Economics," *American Economic Review*, Vol. 58 (March 1968), pp. 147–148.

in value of the external claims will tend to reduce consumption. The rising price level has reduced the value of accumulated savings. A falling price level increases the value of external claims and thus works to increase consumption demand.

Price changes may set off other forces, however, which are more important influences on consumption than these asset effects. A changing price level almost inevitably affects expectations of consumers regarding future prices. If the price rise is expected to continue, the rise itself may induce consumption on the basis that a purchase now will be cheaper than a purchase deferred. This is a way in which a rising price level is self-reinforcing. Others may feel the necessity to reduce their purchases in the face of rising prices so as to have more money to finance the increased outlays that will be necessary. If a rising price level is expected to be reversed, it may discourage purchases by consumers who expect to wait out the higher-price period. Because of the above possibilities, there is no clear way to analyze the effects of price changes on consumption demand.

Changes in the money value of claims arise from changes in interest rates. The money value of a claim at any one time is, to its holder, the price at which it can be sold for money. At its origination a bond or other loan contract states the amount of money which its holder will receive at the expiration of the loan period. If the holder wishes to realize value on the bond prior to that date, he must sell it to someone else. Such transactions lead to the determination of current prices on bonds, and holders of bonds use such market prices in judging the money value of their own bonds.

A rise in the rate of interest on new loans decreases prices of outstanding bonds and new bonds. A falling rate of interest is associated with rising bond prices. On the basis of asset prices we can assume that falling interest rates stimulate consumption demand and rising interest rates work in the other direction. This is something of a return to the pre-Keynesian view, but does not place complete reliance on interest rates in the consumption-saving decision. As with other influences on consumption aside from income, we can say interest rates may cause a shift in the schedule of consumption-income relationships.

Aside from the effects through prices of existing assets, interest rates may work directly to affect the incentive to save. The larger the interest rate, the greater is the reward for saving. On the other hand, if the saver is seeking a fixed sum in the future, as in retirement accumulation, the larger interest rate allows for the accumulation of this sum with a smaller amount of initial saving.

ASSET LIQUIDITY

The previous classification of claims—real, external, and internal—sought to isolate those claims which were net of liabilities. Another classification looks at the liquidity of the claim, meaning the readiness with which the holder can convert the claim to current output. This classification is closely related to the interest rate effect, since in general the more liquid an asset is the less sensitive it is to changes in bond prices.

The most liquid asset is money, which by definition the community always accepts in payment for goods. Claims, such as savings deposits, which are readily converted to money at a fixed amount, are probably the next most liquid. Short-term bonds are more liquid than long-term bonds, which are more liquid than land. A change in the composition of assets, even if the total is unchanged, can affect demand. A rise in liquid assets relative to illiquid tends to stimulate demand. The effect of liquidity on demand would clearly seem to be true for external claims, and in using this classification we can no longer assume that internal claims are neutralizing. A significant way by which the liquidity of internal claims may rise is through financial intermediation. If a bank buys bonds issued by a company, it pays for the bonds by issuing deposits to the seller of the bonds. The public now holds money whereas it formerly held bonds. The corporation has not increased the liquidity of its liability. It is true that the bank has increased its liquid liabilities, but by the nature of its operation it need not assume that this liquid claim will be exercised. The essence of financial intermediation involves the issuance of liquid liabilities and the acquisition of less liquid claims. These claims are often of such a nature that the holder can redeem them without fluctuations in price. Financial intermediation serves to increase the liquidity of the economy and to insulate certain claim holders from fluctuations in the prices of their assets. The institutions experience fluctuations in their asset prices, but over time they can earn a net difference between rates paid on liabilities and earnings on assets. Since their calculations assume certain asset-price fluctuations, such short-run fluctuations do not necessarily influence their economic behavior. Because of intermediation the persons who make consumption decisions are not necessarily the groups which hold variable price assets. Instead they hold insurance claims, fixed-value retirement plans, and savings accounts in financial institutions. The institutions in turn hold bonds, mortgages, and loans.

The most liquid of the asset classification—money—has histori-

cally received the most attention in economic analysis. Money includes, as a minimum, assets directly used as a medium of exchange,
which at the present time consists of currency claims on the government and bank deposits which are transferable by check. Some
economists view the quantity of money as the most important
influence on consumer demand. Consumers have some desired
relationship between their money balances and their annual expenditures. This demand for money, as a function of expenditures, is
relatively stable. Short-run fluctuations in the ratio of money to
expenditures may occur, where some income changes may be
considered transient, but over the long run the money stock exerts a
causal influence over expenditures. The theory includes nonconsumer
expenditures, but the most significant effect quantitatively is on
consumption.

If there is a desired relationship between the quantity of money
and expenditures, then a type of money multiplier is operative.

$$\text{Expenditures} = \frac{\text{Money stock } M}{\text{Desired money-to-expenditures ratio } M/Y}$$

$$= M \times \frac{1}{M/Y}$$

As with the investment multiplier described earlier, there is no
clear way to test this hypothesis empirically. The money demand
function is assumed to be an *ex ante*, behavioral function to describe
the way that a particular income level is reached. When we look at an
actual money to income ratio we do not know if there was a cause-
effect relationship or if the relationship which prevailed was an
equilibrium one.

The observed ratio of money to income has fluctuated cyclically
and has shown long-run drifts both upward and downward. This
would be inconsistent with a rather naïve version of the theory,
which holds an assumed constant ratio of desired money balances to
income. Contemporary versions of the theory assume that the desired
ratio will be different at different levels of income per capita, and that
the public has a long-run concept of income which differs from the
actual, observed income in any one period.

With respect to per capita income, it is assumed that the desired
ratio will rise with rises in income. By this interpretation money is
considered a luxury-good type of asset; the larger is per capita income,
the greater the desire to hold money. The theory also allows for
occasional fundamental changes in the desired ratio, as in the last two
decades, when confidence in future income has caused the public to
reduce its precautionary balances.

With respect to the long-run concept of income, the public is assumed to regard "permanent" income differently from actual income. If there is a rise in actual income, permanent income will rise by less, on the assumption that the rise is partly transient. The observed money-to-income ratio may thus fall, even though the public is in equilibrium with respect to its ratio of money to permanent income. This explains why the observed money-to-income ratio tends to fall in the expansion phase of the business cycle and rise in the recession phase.

Example of Money–Expenditure Equilibrium

Money stock $M = 125$

Money demand $= 1/4$ of annual expenditures, Y

$$Y = \frac{M}{1/4}$$

Equilibrium $Y = \frac{125}{1/4} = 500$

CONSUMER BORROWING

Increased availability of borrowing for consumption can have the effect of increasing consumption demand if the borrowing of one group does not have the effect of decreasing the consumption function of another group. Consumer borrowing is a means by which those who desire saving can increase their assets without the need for an equal amount of investment. The dissaving of one group is the means of saving of the other group. The amount of investment required to support a given income level is less as a result of the dissaving.

An important means by which savers have been able to take claims on dissavers is through financial intermediation. Savers are willing to hold increased claims on banks, and banks in turn hold claims on consumers. Sales finance companies issue bonds held by savers, and in turn the companies lend to consumers. There is no reason to believe these facilities have necessarily increased desired saving out of income. If this is true, the consumption demand of dissavers has risen but the consumption demand of savers has not fallen.

To show the possible effects of consumer credit we can contrast demand before and after its availability, assuming perhaps that a financial institution intervenes. Before consumer credit, only investment expenditures are possible on a deficit basis. All savers run surpluses on business enterprises which are investing. With consumer credit, an additional form of deficit spending becomes possible. The excess of consumption over income of one group will give rise to an excess of income over consumption in the other group, taken in the form of claims on the financial institution. This analysis merely states what a tendency might be with the imposition of consumer credit, but the actual result will depend upon circumstances at the time. If the economy is already fully employed, then a true increase in output is ruled out by definition, and there are many possibilities for the resulting redistribution of output that might follow. In the long run we can say, however, that it appears that the possibilities of demand falling below full employment output are less with consumer credit than without it. Although in some periods the running of consumer deficits might reduce business deficits for investment, in the long run investment demand too is stimulated, since the demand for investment goods is derived from the demand for consumer goods which it produces.

It is also probable that consumer credit causes some shift in the composition of demand. Larger outlays, especially for durable household goods, are more susceptible to credit purchases; thus demand for automobiles, say, may have risen, causing a fall in the demand for public-type transportation services.

SUMMARY

Assets and income determine the ability of consumers to make consumption expenditures. Keynesian theory holds that consumption is functionally related to income, and that income is determined by nonconsumption expenditures. If only consumption and investment are considered, then expenditures are equal to investment divided by one minus the desired consumption-to-income ratio. An alternative expression is investment divided by the desired saving ratio. Total income is a multiple of investment expenditures because of the induced consumption effect of investment income.

The economy's net assets (not matched by liabilities) consist of real wealth and claims held on the government and foreigners. These assets grow as a result of saving out of output. The larger the stock of such assets, the less the incentive to engage in further saving. The value of these claims fluctuates inversely with the rate of interest. The asset effect of a rise in the rate of interest is to discourage consumption, and a fall in the rate of interest has the opposite effects. Changes in the price level affect the value of claims in terms of present goods, but they do not affect the value of real wealth because its price also fluctuates. The goods value of claims varies inversely with the price level. The greater the liquidity of claims, the greater is the effect on consumption demand. Financial intermediaries increase the liquidity of claims. Money is the most liquid of claims, and some economists hold that the quantity of money, rather than total claims or income, exerts the principal effect on demand. If spenders desire a stable relationship between money holdings and annual expenditures, then a change in the money stock will tend to cause a proportionate change in spending. Consumer borrowing through financial intermediaries tends to increase total consumption demand if it provides an outlet for saving of some groups in the economy without increasing the proportion of income which they wish to save.

The consumption-income relationship is the most widely used approach in economic analysis. It recognizes, however, that the desired proportion of consumption to income may shift, and that changes in assets are an important influence that may cause such a shift.

SELECTED REFERENCES

Burk, Marguerite, *Consumption Economics*. New York: Wiley, 1968.
Duesenberry, James, *Income, Saving and the Theory of Consumer Behavior*. New York: Oxford U. P., 1949.
Friedman, Milton, *A Theory of the Consumption Function*. Princeton, N.J.: Princeton U. P., 1957.
Goldsmith, Raymond, *A Study of Savings in the United States*, Vol. I. Princeton, N.J.: Princeton U. P., 1955.
Katona, George, *The Mass-Consumption Society*. New York: McGraw-Hill, 1964.
Suits, Dan, "The Determinants of Consumer Expenditures," *Impacts of Monetary Policy*. Englewood Cliffs, N.J.: Prentice-Hall, 1963.

DISCUSSION QUESTIONS

1. Explain the route by which a rise in investment affects income.
2. "The multiplier works for reductions as well as increases in income." Explain.
3. If saving and investing are always equal, why does a rise in the saving function not lead to a multiple rise in income?
4. How will the ratio of consumption to actual income behave when all of the following conditions are present. (a) income is rising, (b) permanent income rises less than actual income, and (c) desired consumption to permanent income is constant.

5. How will redistribution of income toward greater equality tend to affect aggregate consumption out of income?

6. Will a rise in per capita assets tend to affect consumption in the same way as a proportionate rise in both assets and population?

7. How will expectations of rising prices affect the consumption function?

8. If money creation causes additional consumption, what is the effect on income? On the consumption-income ratio?

5

Investment and Rates of Return

A country's total income accrues to the factors of production which create its output. The income to capital is in two forms, interest and profit, and it is the expectation of return that motivates capital accumulation. This chapter considers interest and profit and their relation to demand for capital goods.

Interest represents the excess of repayment over borrowing in a loan contract, and it is customary to arrange the contract in money amounts rather than real goods. Parties to the contract agree on the amount of interest when arranging the loan. The government may designate that claims constitute "legal tender," which means that the borrower can always discharge his debts in this form. Normally legal tender is the money of the government, but in most cases lenders are willing to accept bank deposits in settlement of debt.

Total return to capital is the excess of the value of output of capital during its life over the amount of capital. It is convenient to consider this return too in terms of the money value of output, but the concept is real rather than monetary. Capital requires the utilization of real resources for its creation. A capital good is beneficial to society only if it returns an output with a value in excess of the resources it costs. The capital and its output are necessarily two different economic goods, and thus to compare them it is convenient to convert the two goods to their values to society as determined in the market. A house is capital and its output is living accommodations. It is difficult and not too meaningful to compare one to the other without converting to a common unit of measure. It is useful to remember, however, that the capital and output are two distinct goods, though this is often obscure when the output is an intangible service, as in the case of housing.

Interest and total return to capital are not equal, and the difference is profit. The separation of interest and profit comes about in the following way. A lender possesses claim to current product, which he transfers to the borrower. The borrower uses the claim to acquire capital, which generates a surplus. From this surplus the borrower pays interest, and the remainder is his profit. Interest is contractual and involves no risk (other than default of the obligation) to the borrower. Total return is an estimate, since it involves assumptions about the uncertain future. The difference between total return and interest—profit—is the reward for risk-taking, and the risk-taker is known as the *entrepreneur.* Even if the entrepreneur acquires capital with his own saving (excess of his production over consumption), the total return still consists of profit and interest— the interest which he could otherwise have received by making his saving available to others.

Some economic theorists have used the term *normal profit* in the same way that interest has been used here. It is the return on capital necessary for its continued employment. Any return above this amount is an unpredictable bounty. Profit is the result of uncertainty and would not exist in a static economy without growth or change. In distinguishing between profit and interest it may be instructive to note that in a world of perfect competition profit, as defined here, would not exist. In perfect competition the factors of production are perfectly mobile. If any firm earned profit, it would be earning a higher rate of return on capital than other firms. This differential would necessarily attract capital to the industry until the abnormal return is eliminated. Profit means that the price of a good exceeds its true cost, where cost includes an interest return on capital, and in competition this higher price could not exist.

Frank H. Knight (b. 1885) described the above theory in the following terms:

> The primary attribute of competition, universally recognized and evident at a glance, is the "tendency" to eliminate profit or loss, and bring the value of economic goods to equality with their cost. Or, since costs are in the large identical with the distributive shares other than profit, we may express the same principle by saying that the tendency is toward a remainderless distribution of products among the agencies contributing to their production. But in actual society, cost and value only "tend" to equality; it is only by an occasional accident that they are precisely equal in fact; they are usually separated by a margin of "profit," positive or negative.[1]

The entrepreneur who receives profit may be an individual or a corporation. The corporation may borrow for investment or may save on behalf of its owner-shareholders as it "retains earnings," i.e., fails to make available to them all of its income for a given period.

[1] *Risk, Uncertainty and Profit* (New York: Harper, 1921), pp. 18–19.

Although the surplus of capital is the source of interest for a large portion of loan contracts, it is not the only way by which interest payments may arise. In other words, the business sector is not the only deficit sector in the economy. Some households consume in excess of income by borrowing from surplus households in the economy. When these borrowers repay interest, they are transferring a portion of their income from current production to the lender. This receipt of interest is not true income from current production, since the wage or other payment from which it arose was the true income component of production. The interest, as well as the principal repayment, is merely a transfer of this income. Governments, too, pay interest, but since the government does not create product, its interest payments must come from current production elsewhere in the economy. Recipients of current income transfer a portion of it to the government—through taxes or loans—and the government uses the transfer to pay interest. Interest, as a return to a factor of production, arises only from business borrowing, and it is this interest which the present chapter considers.

MEANS OF MEASUREMENT

Capital produces goods over its life, and borrowers arrange loans for definite time periods or perpetuity. Time is a necessary function in considering interest or return on capital, and the unit of measure in common use is the year. The measurement compares one value to another—capital to its annual output or lending to interest—in the form of a ratio. Thus both interest and profit are in percent per annum. Since the entrepreneur compares interest with return on capital, it is necessary to express the two on comparable bases. The exposition of the measurement which follows is for general understanding and consequently does not discuss refined measures.

Interest is the excess of the amount repaid over the amount lent (principal), converted to an annual basis. The principal may vary over the life of the loan, as in the case where the contract calls for scheduled repayments over a period of time. It is thus necessary to consider the average annual amount of the loan outstanding rather than the total sum lent in computing the ratio of interest to loan. The payment of the interest portion of the contract also may occur in uneven amounts over the life of the loan. Thus percent interest is roughly:

$$\frac{\text{Average annual interest payment}}{\text{Average annual principal outstanding}} \times 100$$

Interest Example

Terms of contract: 2400 pesos to be repaid in 24 monthly install-
ments of 100 pesos each, plus 10 pesos interest per month.

$$\frac{\text{Average annual interest}}{\text{Average annual principal*}} = \frac{120}{1200} \times 100 = 10\% \text{ per annum interest}$$

*2400 pesos is outstanding the first month, but by the 24th month only
100 pesos is outstanding. The average amount outstanding over the period is
about one-half, or 1200.

The expected return on capital involves an estimate of the net
output of the capital as a percent of the average outstanding value of
the capital. The actual return on existing capital may provide a starting point, but it is the expected return on capital to be installed
which actually motivates the investment decision. Thus the entrepreneur considers expected increments of output associated with increments of capital, a concept known as the "marginal" efficiency of
capital. The entrepreneur takes the monetary cost of capital, called
its *supply price*, and compares it with the net monetary proceeds
expected over the life of the capital. A computation analogous to the
treatment of interest follows.

First, estimate the additional physical output resulting from the
capital. The basis for this estimate is the output of existing similar
capital with adjustments for changes in scale of operation. For instance, doubling textile machines in a factory may not double output
because of the effects of the changing scale of operations on the
efficiency of the total plant. The relevant concept is the marginal
one—the change in output associated with the change in capital.

Second, estimate the price at which total output will exchange in
the market. It may be necessary to lower prices of all output of the
good in question in order to dispose of the additional supplies. This
follows from the concept of *diminishing marginal utility*—the value
of additional amounts of a given good to an individual diminishes as he
acquires more of the good in question. From these price and output
estimates, calculate total revenue (price times output) expected with
and without the new capital. The computation then provides the
data for estimating the change in revenue.

Third, estimate the change in costs that the new output will
entail. These include all expenditures necessary to bring forth the
output (such as labor, raw materials, fuel, etc.) as well as the cost

of the capital good (since the excess over cost is the return). Do not include interest or profit as costs, since these are forms of the return on capital, the measure sought. (Remember, however, that the wages of management are labor costs, not profit.) Again, it is necessary to employ the marginal concept in making the estimates. It is not sufficient, for example, to multiply current wage rates times new labor needed, since it may be necessary to raise wage rates for all laborers in order to attract the new labor. The marginal wage costs per unit of output may thus be higher than existing unit wage costs. This is the way in which the law of variable proportions manifests itself to the producer. The addition to capital increases the cost of factors which are in fixed supply.

Fourth, subtract incremental costs from incremental revenue to derive the net revenue from the addition of capital. It is this surplus that is comparable to interest. Divide this surplus by the number of years of life of the capital to determine the annual average.

Fifth, determine the average annual value of the capital. If the capital wears out (depreciates in value) uniformly over its life, the average value will be about one-half the purchase price. This adjustment is necessary because the capital earns back its cost over its life, rather than in a lump sum at the end, similar to scheduled loan repayments.

Sixth, divide the average annual net revenue by the average annual value of the capital, and multiply by 100. The result is the percent per annum expected return from employment of the additional capital.

The above exposition assumes uniform distribution over time of the revenue from the capital and of the capital depreciation. Refined techniques are necessary for less rigorous assumptions, but the purpose here is only to illustrate the general nature of return on capital and its comparability to interest.

As the entrepreneur views the investment possibilities facing him, he sees that the larger the investment he undertakes, the smaller will be the marginal rate of return. If we plotted on a graph the expected rate of return on the vertical axis and the possible investment on the horizontal, the curve would slope downward as the amount of investment increases. The sum of all producers' expectations would have a similar shape and would yield for us the expected rates of return at each investment level for the economy as a whole. This is called the *marginal efficiency of capital schedule*, showing for each increment of capital (investment) the expected return.

Any schedule other than a downward-sloping schedule would seem unreasonable for the economy as a whole. An upward-sloping

---

Marginal Efficiency of Capital Example

A machine costs 100,000 francs and will last 10 years.

Expected gross revenue: 300,000 francs
Expected costs, including 100,000 franc purchase price:
200,000 francs
Expected net revenue: 100,000 francs
Average annual net revenue: 10,000 francs
Average value of machine, assuming uniform depreciation over time:
50,000 francs
Rate of return:

$$\frac{10,000}{50,000} \times 100 = 20\%$$

---

schedule would mean that the greater the amount of capital in the economy, the higher its rate of return. It would mean, for example, that if we tripled the number of power generators in the economy we would more than triple the monetary value of the output of electrical power. Given the laws of diminishing marginal utility and variable proportions (diminishing returns), this would surely be unlikely.

Remember that the downward-sloping schedule does not refer to the demand for capital goods. Obviously the demand for capital goods is not going to rise as the rate of return falls. The schedule looks at given amounts of investment and the reates of return that would be associated with each.

INVESTMENT DEMAND

Given their expected rates of return, entrepreneurs will compare the return with prevailing interest rates. As long as expected rates of return exceed interest rates, there will be an inducement to investment. It is the relation, then, between the marginal efficiency of capital and interest rates that determines the inducement to investment. As investment continues, the rates of return fall as we move along the marginal efficiency of capital schedule. At the same time, as we shall see later, the act of investment tends to raise interest rates. The two forces together are acting to bring interest rates and capital return together.

It is reasonable to question why entrepreneurs would invest until the point where interest rates and the rate of return are equal, since this leaves no share of total return for profit. Definitions explain part of this problem, but it also appears that the tendency for the two to go to equality is not very strong. In other words, the theory is only a rough approximation to entrepreneurial behavior.

As for definitions, the expected rate of return depends upon the manner of entrepreneurial calculation. We assume that expected sales make allowance for risk, and that the figure used is a sort of minimum possibility. If there are any sales above the minimum, then these sales are the source of profit. If only the minimum sales materialize, then the entrepreneur makes the same that he would have made by lending at interest. If he borrows, he makes enough to cover the interest payments and all costs. Remember that profit is the reward for risk-taking. If all risks materialize, there is no reason to expect profit. The method of figuring expected return makes an allowance for such risk. Profit, the residual return, is not truly calculable. If it were, there would be no reason for its existence. Return earned with reasonable certainty is more in the nature of interest than of profit.

These definitions explain why actual return on capital usually exceeds actual interest. It is not actual return that the entrepreneur considers, but anticipated return after allowance for risk.

To some extent, however, the definitions make the equality of interest rates and capital return a truism. They are true by definition because we have defined away any inequality as being the reward for risk. Nevertheless it is expectations and their effect on decisions that we are truly concerned with, and in this respect the measures do provide some basis for studying entrepreneurial behavior. Suppose, for example, that interest rates rise. If this does not change business expectations, then the marginal efficiency of capital schedule, however defined, remains as it was. All comparisons of interest rates and return, with or without risk, must consider this higher cost of borrowing or higher possible return from lending (opportunity cost). It is reasonable to think that there will be switches at the margin away from real capital demand. Entrepreneurs will forgo the least remunerative investment, causing them to either borrow less or lend more, depending upon their claim position.

The treatment of interest and profit used here will serve best for later theoretical treatment, but for some purposes one can consider interest, from the standpoint of the individual entrepreneur, as a given cost. If we treated interest like other costs, then any rise in interest is a rise in costs. The increased cost reduces expected net revenue and thus discourages capital accumulation by reducing the return on capital. It is necessary in this treatment, however, to remember the unique nature of interest costs. Unlike other costs, interest costs are built in for the duration of the loan, which is perhaps the life of the capital. Costs such as labor arise only if the capital is used. A rise in labor costs may not be a great deterrent to the installation of capital because, if product demand falls, it is not necessary to employ the labor. Not so with interest. This cost continues regardless of the level of operation of capital capacity.

Another rather unique feature of interest is its volatile nature. Observation shows that interest rates fluctuate much more than other costs, and we shall examine later the theory as to why this is so. If interest rates rise, there may be some advantage in waiting for a subsequent fall before entering into a long-term contract. Apparent small changes in interest rates have significant cost effects over long periods of time. As Paul Samuelson phrased it,

> . . . take out your sharp pencil and verify the difference it makes for a long-term decision between being able to get money, let us say, at 5 per cent rather than 7 percent. That may mean all the difference between making a profit of $2 million or a profit of $350,000 on a project; and maybe, in view of the risk, a $350,000 return is not suitable.[2]

We can relate the influence of interest rates on investment by constructing a demand schedule. Such a schedule shows the level of investment that would take place at each interest level. A hypothetical example is:

Interest	Investment (monetary value)
1%	15
2	13
3	12
4	11

This example assumes that the higher the interest rate, the less will be investment. If entrepreneurs make the kind of calculation of rate of return discussed earlier, and if they invest to the point of equality between the marginal efficiency of capital and interest rates, then the schedule of interest rates and investment will look exactly like the marginal efficiency of capital schedule. We can at least say that the investment demand schedule derives from the marginal efficiency of capital schedule, if it is not in fact identical to it. It is possible, however, that deviations between the investment return schedule and the investment demand schedule based on interest rates are in fact rather wide, even if we allow for reasonable risk in calculating ex-

2 "The Current State of the Theory of Interest Rates with Special Reference to Mortgage Rates," *Proceedings of the 1960 Conference on Saving and Residential Financing* (Chicago: U.S. Savings and Loan League, 1961).

pected return. Thus the inequality of capital return and interest rates may be more than definitional. In this case investment becomes insensitive to changes in the rate of interest.

Certainly it has been difficult to prove empirically the effect of interest on investment. The reason for this is the theoretical, subjective nature of the marginal efficiency of capital schedule. High interest rates and investment levels have often gone hand in hand, but this may be due to increased expectations (a shift in marginal efficiency expectations at all interest levels) offsetting the higher interest rates. Studies in both the United States and the United Kingdom have failed to show much observable effect of interest rate on investment, and there are some possible theoretical explanations for this. One is the increased tendency of firms in contemporary economies to rely on their own saving, rather than borrowing, as the means for acquiring capital. In this case they view interest in terms of the opportunity forgone from lending their saving, rather than an explicit cost. For these firms the act of investment consists of converting a financial asset, acquired from previous saving, to a real asset. The producing firm which accumulates saving is not, however, motivated to acquire financial claims and maximize interest income. The management of a producing firm is psychologically oriented to production and sales and to maximization of its share of the market, which makes it predisposed to accumulating real rather than financial assets.

A related explanation lies in the increased size of firms and the concentration of markets in a relatively few producers. Because of their market dominance, such firms may view demand conditions for their products with less uncertainty than a firm competing with many producers. An interest increase in such a case may not dissuade a large firm from the real investment. J. Kenneth Galbraith believes such firms often have for periods of time forgone price increases which they could have taken and increased profits.[3] He calls these forgone price increases unliquidated monopoly gains. The existence of such unliquidated gains means that the firm can increase prices if need be to meet higher interest costs.

A third factor which may minimize interest sensitivity is taxes. Businesses pay taxes only on the profit portion of total return, not the interest portion. A rise in interest costs reduces both profits and taxes, with profits falling less than they would without the tax factor. The economic effects of taxes are so far-reaching, however, that singling one aspect out for treatment is of doubtful validity. The general effect of taxes is to reduce net income to all factor returns,

---

[3] "Market Structure and Stabilization Policy," *Review of Economics and Statistics*, Vol. 39 (May 1957), pp. 124-133.

and it is difficult to conclude whether the net effect is to increase or decrease the incentive to risk taking.

PRODUCTIVITY THEORY

Most of this chapter has discussed interest and capital return as though the effects were all one way, with changes in interest causing changes in the return on capital by affecting the incentive to capital accumulation. In fact we must consider the two as being interrelated, and our next step is to examine the opposite influence—the effect of capital return on interest rates.

One theory of interest rates holds that the expected return on capital determines the interest rate. After allowance for risk, the return to a riskless financial or real asset should be the same. This theory holds that market interest rates adjust to the return on capital, rather than the other way around. At any given time the expected return on capital is the same for all foreseeable investment (changes in capital) because the size of the capital stock is large relative to amounts by which it can increase in short periods of time. The expected return is the same as the existing return. Different levels of investment would, as the entrepreneur views it, have about the same expected yield.

Frank Knight, an originator of the productivity theory of interest, summarized it as follows:

> It must be evident that if borrowing and lending of money occur in a situation where opportunity for productive investment is open, the rate of interest on loans will tend to be equal to the theoretical rate of yield on real investment. An intelligent man will not make a loan at a rate lower than he could secure by investing his capital himself—with allowance for uncertainty and for trouble and expense in the two cases; and the borrower for productive purposes will naturally not pay a higher rate than his investment is expected to yield. Finally, if loans are made for purposes other than productive investment, i.e., for consumption, competition will tend to fix the same rate on these.[4]

In this theory the only way that interest changes can occur is through changes in the productivity of capital. A change in the proportion of output allocated to capital (saving) would eventually change productivity, but the change would be slow. An increase in the saving ratio, for example, would increase the accumulation of capital relative to income. This would eventually lower the return on capital and consequently reduce interest rates. The effect would come very slowly because of the large size of past accumulations of

4 "Capital and Interest," *Encyclopaedia Britannica*, 1946. Reprinted in American Economic Association, *Readings in the Theory of Income Distribution* (Philadelphia: Blakiston, 1946), pp. 396-397.

capital relative to annual increments. The productivity theory is a long-run theory of interest and does not attempt to explain short-run aberrations. The theory is also called a *real* theory of interest, since it makes no reference to monetary effects. All saving is forgone current income and is thereby a release of output for investment. It makes no difference in what form the forgone income is represented—be it money or interest-bearing claims—it is nevertheless a release of current output in return for a claim upon future output. The financial act of lending money or holding money is of no material consequence in this real theory.

Other theories of interest, called the *monetary* theories, pay more attention to the composition of assets desired by savers. The money asset in particular plays a prominent role in the determination of interest. Chapter 6 considers the monetary approach to interest theory.

SUMMARY

Income to capital as a factor of production consists conceptually of two forms. If the owner of capital borrows the surpluses of others to acquire the capital, he pays a stipulated interest on the loan, providing the lender with a known return. Any proceeds over the amount of the loan and its interest is profit, a residual return which is the reward for risk-taking. If the capital owner does not borrow but uses his own surplus for investment, there is nevertheless an implicit interest return, since the entrepreneur could alternatively have lent the surplus.

The computation of both interest and profit is on a percent per annum of the amount lent during the year concerned, or the value of the capital for the year concerned. The marginal efficiency of capital is the estimated return, at any one time, for increments to capital. The return is estimated after allowance for risk, and is therefore the interest equivalent of expected return on capital. The potential investor compares the interest-equivalent return with existing interest rates (taken as given) in deciding the feasibility of investment. Entrepreneurs have an incentive to invest to the point where the marginal efficiency of capital and prevailing interest rates are equal. Consequently changes in interest rates will alter the inducement to invest. This is a theoretical relationship, however, and researchers have been unable to verify it by statistical observation.

The productivity theory of interest holds that the direction of causation is from the marginal efficiency of capital to interest rates. At any time the expected return on any realistic range of possible investment is taken as given by the actual productivity of past capital accumulation. Prevailing interest rates adjust to this productivity schedule.

SELECTED REFERENCES

Eisner, Robert, and R. H. Strotz, "Determinants of Business Investment," *Impacts of Monetary Policy.* Englewood Cliffs, N.J.: Prentice-Hall, 1963.

Jean, William, H., *Capital Budgeting: The Economic Evaluation of Investment Projects.* Scranton, Pa.: International Textbook, 1969.

Knight, Frank, *Risk, Uncertainty and Profit.* New York: Harper, 1921.

Meyer, J. R., and E. Kuh, *The Investment Decision.* New York: Cambridge U.P., 1957.

DISCUSSION QUESTIONS

1. Explain the theory that in a static, competitive economy profit would not exist.

2. How does a rise in interest rates affect present values of existing interest-bearing assets?

3. If interest is a part of the return to capital, why is it that a rise in interest rates will not increase the incentive to accumulate capital?

4. Why does the marginal efficiency of capital schedule slope downward and to the right?

5. Why does the rate of interest and the marginal efficiency of capital tend toward equality?

6. Explain the difficulties involved in observing the effects of interest rate changes on capital formation.

7. How do rises in labor costs and in capital costs differ in their effects on entrepreneurial decisions regarding investment?

8. Why are consumer and government interest payments not considered a part of true income, as is business interest?

6

The Theory of Interest

In a simple economy an individual can hold wealth only in the form of goods. In a credit economy he may hold it also in the form of claims on others. These claims may be in a form that is usable at any moment—in the form of money—or in a deferred form as a loan. The existence of these alternatives means that an individual who has more money than he feels a need for at any time can convert it to a deferred claim. It is not necessary that he convert it to goods. The incentive to convert money to loans depends upon the rate of interest, and the determination of the rate of interest for the economy as a whole depends upon the relative supply and demand for money.

Monetary theories of interest employ supply-and-demand analysis similar to the determination of prices in a commodity market. For each commodity there is a schedule of amounts that producers would supply at various prices and a schedule of amounts that the market would buy at various prices. The equilibrium price is the one at which supply equals demand.

The monetary theory of interest to be employed here sets up a supply and demand for money as functions of the interest rate on loans, but there are some differences from the commodity market analysis. Price, on the vertical axis, is in percent rather than dollars per unit. This is because interest payments are a function of both the amount borrowed and the time of borrowing, and interest as a rate takes care of both of these variables. The interest rate in question is a rather generalized concept of the relation which the economy establishes between present and future values. Certain market rates of interest exemplify this relation. Market rates vary greatly, according to such characteristics as the risk of particular loans, and thus it is better to think of the interest rate in question as an average of market rates. The theory developed here is applicable to the general level of interest rates as a whole but does not attempt to explain variations in individual rates.

The quantity of money demanded and supplied is on the horizontal axis in the graphical analysis of market equilibrium, but it is not at all like quantities in a commodity market analysis. The quantity of money refers to the total stock of money at any time, not to the flow into a market. Money is defined as demand deposits and currency. The rate of interest does not refer to the price of the stock of money in question, because money, to its holder, bears no interest.[1] The theory therefore relates the supply and demand for money to the price of something else—loan assets—which are far larger in amount than money itself. It is quite important to remember that the supply and demand for money does not refer to the supply and demand for lending. It refers to the stock of money in the economy relative to the economy's need for money.

Like any market theory of prices, the theory looks at the market situation at a moment in time to describe the various forces that converge to set the equilibrium interest rate. We are looking at these forces in the *ex ante* sense, realizing that *ex post* supply and demand are always equal. The theory says it is the rate of interest that effects this equilibrium. That rate of interest itself may bring forth forces which change the underlying demand and supply curves, but these forces presumably change more slowly than the rate of interest. The things in particular that we must hold fixed while analyzing interest-rate equilibrium are total income, prices, and the amount of assets outstanding.

The necessity of holding these variables fixed emphasizes the static, short-period nature of the analysis. The aggregate economic situation is a dynamic one, and we can justify static assumptions only on grounds that we are trying to look at one variable at a time. Static assumptions also hold in commodity price theory, but they are not so serious there because any one commodity may not exert a profound influence on the whole of the economy. In analyzing the potato market, for instance, it is not unreasonable to assume that the price of potatoes will not seriously affect income and thereby affect the supply-and-demand curves. We do not make this assumption with respect to interest rates. The cost of borrowing is indeed a pervasive influence in the economy. We are only saying that in the market period analyzed income, price and asset expectations are held stable, but that does not rule out a feedback mechanism by which these variables would respond to interest rates in a future period.

In viewing supply-demand equilibrium we take the supply of

---

[1] The accuracy of this statement depends upon the definition of money employed. For beginning analysis it is better to exclude interest-bearing claims as a matter of definition.

money as a given factor. It is not functionally related to interest rates. This assumption follows from the role of the government as money supplier. Money consists of a transferable claim on the government or a transferable claim on the banking system. The government issues one of the claims and regulates the amount of money deposits which the banks can issue. Government money and deposits are interconvertible, but the government can compensate for any rise in one by an offsetting fall in the other. Consequently the total money supply is a government decision. It is not a decision which is part of the market forces, and is therefore exogenous, or outside the market.

The economy's demand for a stock of money is inversely related to the rate of interest. The lower are interest rates, the larger is the public's desire for the readily usable claim, money. There are a number of reasons why the demand for money behaves in this way.

Assets. Money is a component of the total assets of the economy. Although it pays no explicit rate of return, its holding yields utility in the form of ability to make purchases readily. Holders of assets can be expected to keep some portion of their assets in the form of money. Money is in fact used in the sale and purchase of other assets, and this factor alone might cause some positive relation to exist between the size of assets and the demand for money.

The total value of assets falls as interest rates rise, and vice versa. The present value of an asset is in a rough sense its future value (amount to be repaid at maturity and amount of scheduled interest payments) less whatever amount is necessary to yield a given rate of return. A rise in interest rates means that the present or market value of the asset falls. Consequently any money demand based upon the total value of assets will vary inversely with the rate of interest. Although we can hypothesize this as the general nature of the relation that prevails, there is some doubt as to how strong this effect is. Where the economy is accustomed to interest-rate fluctuations, it may not attempt to adjust its portfolio in the short run to changes in the market value of assets.

Payments Effect. A principal motive for holding money is to have a claim which can be used to make payments. This is the medium-of-exchange function of money, and its most important reason for being. Since the amount of expenditures (or income) is taken as given, we assume no change in this transactions demand for money in the short run as a result of changes in the volume of expenditures. However, even with a given volume of expenditures the economy does not necessarily require a given volume of money. This is because an individual does not have to acquire money holdings until just the instant before he makes a money payment. The greater the interest rate the greater the incentive to postpone the actual acquisition of money until necessary. The spender can hold interest-bearing assets until the time of the scheduled money payment, provided the interest return exceeds the fees involved in the sale and purchase of assets. For this reason the average money balances demanded over a period of time to make scheduled payments will vary inversely with the rate of interest.

Effect of Interest on Transactions Balances

Assumptions: An individual receives on the average $2,000 on the first of the month and makes a $2,000 payment at the end of the month.

Transactions cost of placing $2,000 in an interest asset: $10.

At 6% per annum, interest earning will equal transactions cost:

$$\$2,000 \times .06 \times 1/12 = \$10$$

A rise in interest rates above 6% will eliminate this transaction demand for money except for the brief period before and after its conversion to an interest asset.

Speculative Effect. Since money and interest-bearing assets are alternative forms of holding wealth for the individual, the decision as to which of these assets to hold depends upon one's assessment as to the future values of each. If money is desired in addition to its need for transactions, then it is serving a store-of-wealth function—a function which other assets can also hold. Why, then, hold money, which yields no rate of return? The answer to that question is that the present value of interest-bearing claims fluctuates along with the current rate of interest. For this reason interest-bearing claims fluctuate in their money values, whereas money itself does not. If one expects that the prices of assets will fall in the future, then he is better off to hold money. If he expects them to rise, he is better off to hold assets. The higher interest rates are now the greater is the possibility they will fall in the future, and if they do, asset prices will rise. Consequently, at high interest rates the public prefers to hold interest assets—its demand for money is low. The speculative demand for money varies inversely with the rate of interest.

Relation Between Interest Rates and Bond Prices

Assumption: A bond will mature in 2 years at £2,000 and it provides for no intervening interest payments.

If the interest rate is 8% per annum, the present price of the bond is.

$$\frac{£2,000}{(1.08)^2} = £1,715$$

If the interest rate falls to 6%,

$$\frac{£2,000}{(1.06)^2} = £1,780$$

The general relation is

$$\text{Present price} = \frac{\text{Future payments}}{(1 + \text{interest rate})^n}$$

where n is the years lapsing before future payment. Payment of interest at periodic time intervals and payment of the bond at maturity are in effect separate transactions.

There is an intermediate position which can be taken, if one expects interest rates to rise, and that is to hold fixed-value interest-bearing claims on financial institutions. This possibility reduces the magnitude of the speculative demand for money, but does not negate it. For one thing, this type of asset merely shifts the speculative decision to the financial institution, and it is the institution which then must decide between bonds and money. Another factor that limits to some extent the importance of this type of asset is that it is unavailable in large amounts. An institution cannot accept single, large deposits, pay interest on them, and allow them to be withdrawn at will. The institution counts on stability of deposits by having a multiplicity of smaller depositors. There is no doubt that fixed-value interest-bearing assets have had an important influence in the demand for money, but the point is that they have not completely negated the speculative demand.

The speculative demand arises only from the decision between money and interest-bearing assets. Other types of speculation, such as in the stock market or land, are not a factor. Suppose, for example, that someone expects a land price slump and wishes to be able to buy land when it occurs. He will need assets to trade for the land, but he does not have to hold money. He can hold bonds unless he thinks their price will fall, but in making this decision he is within the framework of the speculative demand. By definition the speculative demand is entirely a function of interest rates and nothing else.

The speculative demand is the most unstable of the money-holding motives discussed. Anything that influences expectations about the future of interest rates can shift the demand curve. Since governmental policy determines the supply of money, the public looks upon the government as an important influence on interest rates, and any governmental move that indicates a change in interest-rate policy will influence the speculative demand.

With a given demand curve for money in relation to interest rates, the interest rate that prevails is then determined by the amount of money which governmental policy allows. A rise in the money stock will tend to lower interest rates, and a fall will tend to raise them. Starting from an equilibrium position, a rise in the money stock creates an excess of money over the amount demanded at the prevailing interest rate. Those holding money will begin lending it out. As they lend they drive up the price of loan assets, forcing down the rate of interest. Their lending does not change the amount of money in existence; it merely passes from lender to borrower. The thing that does change is the rate of interest. As the rate of interest falls, the demand for money rises (moving along the demand function) until equilibrium is restored.

The governmental policy which changes the supply of money will also affect the speculative demand. The rise in money supply signals the government's desire for low interest rates. Expecting lower interest rates, the public will tend to shift into interest-bearing assets and out of money. This reduction in demand reinforces the effect of the increase in supply.

CHANGES IN INCOME

Influences other than interest rates on the demand for money must be shown through a shift in the demand curve. One such influence is output, or income. In a market economy, output enters the expenditures stream and money is the medium for effecting expenditures, giving rise to the transactions demand for money. There are many expenditures in the economy other than those for currently produced output, but national income is used as an indicator of the total transactions demand for money. It is assumed that a rise in national income will be associated with a roughly proportionate rise in other transactions, including trade in existing assets. We can say then that the transactions demand for money is positively related to national income and negatively related to the rate of interest.

It is because of the feedback effect on income that any change in the equilibrium interest rate—caused by a change in demand or supply—is not a permanent equilibrium. To illustrate, we start with a rise in the money stock, which lowers interest rates. As interest rates fall, the lower cost of borrowing encourages investment expenditures, and the higher market price of assets stimulates consumption expenditures. As income rises, the demand for money rises. It may rise to the point where interest rates return to their old level. In this case the whole of the effect of the rise in the money stock has been on income, but the route by which it occurs is the variation in interest rates. Money demand may not rise sufficiently to restore the old interest rate. In this case the effect of the larger money stock is a combination of a rise in expenditures and a fall in the rate of interest.

Since income and the rate of interest are both powerful influences on the demand for money, there are many combinations of the two which are compatible with equilibrium between money demand and money supply. The same demand for money can come from (a) a low rate of interest and a low national income level, or (b) a high rate of interest and a high national income level. All such combinations are shown in the dotted line in Fig. 6-1. In this curve we look at the direction of causation from income to interest rates. With a given money stock, the higher the income level the higher will be the rate of interest. We do not know which income level will result until we know the relation with the other direction of causation, the effect of interest rates on income. The lower the interest rate the greater will be consumption and investment demand. This relationship is shown on the solid line. The equilibrium interest rate and income level is the point of intersection of the two curves.

To show how this equilibrium comes about, let us start from a position on the solid line to the left of the equilibrium one. In this case the interest rate is too high to generate an income level sufficiently high to absorb the given supply of money. (Drop straight down from the solid line to the dotted line to find the interest rate that would absorb the money supply at that income level.) As a consequence there is an excess supply of money at that interest rate and income level. Money holders will begin lending it out, and as they do we begin moving to the right on both lines. The lending causes interest rates to fall, but as this happens product demand increases, bringing along with it money demand. We do not reach equilibrium until the two lines cross.

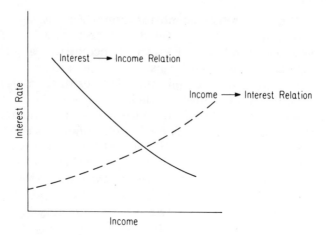

Fig. 6-1. The relationship graphed depicts the simultaneous solution of two equations with two unknowns. The solid line is the equation:

$$e \cdot r = sY$$

where e is the functional relationship of investment to the rate of interest r and s is the desired proportion of saving out of income Y. The equation derives from the necessity that investment must equal desired sY in equilibrium, and investment is negatively related to the interest rate. The broken line is the equation:

$$M = tY + g \cdot r$$

where M is the money stock, t is the transaction demand for money as a function of income, and g is the desired speculative holding of money as a negative function of the interest rate. The equation derives from the fact that in equilibrium money stock must equal money demand. The money stock and the functions in both equations are taken as given variables, and thus the only two unknowns are the rate of interest and income.

ASSET CHANGES

In the initial analysis assets, like income, were assumed fixed. It was the volume of assets—not the value—which was assumed fixed, since the value of assets is directly related to interest rates. It is difficult to quantify the meaning of "volume of assets" in an absolute sense, just as it is difficult to quantify the volume of output. We have to think of volume of assets as the physical volume of existing goods, including land, and the total volume of claims valued at, say, maturity value. Changes in interest rates change the present value of claims, but they do not change the maturity value.

Changes in the volume of assets arise from the public's saving.

This is defined as the public's accumulation of capital and accumulation of claims on foreigners and on the government. A change in the volume of assets should have the same effect on money demand as discussed earlier with respect to the valuation of assets. A rise in assets will tend to increase the demand for money as the public attempts to maintain a balanced portfolio between money and other assets.

Changes in the composition of assets will also affect the demand for money. In general we can say that a shift to assets which have characteristics similar to money will tend to reduce the demand for money. This is because of a substitution effect, as the public substitutes the other asset for money. If the shift is away from money substitutes, then the demand for money rises as the public attempts to restore liquidity by increasing money holdings.

The effect of any change in the supply of money will depend partly upon the way in which this supply affects other assets. There is a variety of ways in which the money stock can change, and their effects upon the demand for money differ.

One important way by which governments create money is to offer it in payment for their own bonds which are already outstanding. The money created is either in the form of deposit claims on the government's central bank or in the form of currency claims payable to bearer. In this kind of transaction the public changes the composition of its claims on the government. If the government bonds extinguished in the process are regarded as money substitutes, then the demand for money will rise along with the increased supply. We would not assume that the demand would rise by the full amount of the supply, since the bonds lost are not likely to be perfect substitutes for money. The shorter the maturity of the bonds, the more closely they serve as a substitute. A government's purchase of its 90-day securities has a less significant effect than its purchases of 50-year bonds.

The government may create money without reducing its bonds by using newly created money to make up the difference between an excess of its expenditures over tax receipts. Whether or not this is a net creation of the public's assets is a highly complicated matter, depending upon what would have been the course of private output in the absence of this government activity. We shall not stop here to analyze the many possibilities, but it is likely that this too would result in a shift of assets held by the public rather than a change in amount. One possibility, for example, is that capital formation will be less as more product flows to the government sector. The public's assets grow in the form of money rather than capital goods, with the result that the supply of money increases more than its demand.

Another way by which money is created is bank purchase of private securities. Generally such a purchase arises from government relaxation of the rules of money creation, allowing the banks to issue increased deposits. As the banks buy private claims, the public substitutes money for holdings of these claims. Such private securities would not likely be close substitutes for money, being such claims as business loans and consumer credit. There is not a fall in money demand compensating for the rise in money supply. Bank-created money tends to reduce interest rates by providing the public with the kind of claim it wants and the borrower with the kind of liability it wants. Liquidity but not total assets is increased.

Current monetary arrangements often merge the two effects described above. If government money acquired from bond sales to the government is deposited in banks, the banks then may create additional deposit liabilities on the basis of the newly acquired government money, which serves as reserves. The two effects are not necessarily tied, and should be analyzed separately. Newly issued government money may not be deposited, banks may not wish to expand on the basis of their new reserves, or the government may change the banks' reserve requirements so that they cannot expand.

An effect similar to bank money creation occurs when the government buys private securities. In this way the public holds a money claim on the government and in turn the government holds a claim on the private borrower. Again there is no net increase in assets but a change in their composition as the public substitutes government money for private claims.

Government monetization of private assets may also result in increased reserves for banks, allowing banks to further expand the public's money holdings. This is the effect of bank discount operations, in which banks sell some of their private assets to the government. The sale increases their holdings of reserves and thus their money expansion capability. The ultimate effect is that the public holds more money and less securities than it otherwise would.

All of these routes indicate that government changes in money will differ in their effects on interest rates according to the way that nonmonetary assets are affected. The less the money change affects assets which are close to money, the greater will be the interest effect of the money stock change.

PRICES

A higher price level raises the money value of transactions and increases the transactions demand for money at all interest rates. In this respect a change in prices enters the analysis in the same way as a change in money income. As far as the transactions demand for money is concerned, it does not matter if the change stems from a change in real output or in prices or in some combination of the two. There is another, more complex way in which price changes affect interest rates, but the analysis is rather imprecise. This effect is through the price expectations which any change in prices generates. If the price level changes (meaning a change in the average money value of all goods), the change gives rise to public expectations about future prices. The public may expect they will stay at the new level, will rise further in the future, or will fall, perhaps to the old level. Under present-day situations the most common expectation is of further rises. This kind of expectation tends to raise the speculative demand for money, and through it the rate of interest. The reason that the speculative demand for money rises is that, at every interest rate, holding bonds becomes less attractive. Interest is fixed in money terms, at the time of lending, and the real value of a given amount of money declines as prices rise. To say that the demand for money rises at all rates of interest because of the price expectation is assuming that the demand for money is functionally related to the public's concept of real interest, i.e., the value in terms of goods of the interest they will receive.

Effect of Price Expectations on Required Interest

Assumption: A loan made for $1,000 for a 5-year period, with principal and interest to be repaid in one lump sum at the end of 5 years.

At 4% per annum, the repayment would be

$$\$1,000 = \frac{X}{(1.04)^5}$$

$$X = \$1,217$$

Assume now the lender expects prices to be 10% higher at the end of 5 years and he requires a repayment that will compensate for this fall in the value of money.

Required payment is:

$$\$1,217 + (.10 \times \$1,217) = \$1,339$$

The rate of interest at this repayment is:

$$\$1,000 = \frac{\$1,339}{(1+r)^5}$$

$$r = 6\%$$

To get a real rate of return of 4%, the lender has charged a contract rate of 6%.

If the demand for money rises because of this price expectation effect, it is the potential moneylenders' way of driving a harder bargain. It is not really that they want to hold money, because the real value of money, too, will fall if prices rise. The holder does not really desire money, but it is a temporary way by which he maximizes his asset position. The speculative demand for money is always of this character.

Another way by which price changes affect interest rates is through the effect on the money value of existing real wealth. The prices of existing capital and land rise along with the prices of newly produced goods because the present value of these factors of production is derived from the expected future value of their output. A similar concept applies to labor, sometimes called "human capital." Part of a person's wealth is his own capacity to produce, and the money value of this production rises along with the price level. A rise in the money valuation of wealth will also tend to raise the demand for money, as the public attempts to maintain a balanced portfolio between real wealth and money. This effect applies only to real wealth; it does not affect claims, because they are fixed in money terms.

SAVING AND INVESTMENT

A classical approach to interest theory relates the interest rate to saving and investment. Saving tends to lower interest rates and investment tends to raise them. The equilibrium interest rate is the one at which saving and investment would be equal.

Interest rates also respond to changes in saving and investment in the monetary approach. Investment is a form of expenditure and therefore gives rise to a transactions demand for money and a tendency to increase interest rates. An independent rise in investment must be explained on the basis of an increase in the expected rate of return on investment. It is in this way that expected rate of return on capital—the important variable in nonmonetary theories of interest—enters the monetary analysis. If the expected return on capital rises, then investment will be higher at all levels of interest rates. In the interest-income graph (Fig. 6-1) the solid line, showing the causal influence of interest rates on income, is shifted to the right, and the equilibrium interest rate rises.

How does a rise in saving affect interest rates in the monetary analysis? First, we must be specific as to the meaning of the term. Do we mean a rise in actual saving or a change in the desired saving-to-income ratio? If the meaning is exclusively a rise in actual saving, then there must have been a rise in investment for this to take place. The rise in saving is a passive result of the rise in investment. The increase in investment tends to raise interest rates.

A rise in the desired saving ratio means a fall in the desired consumption-to-income ratio. This fall represents a decrease in anticipated expenditures, and thus a fall in the demand for money and in interest rates. Suppose now that there is a rise in investment expenditures and at the same time a fall in the desire to consume. Total demand and income possibly remain the same. The community has engaged in greater capital formation and has accommodated this output by consuming less. There has been an increase in desired saving offset by an increase in investment. The consumption of expenditures has changed but not the total, and thus the demand for money remains the same. The interest rate is unaffected.

LOANABLE FUNDS

An alternative monetary approach to interest theory looks at the demand and supply of lending. In the usual form the analysis applies to the flow of lending that would take place in a market period at various levels of interest rates. It assumes that the amount of lending would be greater, the higher is the rate of interest, and the amount of borrowing would be inversely related to the rate of interest. The equilibrium rate is the one at which borrowing and lending would be equal.

The previous analysis was a money-stock approach, looking at the demand and supply of money to hold. The loanable funds is a flow analysis, looking at the amount of money lending. The quantities involved are quite different. Over a period of time some money is held and never lent, while other amounts of money may be lent several times, passing from hand to hand. Despite the different ways of attacking the problem, the two monetary approaches are closely related. As interest rates affect the desire to hold money, they are necessarily affecting the desire to lend money. Generally the loanable funds and the money-stock approaches arrive at the same conclusions about the determinants of interest rates. Let us examine the loanable-funds analysis more carefully in order to compare the two theories.

First we must define the scope of the loanable-funds market under consideration. There are many alternative ways of drawing the limits, but perhaps the most important principle is consistency in the definitions for determining the elements entering supply and demand. The market used here is the net flow of new lending within a nation between households, business, and governments over a time period. We shall exclude borrowing within these sectors by netting them out. Consumer borrowing is offset by consumer saving; business saving is offset by the investment it finances or by the dissaving of some other business. The demand for loan funds then comes from the net loan demands of business and government. The lower the interest rate, the higher will be this loan demand, but we assume that most of this sensitivity comes from business borrowing. The shape of this curve is really the same as the shape of the investment demand curve.[2]

To analyze the supply of loan funds we must look at the sources of money for lending. The first possibility is that the public acquires money for lending through saving. Here we are looking only at the saving of individuals. Business saving is excluded because it is offset by business acquisition of capital. Saving then is the income of individuals less the income which is consumed and which is paid to government through taxes.

In the course of saving, individuals acquire money balances, and they may in turn pass these money balances to business or government. Saving is thus a source of possible money loans. The public may not, however, choose to lend back all of its saving. If it does not, then it is attempting to increase money holdings. This is impossible in the absence of an increase in money supply, but the attempt to do so is one of the factors influencing interest rates.

If the public does choose to increase its money balances, then it is engaging in money hoarding. It is choosing to hold money idle, rather than make it available for spending. After the fact, we measure money hoarding by relating money to expenditures. If expenditures fall and the stock of money remains the same, there has been money hoarding. If the ratio of expenditures to money rises, there has been dishoarding. The hoarding or dishoarding comes about through unwillingness or willingness to lend and therefore to make money balances available for further spending.

Saving, expenditures, and money lending are continuous processes, and yet in a supply-demand analysis we are looking at a moment in time. As market participants enter the time period in question, the facts upon which they have to make their decision are from the most recent past period, not the market period in question. Their saving expectations are therefore carried over from the previous period and are based on that period's income. It is probable that the past period's income is the biggest factor determining their

---

[2] The netting process is somewhat arbitrary. Consumer borrowing could be included, and then consumer lending must enter the supply side. Investment financed by retained earnings could be included in both demand and supply.

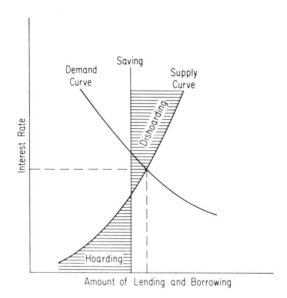

Fig. 6-2

expected saving. Will their planned saving be influenced by interest rates? Probably not. The principal motivation for saving is the reallocation of spending over one's lifetime—or other psychic satisfaction from the acquisition of assets. We assume that saving is functionally related to income, not interest rates. Therefore saving can be taken as a fixed amount, determined by yesterday's income.

Money hoarding, however, is directly related to interest rates. At low interest rates the public would prefer to take their saving in the form of money claims. Hoarding would tend to decrease the supply of lending below saving. At high interest rates the public would be willing to lend some of their previously held money balances. They would be willing through dishoarding to lend more than their saving. Because of the hoarding-dishoarding phenomenon, the total supply curve of loanable funds is positively related to the rate of interest— the higher the rate, the more will be lent.

For simplicity let us assume that taxes equal government spending and there is no government borrowing. We enter the market period with a supply-and-demand curve as in Fig. 6-2, the shaded areas representing net hoarding or dishoarding, measured in each case as the distance from the saving to the total supply curve.

The anticipated saving is based on the previous period's income. The actual supply-demand situation results in borrowing in excess of saving of the previous period, so that there is some dishoarding. This dishoarding has financed increased investment, so that income and expenditures rise. Saving, too, will be higher in the period in question and will be equal to externally financed investment. The dishoarding that took place is measured by the higher expenditures in relation to the given money stock.

A change in the public's hoarding desires is a shift in the supply of loanable funds. An increase in desired hoarding means a shift to the left, and a tendency to higher interest rates. It may seem strange that an increased desire to hold money will raise interest rates, when the holding of money bears no interest. The reason for this paradoxical result is that no new money is available, and the willingness of one person to hold must be matched by the forfeiting of money balances by someone else. It is through interest rates that the economy bids on the available money supply.

The willingness of the community as a whole to take their surpluses (saving) in the form of money can be a factor in reducing interest rates, provided new money is issued to accommodate this demand. But here we are looking not at hoarding-dishoarding, but at a different phenomenon, the supply of money. The supply of new money coming to the market at any time period is another factor influencing the total supply curve of loanable funds. Additions to money are essentially a governmental decision, and therefore we shall not try to functionally relate them to interest rates in a market sense. Any addition to money is therefore an equiproportionate shift to the right in the supply curve of loanable funds and has the tendency to lower interest rates.

An addition to the money stock is a means by which borrowers can acquire money without others having to give up money. New money increases the supply of loanable funds without affecting the demand. The bank supplies loanable funds by creating it. A similar situation occurs in the case of new money which the government issues to finance the excess of its expenditures over taxes. This excess is a part of the total demand for loanable funds, and we can assume it exists independently of the intention to create money. When the government issues new money, it provides the supply of loanable funds to meet its own demand.

Just as money creation increases the supply of loanable funds, money destruction involves an equiproportionate reduction in the supply curve. When banks reduce their deposit liabilities, they sell loan assets for money. Money payments which otherwise would be lent are paid to banks to retire loans or buy existing loan assets held by a bank. Government money destruction may involve an excess of tax payments over government expenditures. The excess then reduces the government's monetary liability. This excess of tax payment reduces the public's saving, which otherwise would flow into loanable funds.

Changes in the amount of money have the same effect as other supply factors, being no more or less powerful in their effects on the economy. As shown by the earlier example, dishoarding can also provide the means for financing a rise in investment expenditures, so that the investment of one period can exceed the saving of the previous period. A rise in the money stock allows more savers in the *ex post* sense to take their surpluses in the form of money. Dishoarding reduces the proportion of saving desired in the form of money.[3]

Having constructed the total supply and demand curve for loanable funds, we can compare the outcome of various influences through this and the money-stock analysis:

- A rise in the propensity to save increases the supply of loanable funds (based on previous period's income) and tends to lower the interest rate. In the money-stock approach the increased propensity to save is the same as a decreased propensity to consume, which lowers the transactions demand for money, and therefore the interest rate.
- An increase in money hoarding desires reduces the supply curve of loanable funds. But an increase in money hoarding is the same thing as an upward shift in the speculative demand curve for money. Through both analyses the rate of interest rises.
- An increase in investment is a shift to the right in the demand curve for loanable funds. An increase in investment also increases the transactions demand for money, by raising expenditures.
- An increase in government expenditures tends to reduce private saving by reducing the amount of product available for allocating between consumption and saving. Government expenditures also affect the transactions demand for money, and thereby interest rates.
- A change in the money stock also is a change in the supply of loanable funds, with similar interest-rate effects.
- An increase in national income increases the transactions demand for money and thereby the interest rate. In the

[3] Hoarding and dishoarding relate an asset—money—to a flow, such as expenditures or saving. In this case the asset in question is demand deposits in banks and currency claims on the government. A switch between the two, say from currency to bank deposits, is not a change in hoarding propenstities because a rise in one offsets a fall in the other. The holding of bank deposits is as much hoarding as the holding of currency. Each of these claims entered loanable funds supply when newly created; neither can reenter except as its holder passes it to someone else in the creation of a claim. Money held as a bank claim is not continually lent; to consider it so is confusing stocks and flows.

loanable-funds theory we have to be specific about the source of this increase. If an increased propensity to consume, it lowers the supply of loanable funds from saving. If an increase in investment, it raises the demand curve for loanable funds.

The debate between advocates of the two theories has been long and involved. Each theory has been modified with time to take into account challenges imposed by the opposition theory. At the present time many, though not all, economists view the two theories as alternative ways of looking at the same underlying phenomena. Generally the analysis of various economic changes will show them to have the same effect on interest rates regardless of which theory is used.

The principal difference in the theories lies in the longer-run effect of saving on the equilibrium interest rate. Under loanable funds a rise in the investment-demand curve will cause some increase in investment and some increase in the rate of interest. This rise in investment will increase income and consequently saving expectations in future periods. The saving curve tends to shift with the investment curve, limiting the long-run effect of the rise in investment on interest rates. This was the objection which Keynes raised when he formulated the money-stock approach to interest analysis. In this theory as now formulated a rise in investment increases the transactions demand for money, and thus the interest rate. This effect remains as long as the higher investment continues, and the resulting rise in interest rates tends to check the higher investment. In the loanable-funds theory saving rises with investment, and the continuation of the higher interest rates is not assured. In any one period the demand and supply curves are independently formulated, but the curves of different time periods are interconnected. The Keynesian approach seems to offer a more determinant solution to the interest rate question, and for that reason is principally employed in this book.

SUMMARY

Monetary theories of interest relate the rate of interest to the relative amounts of money available for lending and borrowing. One approach considers the total stock of money, taken as determined by the government, in relation to the demand for money. The demand for money is inversely related to the rate of interest. The higher rate of interest, the greater the opportunity cost of holding money, which bears no interest. The higher the rate of interest, the greater is the likelihood that interest rates will fall in the future and loan assets will rise in price. The latter effect gives rise to the speculative demand for money.

A change in expenditures will change the demand for money in the same direction because money is used as the transactions medium in expenditures. A change in assets will tend to change money demand in the same direction, unless the assets in question are close substitutes for money. Assets change as a result of saving, a change in the price level, or a change in interest rates. Changes in the price level affect the money value of real assets but not of financial claims. Changes in asset prices resulting from interest rate changes are part of the explanation of the inverse relation between money demand and interest rates. In addition to the effect of prices on asset values, price changes also affect money demand through their effect on price expectations. Expectations of higher prices increase the demand for money at all interest rate levels.

Analysis of the demand and supply of loanable funds provides an alternative explanation of interest rate determination. The supply schedule of loanable funds is the net effect of anticipated saving, the propensity to money hoarding-dishoarding, and money creation or destruction. Money hoarding-dishoarding, is the flow equivalent of the speculative demand for money. The loanable funds and the money stock theories generally come to the same conclusions about the short-term effect of changes in variables, such as the investment demand or the propensity to save, on the rate of interest.

SELECTED REFERENCES

American Economic Association, William Fellner and Bernard F. Haley (eds.), *Readings in the Theory of Income Distribution.* Homewood, Ill.: Irwin, 1946.

Conard, Joseph, *Introduction to the Theory of Interest.* Berkeley: U. of California Press, 1959.

Hahn, F. H., and F. P. R. Brechling (eds.), *The Theory of Interest Rates.* New York: St. Martin's, 1965.

Lutz, Friedrich, *The Theory of Interest.* Chicago: Aldine Publishing, 1967.

Shackle, G. L. S., "Recent Theories Concerning the Nature and Role of Interest," *Surveys of Economic Theory*, Vol. I. New York: St. Martin's, 1966.

DISCUSSION QUESTIONS

1. Explain the difference between the demand for money and the demand for loanable funds.

2. Why is the stock of money assumed not to be a function of interest rates?

3. Why is the holding of money for stock market speculation not considered part of the speculative demand for money?

4. How might each of the following affect interest rates:
   (a) increased expectation of rising prices
   (b) a fall in the stock of money
   (c) a rise in national income

5. Explain why the curve in Fig. 6-1, showing the interest-to-income relationship, slopes downward and to the right. Explain why the income-to-interest line slopes upward.

6. Show the effect on interest rates of an increased desire to hoard money, using (a) the money supply-demand approach and (b) the loanable-funds approach.

7. If the government buys bonds with newly created money, how is the demand for money affected? How are the demand and supply of bonds affected?

7

Asset Differentiation

The monetary theory of interest in its pure form considers two assets—money and long-term bonds. The interest rate on bonds is a function of the demand and supply of money, or alternatively of the demand and supply of bonds. This simplified model requires considerable modification in a system of many types of claims of varying degrees of liquidity. Liquidity is the readiness with which the holder of a claim can convert it to real goods. Money is by definition usable in exchange at any moment and is thus the most liquid asset. Long-term claims are the least liquid. In between these extremes the variety of claims allows for a gradual progression from money to illiquid claims. The British economist R. S. Sayers wrote:

> There is no clear line between purchasing power that carries no interest and interest-earning assets that carry no purchasing power. "Commercial banks" shade into industrial banks, savings banks and building societies, and these into a host of other financial intermediaries; the liabilities of these are close substitutes for each other, so that a clamping down on one group will not create such an abrupt scarcity of liquidity as will have a worthwhile impact on the pressure of total demand.[1]

A listing of some characteristics of claims will indicate the variety of assets which are common in developed economies.

Debt and Equity. If the claimant holds an asset which calls for a fixed payment in the future, it is a "debt" type of claim. The fixed amount may be an annual payment, a lump sum payment at the termination of the contract, or some combination of the two. If the claim represents a share ownership of real capital, it is equity in nature. Common stock is a form of ownership of a business corporation organized for production. The owner of stock shares in the surplus of the corporation, but has no claims to any fixed payment.

Marketable and Nonmarketable. Some borrowers, such as governments and well-known business firms, issue claims by selling them on

[1] "Monetary Thought and Monetary Policy in England," *Economic Journal*, (December 1960). Reprinted in Richard Ward (ed.), *Monetary Theory and Policy* (Scranton, Pa.: International Textbook, 1966) p. 366.

an impersonal market to the highest bidder. The holder of such a claim can normally expect to resell it at any time. Loans negotiated directly between borrower and lender may have no marketability, and the lender may be able to convert the claim to real product only at maturity.

Primary and Intermediary Claims. Primary claims arise when those who have surpluses from current production lend directly to those who have deficits. But it is also common for intermediaries (financial institutions) to borrow from surplus units and lend to deficit units. The chain of lending is thus

Ultimate borrower	Intermediary	Surplus lender
Debt →	Claim deposit liability →	Deposit

Fixed Maturity and Optional Maturity. Most primary claims specify the time at which the lender must repay. Some intermediaries issue claims in which the lender can require repayment of the full maturity value on very short notice or almost on demand. Thus for the holder of the claim there is no fluctuation in the current conversion value of the claim.

Short-Term and Long-Term. Even when the maturity is fixed, the length of terms of loans varies widely. Banks in the United States lend reserves to each other on an overnight basis. At the other extreme some governments issue perpetual bonds, i.e., no fixed maturity date. The value of such a claim arises from the annual fixed payment the government must make to the holder in perpetuity.

Money and Nonmoney. The money asset can be defined as one which can immediately serve the payments function. Liquid and illiquid is a closely related distinction, but the liquid classification would normally apply to a broader range of assets than demand deposits and currency.

Money claims are both primary and intermediary. When the government buys goods by issuing currency notes, it runs a deficit, i.e., acquires more goods than it receives through taxation. The recipient of the currency claim is the surplus unit in the economy. When banks issue demand deposit claims, they use the proceeds to acquire claims on others, say business firms. In this case money is an intermediary claim. The demand deposit holder has a claim on a bank and the bank has a claim on a business firm, the ultimate borrower.

A principal function of intermediaries—banks and others—is to bring together the surplus and deficit units in the economy. John Gurley and Edward Shaw, who have studied extensively the economic role of financial claims, stated:

> Intermediating techniques turn primary securities into indirect securities for the portfolios of ultimate lenders. They give lenders a wide

variety of financial assets particularly suited to their needs, and they also make it less necessary for borrowers to issue these types of securities, which are ill-adapted to their own businesses. They enable spending units to escape the strait jacket of balanced budgets and to order their spendings more efficiently.[2]

CLAIMS AND OUTPUT

In general an economy's claims will grow with its output, but there is no invariable relationship between the two. The organizational structure of the economy in the production and distribution of output is a basic determinant of claim creation. If the economy favors imbalance among its members in spending and income, claim creation will be large in relation to output. When purchasers maintain balance between their expenditures and income, claims do not arise from output. A feudal economy of self-supporting estates would have a small ratio of claims to output. The manorial baron is both saver and investor, and the farm workers can consume no more than their earnings. A democratic manufacturing society with a complex market distribution system aggregates the saving of many into large capital outlays, with growth in claims matching investment. In such economies the greater the importance of capital, as measured by the capital-output ratio, the larger will be the growth in claims relative to output. A large capital-output ratio means that investment is a large proportion of total output, since capital must grow in proportion to output. If different groups in the economy are savers and investors, as they they are likely to be, claim creation will accompany the investment.

Owners of existing capital may use the proceeds of the output of their capital as a source of some investment. In this case the same producer engages in both saving, through "retained earnings," and investing. A factor which will discourage this means of investing is a relatively fast growth rate of the economy. A fast growth rate means generally that investment is large relative to accumulated capital, and producer surpluses are less adequate to accommodate investment. The consequent reliance on external saving to accommodate the investment gives rise to increased claims.

There are some reasons for believing that the ratio of claims to income will eventually fall as an economy reaches a mature state. One cause for such a shift is the apparent tendency for production to shift to service-type industries in the mature stages of growth.[3] A

[2] *Money in a Theory of Finance* (Washington, D.C.: The Brookings Institution, 1960), p. 197. Much of the present chapter draws on this original work.
[3] See Allen G. B. Fisher, *Economic Progress and Social Security* (London: Macmillan, 1946) and Colin Clark, *Conditions of Economic Progress*, 3d ed. (London: Macmillan, 1957).

society first satisfies its primary needs, largely agricultural in nature. The secondary stage concentrates on manufacturing, the transformation of raw materials to products of greater utility. The output of tertiary industries is intangible, such as distribution and medical and educational services. Tertiary activities have a lower capital-output ratio, and because they do not give rise to durable goods, claims are less likely to accompany their production. H. T. Oshima has hypothesized that in advanced capitalism purchases of consumer-type durables increase and the capital-output ratio falls.[4] Households substitute real assets, such as automobiles and houses, for financial assets.

There is some evidence that capital-output ratios have fallen in the United States in this century. However, there are considerable problems in valuation, and the evidence is by no means conclusive.[5]

Financial intermediation is conducive to growth in claims. By offering savers the type of claim they desire, intermediaries facilitate the saving-investment process. In the absence of the intermediary claim, savers might be unwilling to accumulate financial claims, preferring instead to accumulate real goods. The effect of intermediation on claims creation is still greater if we count claims gross, which means including both the saver's claim on the intermediary, and the intermediary's claim on the ultimate borrower.

Government policy influences the growth of intermediation. If the government's share of total output grows, intermediaries are discouraged, since governments largely finance deficits directly rather than through intermediaries. Governments encourage intermediation when they limit creation of their own liability. The public then turns to the intermediaries to issue the type of claim which savers desire. Governments also encourage intermediation by providing various types of regulation and insurance which enhance the safety of the intermediary's liability.

ASSET MARKETS AND PRICES

The valuation of assets offers something of a conceptual problem in analysis of assets and output. As pointed out earlier, output gives rise to claims through the surplus-deficit relationships that accompany output. But the total of claims may also change through changes in their market prices. Fluctuations in asset values thus

[4] "Consumer Asset Formation and the Future of Capitalism," *Economic Journal*, Vol. 71 (1961) pp. 20-35.

[5] For a criticism of available measures, see Paul Anderson, "The Apparent Decline in Capital-Output Ratios," *Quarterly Journal of Economics*, Vol. 75 (November 1961) pp. 615-634.

loosen the link between output and claims. An alternative is to consider the value of claims in terms of original cost. The holder, however, views claims in terms of their current market value, and it is this valuation which influences his economic behavior. Consequently it seems that we have to accept changes in their market valuation as changes in claims outstanding. This is contrary to our treatment of income and output, where we are interested in real rather than monetary changes.

When the public attempts to alter the composition of existing claims, it is the price of claims, rather than their values, which changes. Once a claim comes into existence, it remains outstanding until maturity unless the obligor, the party responsible for fulfilling the claim, wishes to extinguish it earlier. The issuer of a 10-year bond may leave it outstanding for ten years or may extinguish it after five years by purchasing it. The holder of the bond does not have this option. True, the holder may sell a bond, but he does not extinguish it unless he sells it to the original obligor. This fact may seem trivial, but it is important in understanding that the economy's holdings of claims are not necessarily sources of claims to real goods for the economy as a whole. The holder of a claim can convert it to goods only as someone else is willing to give up goods. It is true that an individual claim holder can normally expect to convert it to goods at will (though at an indefinite price), but what is true for the individual is not true for the economy as a whole.

Since claimants as a group cannot destroy claims, it is not possible for the composition of outstanding assets to shift radically from one form to another. One often hears such statements as, "Money is moving from the bond market to the stock market." The statement would seem to imply that bond holders as a group are able to liquidate bonds and increase their holdings of stocks. The only way in which this would be possible is for business firms to issue additional shares and use the proceeds to buy their outstanding bonds. Such mass movements on the part of borrowers do not occur, and consequently statements about shifts in assets are often misleading.

Attempted shifts among assets by their holders occur regularly, but the effects of these shifts are to change their relative market prices, not the volume outstanding. If large numbers of bondholders attempt to shift to shares, the price of shares will rise and the price of bonds will fall. The market reaches equilibrium through changes in relative prices, not through changes in amounts outstanding. One group of assets cannot be regarded as a "source of funds" for another group of assets; for every seller of an asset there must be a buyer.

The primary way in which the distribution of claims changes through such attempted shifts is through the effect on new issues and through the changing valuation of existing claims. If stock prices rise and bond prices fall, there is an increase in the total valuation of stocks and a decrease in the total valuation of shares. These changes may also encourage new share issues and discourage new bond issues, thus leading to some change in the volume outstanding.

ASSETS AND INCOME

Financial intermediaries have created an increasing number of claims with characteristics similar to demand deposits. These near-money claims are of a deposit character, and their value in terms of money does not fluctuate. The chief difference between monetary and nonmonetary intermediary claims are the following. (1) Government policy in many countries regulates the volume of money claims outstanding, but not other intermediary claims. (2) The rate of interest on nonmoney claims is higher than on money claims, which in many countries pay no interest at all. (3) Money claims are transferable on order (by check), while nonmoney claims often are not. (4) Institutions often limit the size of any one holder's interest-bearing deposits and in other ways limit them to individual, as opposed to business, usage. From the standpoint of the holder, the principal advantage of the money claim is the usability as a means of payment; the principal advantage of other intermediary claims is the earning of interest without forgoing the right to redeem the asset virtually at will.

Monetary theories of interest look at the composition of assets between bonds and money; as the composition becomes more complex it is necessary to modify the monetary theories accordingly. The liquidity preference theory, in its original form, was an analysis of demand and supply for "liquidity," not necessarily money. Keynes said:

> . . . We can draw the line between "money" and "debts" at whatever point is most convenient for handling a particular problem. For example, we can treat as *money* any command over general purchasing power which the owner has not parted with for a period in excess of three months, and as *debt* what cannot be recovered for a longer period than this; or we can substitute for "three months" one month or three days or three hours or any other period; or we can exclude from *money* whatever is not legal tender on the spot.[6]

One way of revising the money approach to interest is to broaden it to a "liquidity" theory. The interest rate is a function of the demand and supply of liquid assets—money plus other assets which allow the holder to maintain a fixed-value claim. The demand for

---

[6] John Maynard Keynes, *The General Theory of Employment, Interest, and Money* (New York: Harcourt, 1936), p. 167 n.

such assets is inversely related to the rate of interest, as is money. The lower the rate of interest, the greater is the demand for fixed-value claims. The supply of such claims depends upon government policy. The government could control the supply of all such claims, but governments do not normally exercise such control. Governments do control the amount of money issue, and conceivably could determine the total of liquid assets by altering the money stock to offset changes that might occur independently in other liquid assets. Direct control of intermediary assets, if instituted, would lessen the fluctuations required in money to control the total.

Suppose now that there is an increase in demand for the total of liquid assets at all interest rates. This means that the public is attempting to shift out of nonliquid assets, thus reducing their price and raising the interest. Equilibrium will occur at a higher interest rate if the supply of liquid assets is unchanged. Alternatively, the government might allow the supply of liquid assets to rise. The rise in interest rates is considerably less because the intermediaries then buy bonds or other loan assets as they increase their deposit liabilities. Their incremental demand for assets offsets the incremental supply by those who wish to acquire deposits.

Suppose the public desires to shift from savings deposits to money deposits. If governmental policy keeps the total unchanged, then demand deposits will expand by the amount desired and savings deposits will fall. Since there is no change in the demand or supply of liquidity, interest rates do not change. Put another way, the monetary and banking system holds the same amount of securities as before the shift, and thus the demand for securities does not fall.

The reasonableness of treating all liquid assets together lies in the similarity of their characteristics. The demand deposit holder who shifts to nonmoney claims is really not forfeiting much liquidity. Consequently the act is not really an increase in his willingness to lend, i.e., to transfer purchasing power to others. If he had shifted the demand deposit to bonds, he would then have forfeited liquidity for the duration of the bond, an act which fundamentally alters the availability of purchasing power to those who wish to run deficit income positions.

The principal difficulty with the liquidity approach is the assumption that government policy determines total liquid assets. There is some advantage in retaining the monetary analysis of interest rates if government policy largely concerns itself with money control as opposed to liquidity control. If we return to analysis of the demand and supply of money, we must recognize the effects of liquid assets on the demand for money. Since these assets serve much of the function of money, we assume that they reduce the demand

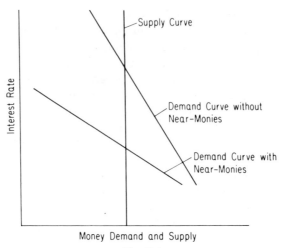

Money Demand and Supply

Fig. 7-1

for money. In general we can say the greater the availability of such assets, the less will be the demand for money.

Let us illustrate with two demand curves for money—one assuming money is the only truly liquid asset and the other that liquid near-monies are available (Fig. 7-1).

The demand curve is both lower with the near-monies and more elastic, i.e., more responsive to interest changes. A small change in interest rates will reduce the demand for money by causing the public to shift to near-money assets which are only slightly less liquid than money.

Suppose now that the public decides to shift from bonds to savings deposits. This entails no change in money demand or supply and is neutral on the interest rate, provided the expansion in saving deposits can take place. If the government reduces the money supply as a result of the expansion, the interest rate rises. In the liquidity analysis we would have said that the shift out of bonds was an increase in the demand for liquidity, with a resulting rise in interest rates. Supply does not increase with demand since, by hypothesis, demand deposits contract to offset increases in savings deposits.

The choice of a method of analysis largely depends upon the manner in which the government exercises control. The liquidity analysis does have the advantage of looking directly at movements in a wider range of assets as a causal factor in interest changes. In many countries, however, the money analysis may be closer to the way that the government actually formulates policy. Either analysis requires a judgment about the nature of particular assets in the country concerned, but the liquidity analysis recognizes this more explicitly.

DEPOSIT RATES

In both the money and the liquidity analyses of interest rates we have hypothesized certain relations between interest rates and supply-demand on the assumption of other things fixed, such as income and prices. One of the things assumed fixed is the rate of interest on the asset in question—money in the monetary analysis and deposit-type assets in the liquidity analysis. For example, we have assumed that as the interest rate rises, the demand for liquid assets falls, where the interest rate in question is the rate on non-liquid debt, bonds. If the rate on liquid assets also rises, then there is no necessary reason why the demand for them should fall. Let us call the liquid-asset rate the deposit rate, since deposits are the principal type of assets we have included in the analysis. The necessity to consider the deposit rate arises largely from near-money deposits, but in some countries the demand deposit component of money also carries interest, and it is possible that the practice will become more widespread in time.

Monetary theories of interest are a short-run, *ex ante* type of analysis, and for this reason it is not unreasonable to work with an assumed fixed deposit rate. Financial institutions have found it impractical, or at least unnecessary, to alter deposit rates on a day-by-day or week-to-week basis. Even if they were able to do so, however, we can make certain hypotheses about the nature of the deposit rates which will allow us to incorporate them in monetary interest theories.

Let us take the case of the demand for liquid assets, or for money if we admit demand deposit interest rates. With a fixed deposit rate the demand for deposits fall as the rate of interest on bonds rises because the spread between deposit rates and bond rates widens. Suppose now that we allow for the possibility that the deposit rate also rises. In this case the demand for deposits falls only if the deposit rate rises less than the bond rate. Our hypothesis is that the deposit rate does rise less, for the following reason. A rising bond rate applies only to new loans (bond sales), not to those outstanding. Deposit rates, however, necessarily apply to the total of deposits. (If they did not, depositors would redeem "old" ones and buy "new" ones.) Institutions, however, will earn the higher bond rate only on new loans, and thus cannot increase proportionately the rate on total deposits. Graphically we can depict the effect on the demand curve in Fig. 7-2.

We can also use the hypothesis for considering a supply curve which shows some response to interest rates. Let us assume a government policy which fixes the supply of currency and demand deposits

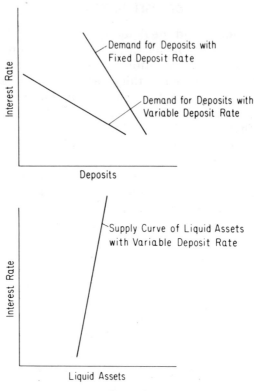

Fig. 7-2

but does not fix other deposits. Under these conditions the higher the bond rate the greater will be the willingness of deposit institutions to sell claims against themselves. To do so the institutions offer higher and higher deposit rates on these claims. The supply curve of liquid assets thus looks as in Fig. 7-2. The amount of deposit assets shown at zero interest rate represents the stock of such assets already existing prior to the market period under consideration. Even at zero interest on new loans, the institutions still maintain their existing deposits, which sustain loans already negotiated. In addition government money issues are a fixed amount regardless of interest rates. The stock of existing assets is a legacy left over from the past. At anything other than zero interest on new loans, there is an incentive to supply additional deposit claims.

As this analysis shows, the deposit rate itself is of some importance in determining the ultimate bond rate. It is for this reason that some economists advocate government control of deposit rates. In many countries demand deposit interest does not exist, by bank agreements or legal directive, and other deposit rates are subject to ceilings. The existence of such control forestalls financial institutions from increasing the supply of deposits. If the government is trying to raise bond interest rates, control of the deposit rate is one way of preventing institutions from raising supplies of deposits. On the other hand, the failure of deposit rates to rise with bond rates reduces demand for existing deposits, a factor which works against interest increases. It is obvious that control of deposit rates may make government interest policy more powerful, but it surely does not make it any less complex.

TERM STRUCTURE

In the monetary and liquidity theories of interest the principal determinant of demand for liquid assets was expectations about future interest rates. If the public expects interest rates to rise, they prefer to hold assets in a form that will not fall in value. As they attempt to acquire such assets, they reduce their demand for bonds, and the interest rate adjusts until there is equilibrium between demand and supply of liquid assets.

This same expectations phenomenon offers an explanation for the differences in interest rates that are found at any one time on securities of different maturity periods. These differences make up the term structure, or maturity structure, of interest rates. The structure shows the per annum yield to maturity on bonds of various terms, say one to thirty years, facing a bond buyer at any one time. The expectations theory holds that it is the relative strengths of lender and borrower expectations about the timing of future interest rate changes that determines any existing yield structure.

Let us first look at the theory from the standpoint of the individual and then consider the economy as a whole. The person who decides that interest rates will rise in the future has a number of opportunities open to him. If he expects the rise to come within a short period of time, he will prefer to hold money balances until the rise occurs. If the rise does come, he incurs no loss on his liquid claims and can convert them to the high-yielding bonds. Suppose, however, that he expects the rise to come in about one year. In this case he may buy a one-year security, allowing him to earn some interest while awaiting the higher rates. He would not buy a long-term bond, since he expects its price to fall well before the bond matures.

The lender has been willing to forgo some, but not much, liquidity, in moving from idle balances. The timidity of his move from idle balances has led him to exert a downward influence on relatively liquid securities but not directly on the long-term, illiquid securities.

In the final analysis it is liquidity preference that explains both the bond rate and the term structure of rates.

A borrower has the same kind of considerations. If a borrower expects interest rates to fall in the future, he may be willing to pay a very high rate on one-year securities, hoping to be able to finance later on a long-term basis at a lower rate than currently prevailing on long-term lending.

The relative strengths of borrower and lender expectations about future interest rates determine the term structure. This may appear to leave the maturity structure in a chaotic state, but actually the forces have tended to work rather systematically in the United States in the absence of war and depression. When interest rates in general are relatively high, the short rate tends to exceed the long rate. Expectations of a fall increase the demand for short-term borrowing and the supply of long-term lending. For opposite reasons, when interest rates are relatively low by historical standards, short rates tend to drop below long rates.

Both short- and long-term rates enter the liquidity function in a manner shown in Fig. 7-3. In the example a 4 percent long rate and a

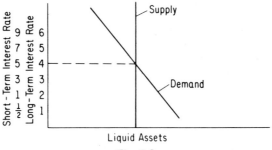

Fig. 7-3

5 percent short rate bring equilibrium between the demand and supply of liquidity. Lending and borrowing will switch between short and long until the yield structure reaches this relationship. Any given change in the equilibrium long rate, say from 4 to 5 percent, will bring a greater change in the equilibrium short rate (5 to 7 percent). The hypothetical schedule shows only the rates on two maturities for illustrative purposes, but the expectations effect is an explanation for the entire term structure.

SUMMARY

Contemporary economies create a wide variety of assets. Claims vary according to time to maturity, marketability, liquidity, and the extent of intermediation between borrower and lender. Factors conducive to claim creation are a fast growth rate of output, a large capital-to-output ratio, and the development of intermediating techniques.

Intermediary claims offer their holder a way of earning interest while retaining the option to redeem the claim. One approach to interest theory treats the interest rate as determined by the supply and demand for liquid assets—money plus other intermediary claims. An alternative method is to treat intermediary assets as a reduction in the demand for money (currency and demand deposits.) Government policy can determine the total of liquid assets by varying money to offset changes in intermediary assets.

Any increase in the deposit rate on liquid assets tends to increase the demand for them, where the demand schedule is a function of interest rates on other assets. This effect will tend to increase the interest rate on other assets unless the government also allows the supply of liquid assets to rise. The complicating effect of deposit rates on other interest rates is one reason that governments control deposit rates to some extent.

Expectations about the future timing and direction of interest-rate changes provide an explanation for different rates prevailing on securities which differ only in their terms to maturity. Short-term rates tend to exceed long-term rates when interest rates in general are relatively high. The opposite relationship holds when interest rates are low relative to their long-run normal.

SELECTED REFERENCES

Ball, R. J., *Inflation and the Theory of Money.* Chicago: Aldine Publishing, 1965.

Gurley, John G., and Edward S. Shaw, *Money in a Theory of Finance.* Washington, D.C.: Brookings Institution, 1960.

Hester, Donald, and James Tobin, *Financial Markets and Economic Activity.* New York: Wiley, 1967.

Johnson, H. G., "Monetary Theory and Policy," *Surveys of Economic Theory,* Vol. I. New York: St. Martin's, 1966.

DISCUSSION QUESTIONS

1. What role do financial intermediaries play in the economy?

2. What differences would you expect between the United States and Australia in the effect of economic growth on the growth of claims?

3. What is the effect on claim creation of an increased role of government in the economy?

4. How does the availability of near-money assets affect the demand for money? The supply of money?

5. State the arguments for government control of the rate of interest paid on savings deposits.

6. Suppose short-term rates exceed long-term rates. How can this relationship be explained theoretically?

8

Prices

In modern economic systems the prices of goods are expressed in terms of their money values. Though relative prices are the means by which economies guide the allocation of resources, it is somewhat paradoxial that it makes no difference what the price *level* is. The economy is indifferent to its price level, the average money values of all goods traded. One price level will serve the economy just as well as another.

A means of illustrating the neutrality of price is an imaginary doubling of all prices and a doubling of the money values of all outstanding claims. The doubled price doubles everyone's cost, but at the same time it doubles incomes, since all payments give rise to equivalent receipts. The doubling of claim values leaves the holders unaffected in command over present goods, and the obligation of debtors is unchanged in terms of present goods. When prices, income, and assets all change proportionately, no one is better or worse off.

The effects of a price rise will differ in accord with whether or not it is anticipated. If it is not anticipated, it will not be reflected in interest rates, with the result that real interest is lowered if prices rise, and in some cases may even be negative. Similar considerations are involved in rental contracts, and even in wage contracts if their duration is very long. Widespread expectations of rising prices have on occasion brought forth special clauses in contracts to adjust the terms in accord with any rise in prices, sometimes called "escalation" clauses or "index" clauses. Such clauses became widespread in the Finnish price advances of the mid-1960's, and were estimated to be contained at one time in one-half of the outstanding bonds in the country.

The uneven incidence of price changes is likely to result in those with the strongest economic bargaining power gaining in periods of price rises. Some studies have shown in the United States that the postwar rise in prices was regressive, in the sense that those in the lower-income classes suffered a decline in their net worth (real value of assets minus liabilities), while the upper-income classes gained.[1] This negative redistribution of wealth is perhaps the greatest cost to society of unstable prices. One of the means of stopping price rises is higher rates of taxation (to reduce aggregate demand), and rates can be set to avoid unwanted redistributions.

Although any price level will do as well as another, *changes* in the price level do indeed have important economic consequences. The reason for this is that, unlike the assumptions of our imaginary doubling, changes in prices do not affect everyone the same way. For one thing, price and income changes are not generally uniformly distributed. Some prices are more sensitive to change than others. Some types of income are more sensitive than others. Wages of nonproduction workers, for example, tend to change less readily than profits. In a period of rising prices profits will rise relative to these wages and there is a redistribution of income. The goods value of profits is higher and the goods value of wages lower.

Another reason that price changes involve a redistribution of wealth is that claims outstanding are fixed in money values. We applied our imaginary doubling to claim values, but in an actual situation of price changes they would remain fixed in money terms. With a rise in prices the goods value of claims falls. The lender may actually get back less than he lent unless the interest rate is sufficiently high to compensate. Losses involved in holding claims (including money) in the case of price rises make it difficult for the price rise to be contained. If the public expects further increases, they choose to hold real goods rather then claims. In the course of acquiring goods they bid up their prices, tending to reinforce the initial situation.

MEASURING PRICES

Because the price level per se is inconsequential, we do not attempt an absolute measure of prices in the aggregate. It would be possible to take a collection of goods and express the money value of the goods, but the resulting figure would have little meaning in an absolute sense. Employment of the bundle of goods becomes more useful, however, if we measure changes in its prices, rather than the price level, and express the figures in terms of *index numbers*.

An index number measures one quantity as a percent of another

[1] These results are summarized by Martin Bronfenbrenner and F. D. Holzman, "A Survey of Inflation Theory," *Surveys of Economic Theory*, Vol. I (New York: St. Martin's, 1966), pp. 94-100.

quantity. We take a collection of goods and aggregate their value in monetary units at any one time. At a later time we aggregate the monetary value of this same collection in terms of the prices then prevailing. Let us assume that the aggregate in the first period is valued at 2 million krona and in the second period at 2.1 million. The index number is then $\frac{2.1}{2.0}$, or 105. (The sign (%) percent is implied when the number is expressed as an index.) This means that prices in the latter period are 105 percent of their value in the base period, or that they have risen by 5 percent.

Note that we have taken a specific collection of goods from the economy and priced them in two different periods. We cannot infer that goods not included have risen by the same percent, or even that each good in the collection has risen the same as the average. If we are to attempt to make this figure representative of the economy as a whole, we must be careful to take a sample of goods which is characteristic of those traded in the economy. We must also be careful in choosing the quantity of each of the goods we put in the sample, and again we must make the quantity representative of the quantities which the economy actually purchases. In calculating price changes the quantities must be kept the same throughout the periods of comparison. Otherwise the change in total money value of the collection between two time periods would consist of changes in both quantity and price, and we would not have a true measure of price change.

One serious problem in observing price movements is changes in the composition of purchases. If the collection of goods is representative of the economy's purchases in the first period, it may not be representative in the second period, since demand may shift between periods. There is no real solution to this problem, which is inherent in intertemporal comparisons. If the time periods are not far distant, say from one year to the next, the distortion involved in keeping relative quantities fixed is probably not great. The greater the time span, the less meaningful the index number comparisons become. There is no meaningful way to compare prices now with those prevailing in World War I; the goods traded now are not the same goods as those traded then.

The relative importance given to each good in the index is called its "weight." In computing the index each price is expressed as a ratio to the price in the base year. But it is not reasonable to sum these prices and divide by the number of prices, because by this procedure each price would contribute equal weight to the average index. The practice is to assign weights based upon the proportion of total expenditures which the good in question accounts for in some given time period. The price index for that good is then weighted by the proportion it accounts for in total spending. When the prices of all goods are computed, then the weights necessarily add to 100 percent.

	(1) Price Change from Base Year, Percent	(2) Price Index	(3) Weight*	Column 2 X Column 3
Category of Good				
Transpor- tation	5	1.05	.10	.105
Food	3	1.03	.20	.206
Housing	2	1.02	.20	.204
Household durables	4	1.04	.10	.104
Other	1	1.01	.40	.404
		Totals	1.00	1.023†

Weighting of Hypothetical Price Index

*Proportion of expenditures of this category to total expenditures in a given period of time.
†Ratio of current prices to prices in the base year.

The term *inflation* normally refers to a rise in the price index. Whether or not an inflation exists depends upon the severity of the rise and the span of time over which increases are occurring, but there is no general agreement as to what magnitudes constitute inflation. In the past three decades the general course of price movements throughout the world has been upward, and we have come to think of some degree of inflation as being the expected course of events. Economists even refer to aggregate price theory as the theory of inflation. The term *deflation* is not used exclusively to refer to a fall in prices, which seldom occurs. Deflation, or a deflationary economy, may refer to the presence of unemployed resources in the economy, whether or not price decreases occur.

MONEY ILLUSION

A rise in prices is the same thing as a fall in the value of the monetary unit in terms of goods. If the monetary unit is worth 1 in the base period and prices rise 5 percent, then in the latter period it becomes worth 1/1.05, or .952, in terms of its base year value. Economists use the term "money illusion" to refer to economic behavior which overlooks changes in the value of money in making decisions involving money. J. M. Keynes believed that labor exhibited such behavior: "Whilst workers will usually resist a reduction of money wages, it is not their practice to withdraw their labor whenever there is a rise in the price of wage-goods."[2] A person who holds goods or land which rise in price may consider he has made a nice speculative gain. But if this gain is the result of a general price rise, the money he gets is worth less than the money he originally used to buy the goods. The gain turns out to be illusory, except in the relative sense that if he had held money, instead of goods, the money would have actually fallen in value.

Those who consider the interest rate a true measure of the return on an asset suffer from money illusion if prices are changing. The money used to acquire the asset may have greater value than the money received under the fixed amount repayment terms. The real rate of return must make allowance for the rising price level.

An extreme form of money illusion occurs when money income for the society as a whole is taken to be synonymous with real income. This type of money illusion is associated with military expenditures, especially when they assume wartime proportions. War production reduces real income because it diverts resources that would otherwise flow to economic satisfaction. But because the initial expenditure by government results in money income to the public, such expenditures receive the undeserved reputation of "lifting the economy." Concern over real income, as opposed to money income, would destroy this money illusion.

PRICE THEORY

Because prices are important in a relative sense only, there is no way of specifying what the price *level* of the economy should be. One price level can result in equilibrium just as well as another. Suppose we had an economy in which we knew the total volume of physical output, the propensity to consume out of output, the real rate of return on capital, and all other real variables. We still could not determine the price level. If we added financial assets, including money, as known variables, we then would have something on which to hang a price level, but these financial assets, expressed in the monetary unit, cannot be taken as independent of the price level. At

[2] *The General Theory of Employment, Interest and Money* (New York: Harcourt, 1936).

the time of creation the money value of the assets arose directly from the price level than prevailing.

Although we cannot specify an equilibrium price level in the abstract, we can analyze forces leading to price changes. In any period there is some price level inherited from the past, and there are some outstanding claims which resulted from previous price levels. Changes in economic variables may require changes in the price level to restore equilibrium. Economists have not settled on any one approach to the analysis, but generally it centers on the relation between aggregate demand and the economy's capacity to produce. The problem is necessarily one of dynamic equilibrium. As Gardner Ackley has stated:

> . . . We define inflation as *rising prices*, not as "high" prices. In some sense, then, inflation is a disequilibrium state; it must be analyzed dynamically rather than with the tools of statics. . . . As with other parts of dynamic analysis, the study of rates of inflation is both complex and relatively underdeveloped.[3]

The theory relates the rate of change of prices to the rate of change of other variables in the economy. One important variable is the rate of change of aggregate supply. Through growth in the size of the labor force and capital and through growth in productivity, there is ordinarily some rise in the capacity to produce over time. Second, consider the growth rate in aggregate demand, which consists of consumption, government, business, and foreign demand. As a starting point we assume that the change in prices is the result of the relationship of these two growth rates. If the growth in aggregate demand exceeds the growth rate in potential output, then a price rise is the result. In an *ex post* sense, this is definitionally true. If total expenditures grow at 6 percent, but output grows only at 4 percent, then prices must have risen approximately 2 percent. The theory says somewhat more than this. It takes potential output growth as a given factor, and states that the inflation can be explained by the excess demand growth rate.

How about the case in which growth in demand is less than the growth in supply? Here we are not so inclined to believe that the result will be falling prices, for contemporary economies display tendencies toward downward price rigidity. Firms tend to curtail output rather than reduce prices to dispose of output. They are willing to operate at excess capacity because they believe that this is in their long-run interest. In industries dominated by a few sellers—and this seems to be increasingly the case—a fall in prices is seen as futile because the few other firms in the industry will do the same thing.

[3] *Macroeconomic Theory* (New York: Macmillan, 1961) pp. 421-422.

Labor, too seems to have a downward rigidity in wages. Trade unions may not insist on wage rises during periods of deficient demand, but they are unwilling to accept cuts. Consequently an excess of growth in capacity output over growth in demand may result more in price stability rather than actual decreases.

The aggregate price theory as outlined is known as a *demand-pull theory of secular inflation.* It asserts that the tendency to price rises has occured as a result of the excess growth of demand over supply. Prices rise during periods of excess demand growth, but they do not fall during periods of excess growth of output potential over demand. Consequently over the long run there is a tendency toward secular inflation—a persistent upward drift in prices.

Experience indicates, however, that even the maintenance of balanced growth between demand and supply will not assure a stable price level. There have been periods in which total expenditures did not grow at the rate of total output, and still prices have risen. This behavior is consistent with an explanation called *cost-push inflation.*

Each participant in the economy attempts to increase the share of output which he receives. The business sector seeks to increase the spread of earnings over cost; labor attempts to increases its wages. Other groups, such as farmers or pensioners, are also included in the theory. Increases in wages, profits, or other compensation will result in real gains to the recipients, provided the prices which they pay for their own purchases remain stable. Individually any one producer—business or labor—is not concerned about the effect of his own return on total prices, but each case of attempted price rise tends to increase the general price level. The result of these individual efforts is that aggregate prices rise, and the gain that was sought does not actually materialize. Increased prices offset increased money income. Even the realization of this does not stop the attempted gains; then it becomes necessary to get the larger money return just to keep from falling behind.

Some theorists place principal reliance upon cost as the determining factor, with aggregate demand playing a distinctly minor role. In this view prices in contemporary capitalist systems do not emerge from the interplay in the market of supply and demand, but instead are fixed by the corporate producers on the basis of a markup to assure normal profits. Sensitivity to demand implies price instability, and this is incompatible with the necessity for long-run planning in a complex industrial organization. John Kenneth Galbraith has interpreted the business view as follows:

> Price competition with its attendant dangers must be prevented. Prices must be low enough to facilitate the recruitment of customers and the

expansion of sales and at the same time high enough to provide earnings
to finance growth and keep the stockholders content.[4]

In this framework increases in prices must largely originate with
rises in labor costs. Other economists believe that both cost-push and
demand-pull are important in inflation. The belief is that the continuation of relatively strong demand is necessary for cost-push to be
operative, but demand does not have to rise at a faster rate than
output. It merely has to be permissively strong.

In the past three decades the economy's participants have come
to count on continuance of strong total demand, and this attitude
results at least partly from political commitments to maintain employment at high levels. In this climate cost push can be operative
even if demand is growing at a rate no greater than output growth.

Another approach to the explanation of inflation says that comparison of aggregate supply-and-demand growth masks underlying
tendencies that may be causing price movements. Let us take a case
of balanced growth in which excess demand in one sector is offset by
sluggish demand elsewhere. In the buoyant sector prices tend to rise
because of the difficulty of transferring resources from the sectors
where demand is weak. Labor is not easily retrained, and capital
often cannot serve multiple purposes. Although prices in one sector
rise, downward rigidity in other sectors cause these prices at first to
remain stable. Then the higher prices from the expanding sector
bring forth demands for higher wages throughout the economy.

We have here a variety of approaches to the explanation of price
movements, and they are not necessarily inconsistent. The principal
force causing a price movement may vary at different times, and only
through an analysis of the circumstances of a particular inflation can
this force be estimated. None of these theories is necessarily applicable as a prediction of persistent price change in the absence of
special assumptions. The theory of secular inflation, as noted, hypothesizes that there will be periods of excess demand and rising
prices, with intermittent periods of relative price stability. Though
this seems to fit the facts of recent years, conditions could easily
change. One possible factor which could cause such change is a rapid
rise in the rate of potential output growth.

Technological advance increases the productivity of labor and
lowers the real cost of a given output of goods. The decrease in real
cost could result in lower money cost if it were not for increases in
money returns to the factors of production. In some cases in which
technological advance has been great, such as telephonic communica-
tion, there have been some decreases in prices. With rapid advances in
automation it is not inconceivable that productivity advances could

---

[4] *The New Industrial State* (Boston: Houghton Mifflin, 1967), p. 189.

eventually bring persistently falling prices. Rising money returns or falling goods price are alternative ways in which the benefits of productivity accrue to the factors of production. If rising money returns are the route, then productivity gains tend to accrue to those in the strongest bargaining position—highly organized labor and monopolistic industrial owners. If falling prices are the route, the benefits are initially more widely diffused.

MONEY AND PRICES

The theory of prices which compares growth rates of demand and supply can alternatively be expressed as the growth of money expenditures relative to the growth in output. Since the stock of money is used in making money expenditures, it might be hypothesized that there is a close relation between the amount of money in the economy and the amount of money expenditures. If this hypothesis is true, then we can narrow our theoretical focus to the relation between the growth of money and goods rather than money expenditures and goods. This approach—which has a centuries-old history—is called the *quantity theory of money*. According to this theory, prices (which are denominated in units of money) are the result of the relation between the number of units of money in the economy relative to units of output.

The quantity of money and money expenditures are not synonymous. A given amount of money can be held idle during a period, it can be used frequently, or it can be used little. Money and its use (called its *velocity*) are related definitionally:

$$\frac{\text{Velocity}}{\text{during a period}} = \frac{\text{Money expenditures during the period}}{\text{Quantity of money outstanding over the period}}$$

It follows then that money times its velocity equals money expenditures. The quantity theory of money assumes some stability in the velocity of money.

The quantity theory holds that the demand for goods, as represented by money expenditures, stands in some constant relationship to the amount of money. Goods demand cannot rise and fall of its own accord, because this would imply changes in the relationship of expenditures and money. Rises in prices are the result of increases in demand caused by increases in money. Demand-pull theories start with the increases in demand, without assigning a causal connection with changes in money.

To illustrate the operation of the quantity theory, we hypothesize a doubling of the quantity of money, leaving other variables unchanged. If the economy was in equilibrium with its old level of money holdings, it is no longer in equilibrium with the doubled amount of money. Money holders will then proceed to spend, but this does not reduce the amount of money; it merely changes hands. The spending increases demand and prices, and the economy will not return to equilibrium until it has doubled the value of goods, or output.

It is important to note that it is not the quantity of money per se that determines prices, but the quantity in relation to the output of goods. A rising quantity of money does not mean a rising price level under this theory unless it exceeds the rise in output. According to Milton Friedman:

> There is perhaps no empirical regularity among economic phenomena that is based so much on evidence from so wide a range of circumstances as the connection between substantial changes in the stock of money and in the level of prices. To the best of my knowledge there is no instance in which a substantial change in the stock of money per unit of output has occurred without a substantial change in the level of prices in the same direction. Conversely, I know of no instance in which there has been a substantial change in the level of prices without a substantial change in the stock of money per unit of output in the same direction.[5]

The quantity theory is really a theory of the demand for money, and it hypothesizes that the demand for money bears a stable relation to the volume of expenditures. If the volume of money rises, expenditures rise. If the output of goods upon which expenditures are made is unchanged, then the rise in expenditures means a rise in prices. In equation form we can say

$$\underset{\text{Demand for money}}{M_d} = \underset{\text{Given function}}{F_m} \times \underset{\text{Expenditures}}{Y}$$

and

$$\underset{\text{Expenditures}}{Y} = \underset{\text{Prices}}{P} \times \underset{\text{Output}}{O}$$

If the money stock and the money demand functions are taken to be the given variables, and money demand equals money supply M;

$$PO = \frac{M}{F_m}$$

[5] From a statement to the Joint Economic Committee, U.S. Congress, 1958. Reprinted in Edwin Dean (ed.), *The Controversy over the Quantity Theory of Money* (Boston: Health, 1965), pp. 89-90.

When output is given, then

$$P = \frac{M}{F_m\,O}$$

This equation says that the price level is directly related to the quantity of money and inversely related to the quantity of output and the demand for money.

The crucial assumption is the stability of money demand relative to expenditures. The theory does not in fact state that it is an absolute constant, but that it displays a long-run tendency to stability. Contemporary quantity theorists hold that the demand for money, in fact, rises more than proportionately to income (or expenditures). In this case a rise in the money stock will increase expenditures, but less than proportionately.

The quantity theory is not necessarily inconsistent with the other explanations of price movements which have been discussed, but special assumptions are sometimes necessary to make the theories compatible. Let us compare theories, starting with the case in which demand for goods grows at a greater rate than potential output. The quantity theory would deny that this could happen for any prolonged period of time except as a rise in the money stock takes place. If the money stock did not rise, then a rise in expenditures would necessarily mean a fall in the ratio of money to expenditures. Some would say the economy could tolerate this—that money demand is not a stable function of expenditures—whereas the quantity theorist would consider this a disequilibrium situation if the rise in expenditures were long continued.

In the case of cost-push inflation the rise in prices with output stable would necessarily mean a rise in aggregate expenditures. With an unchanged money stock, the money/expenditures ratio would fall. The quantity theory would deny that this could happen except as a transitory situation. Cost push becomes valid only if there is an accommodating rise in the money stock. We can then no longer distinguish between a rise in the money stock or a cost push as the causal factor.

MONETARY POLICY

The strict quantity theory of money indicates a direct relation between the money supply and prices. The influence of monetary policy can also be shown even if the strict version is not accepted.

The quantity theorist says changes in money directly influence desired expenditures and thereby prices, depending upon changes in real output. The alternative way by which monetary policy is explained is through interest rates. Monetary policy changes interest rates and changes in interest rates may in turn affect demand and thereby prices. In this explanation monetary policy has a tendency to increase or decrease prices, but only indirectly.

Those who reject the quantity theory contend that money does not necessarily lead to spending. An increase in the money supply may lead instead to more lending and a fall in the rate of interest. Through the lower interest rate the demand for money increases, and the *ex post* observed effect is a fall in velocity. The quantity theory holds that the demand for money rises as a result of a rise in expenditures and that the interest rate effect is not important.[6] A rise in expenditures would be necessary to restore equilibrium between money demand and money supply.

In time the interest-rate changes may spill over into the commodity market, but the results are not as certain as the quantity theory would indicate. The fall in interest rates raises the price of fixed payment claims because of the inverse relationship between claim prices and interest rates. As the prices of financial assets rise, they become relatively less attractive compared to real goods and claims on real goods in the form of corporate shares. The public then tends to acquire real capital, driving up its price and lowering its rate of return. At the same time the increase in the market price of assets may induce consumption spending. As the demand for capital and consumer goods rises, their prices will also tend to rise unless the supply of goods can rise accordingly.

The relation between money and prices is not ignored even if the quantity theory of money is rejected. The route is through the effect of the changing money stock on the growth in aggregate demand and its relationship to the growth in aggregate supply. The effect on aggregate demand comes through interest rates and asset prices rather than directly.

SUMMARY

The value of a given unit of money is the goods it will buy. Changes in the value of money are the reciprocal of the price index, which measures percent changes in the money value of goods. Failure to allow for changes in the value of money in economic behavior is called money illusion.

---

[6] "Empirical evidence suggests that interest rates have a systematic effect in the expected direction but that the effect is not large in magnitude." Milton Friedman, Statement to the Joint Economic Committee, U.S. Congress, 1958. Reprinted in Warren Smith and Ronald Teigen (eds.), *Readings in Money, National Income and Stabilization Policy* (Homewood, Ill.: Irwin, 1965), p. 84.

The economy is indifferent to its price level, but once a price level is set, changes in prices involve redistribution of wealth, since the change does not affect all economic units in the same way. The demand-pull theory of inflation holds that price rises are the result of growth in demand over growth in output potential. The cost-push theory holds that attempts by producers (including labor) to increase their individual returns leads to increased prices, even if demand does not grow faster than supply. The quantity theory of money holds that price changes are proportionate to changes in the quantity of money per unit of output.

According to the quantity theory, the economy restores equilibrium after a change in money by a change in expenditures. The alternative explanation is that interest rates restore equilibrium, but that the change in interest rates may then affect expenditures in the same direction as indicated by the quantity theory.

SELECTED REFERENCES

Ackley, Gardner, *Macroeconomic Theory.* New York: Macmillan, 1961.

Bronfenbrenner, Martin, and Franklyn D. Holzman. "A Survey of Inflation Theory," *Surveys of Economic Theory*, Vol. I. New York: St. Martin's, 1966.

Friedman, Milton (ed.), *Studies in the Quantity Theory of Money.* Chicago: U. of Chicago Press, 1956.

Patinkin, Don, *Money, Interest and Prices.* New York: Harper, 1956.

DISCUSSION QUESTIONS

1. What are some redistributions of purchasing power that might be expected in an inflationary situation?

2. It has been said that inflation is not serious as long as interest rates accommodate to the rising prices. What is the basis for this statement?

3. Stock shares are generally favored over bonds in periods of expected inflation, with consequent readjustment in the relative prices of the two. What is the reason for this preference?

4. What forces in the economy tend to prevent downward price adjustments?

5. What prices in the economy have fallen in recent years, and what is the explanation for this fall?

6. Why do some economists believe that wage increases are the principal active force in cost-push inflation?

7. What is the relation between the demand-pull theory of inflation and the quantity theory of money?

9

Dynamic Equilibrium

Economic analysis employs extensively the concept of *equilibrium*. The economic system and its components reach equilibrium through the mutual adjustment of variables such as prices and the income-consumption relationship. In a given market, for example, supply will rise with price and demand will fall with price. Equilibrium occurs only at the one price at which supply equals demand. In a similar way, the interest rate equilibrates supply and demand for money.

Many variables enter into the determination of the equilibrium level of national income. Desired saving must equal desired investment; the return on capital must equal the interest rate; money demand must equal money supply, and so on. An equilibrium condition at one time, however, does not mean that equilibrium will be continuous. The nature of the economic and social system seems to dictate a moving equilibrium. In other words, there is an equilibrium growth rate as well as an equilibrium income level at any one time.

There are at least two important factors in the economy which indicate output growth as a condition for equilibrium. One of these is population. The economist can virtually take increases in population as a given sociological factor. Increases in population mean increases in the labor force, and consequently increases in the full-employment output. The other factor disturbing static equilibrium arises from the nature of capital. We shall examine these two growth factors—population and capital—and the relation between the two.[1]

INVESTMENT AND CAPACITY

In any one time period an economy normally devotes a portion of its output to capital formation, which is the investment compo-

[1] The theories treated in this chapter originated with Sir Roy Harrod and Evsey Domar. See Harrod, *Economic Essays* (London: Macmillan, 1952), and Domar, *Essays in the Theory of Economic Growth* (New York: Oxford U.P., 1957).

nent of national income. Investment is the form in which the economy saves. Since equilibrium normally calls for some positive saving, some investment is necessary if equilibrium is to prevail. If investment is a portion of the output of a period, it necessarily follows that at the end of the period the nation's capital stock will be larger than at the beginning. Since the purpose of capital is further production, the rise in capital means that the economy's capacity to produce has increased. In this sense the increase in capital has caused a disturbance to equilibrium. If capital was just adequate to produce the output of the period, then the larger capital stock calls for a larger output if that capital is to be used. Regardless of what the output level is at any one time, if any component of it is investment, then output must rise if it is to absorb the capacity of that investment. If it does not, then the economy is in disequilibrium for it is not using its capital stock. The existence of capital, therefore, contradicts the idea of a stationary equilibrium. Equilibrium can be defined only in a moving or dynamic sense. There may be an equilibrium growth rate but not an equilibrium output level.

We can quantify the capital-growth relationship with certain hypothetical assumptions, though the reader should remember that these assumptions imply a rigidity which in fact does not prevail. The purpose is merely to illustrate underlying tendencies in the economy. Suppose that a truck hauls 150,000 ton-miles a year. If a producer expects to haul additional tonnage, he must first obtain an additional truck, which represents investment. His total output must then rise to 300,000 ton-miles, or else the capital is being underutilized. Only if he is able to utilize his investment is the entrepeneur satisfied with his investment decisions. If conditions of demand do not allow him to utilize the newly installed capital, he will not wish to install additional capital.

We can broaden this individual situation to the economy as a whole, but then we have to use the monetary valuation of output and capital in order to employ common terms. We are now aggregating the capital-output relationships desired by all producers. Since this differs for individual producers, the aggregate capital-output relationship will vary, depending upon the type of capital installed. For illustrative purposes, however, we shall assume a *desired capital-output ratio* that is relatively constant.

Suppose that entrepreneurs desire a capital-output ratio of 2:1. For entrepreneurs to be in equilibrium, the monetary value of output must be at least one-half the monetary value of the capital stock. If this desired capital-output ratio is always the same, then any addition to capital requires a subsequent addition to output of one-half this amount. We can with this formula define the equilibrium growth in output.

Let Y = output
      I = investment
      Cr = capital-output ratio desired

Then

$$\text{Change in } Y = \frac{I}{Cr}$$

The investment of one period requires that output be higher in the next. The required addition to output is investment divided by the capital-output ratio. This formula stresses the capacity creating effects of investment.

INVESTMENT AND INCOME

Investment is a source of capacity in future periods, but it is a source of income in the period produced. A simplified view of the income-generating effects of investment emerges if we make certain hypotheses about economic behavior. Again, it is not necessary that these specifications be rigidly fulfilled to confirm the underlying tendencies. Let us assume that all consumption is a functional relationship to income, and that this relationship is stable. In that case all of income is the result of the working of the investment multiplier.

$$\text{Income} = \text{Investment} \times \frac{1}{1 - \text{consumption ratio}}$$

$$= \frac{\text{Investment}}{\text{Saving ratio}}$$

$$\text{Income} \times \text{Saving ratio} = \text{Investment}$$

We now have an expression for investment which relates investment to income. Equilibrium is established by income rising to the point where saving at that income level is equal to the given investment. Let us substitute this expression for investment in the earlier formula expressing the relation between capital and income.

$$\text{Change in } Y = \frac{I}{Cr}$$

$$= \frac{sY}{Cr}$$

where s is the desired saving ratio. Dividing both sides of the equation by Y, we obtain

$$\frac{\text{Change in } Y}{Y} = \frac{s}{Cr}$$

The left-hand side of the equation is the growth rate of income. Thus we have succeeded in defining an equilibrium growth rate without reference to any actual income level. An actual income level is not necessary as long as the saving ratio and the desired capital-output ratio are specified.

A similar approach to the problem starts with asking what the equilibrium growth rate, $\dfrac{\text{change in } Y}{Y}$, is. The required change in Y is I/Cr and Y in the base period is I/s. Substituting,

$$\frac{I/Cr}{I/s} = \frac{s}{Cr}$$

The growth rate is thus directly related to the desired saving ratio and inversely related to the desired capital-output ratio. The more an economy wishes to save out of output the greater must be its growth rate to absorb the additional capacity generated by the saving. The greater the capital needed relative to output the smaller will be the growth rate required to utilize capital.

Under the assumptions of this example, there is only one source of growth in demand, and that is growth in investment. Consumption, remember, is a passive factor which responds to income. Consequently the growth rate specified for total income must also be the growth rate of investment, since income is always a constant multiple $1/s$ of investment. Investment and income must rise at the rate of s/Cr for the economy to remain in equilibrium. We call this unique rate the *warranted growth rate*.

CAPITAL-STOCK ADJUSTMENT

If the economy departs from the warranted growth rate, under the specifications of the example used here there are no forces which tend to restore equilibrium. Any departure from the growth rate creates an unstable situation. This occurs because producers attempt to adjust their capital stock to changes in output. In so doing they change output and further aggravate the maladjustment of capital stock to output. If, for example, investment grows in some period at a rate greater than the equilibrium growth rate, the resulting growth in output causes capital to be short relative to output. Producers respond by further increasing investment. But output rises still more than capital, and the attempt at capital-stock adjustment fails. Likewise, if investment falls below the equilibrium rate, the capital-stock adjustment principle will cause entrepreneurs to continue reducing investment. If the upward or downward spiral is to stop, forces other than those specified in the example must come into play.

Example of Fulfillment of Warranted Growth Rate

Desired ratio of saving to income = 0.10

Desired capital-output ratio = 2.0

Warranted growth rate = $\dfrac{0.10}{2}$ = 0.05

Output	Investment	Capital-Stock (beginning of period)	Capital-Output Ratio
100.00	10.000	200.0	2
105.00	10.500	210.0	2
110.25	11.025	220.5	2

Disequilibrium Arising from Investment Increase
in Excess of Warranted Growth Rate

100	10	200	2
110	11*	210	210/110 = 19†
150	15‡	221	221/150 = 15†

*An assumed 10% rise in investment.
†The rise in investment decreases the ratio belowed desired level.
‡Assumed acceleration of investment in an attempt to restore capital-output ratio.

Disequilibrium Arising from Investment
below Warranted Growth Rate

100	10.0	200	2.00
103	10.3*	210	2.04†
100	10.0‡	220	2.20†

*An assumed 3% rise in investment.
†Investment is inadequate to maintain level of output which achieves the desired capital-output ratio.
‡Assumed fall in investment resulting from excessive capital-output ratio.

In order to allow for the possibility of a rise in income which violates the capital-output ratio, we can assume that the ratio is not rigidly determined by technological requirements but is the desired long-run position of producers. They may have, say, some excess capacity which they desire, and in the short-run a rise in output reduces excess capacity. This reduction then motivates producers to order more capital equipment to restore productive capacity. Alternatively, if there is no excess capacity, the rise in demand causes a rise in money expenditures and income through a rise in prices rather than real output. The rise in prices improves the profit position of producers, and this too stimulates demand for more capital. It is important, then, to realize that the capital-output ratio assumed is not a constant that must always be fulfilled but is a kind of target toward which adjustment is taking place, and the economy is not in true equilibrium when it is not fulfilled.

The incentive to invest comes from the expected return on capital. Analysis of the effect of output on investment is not inconsistent with this view. Sales in the present influence expected sales in the future. If sales rise relative to existing capital, expectations of capital return rise at all levels of investment. Entrepreneurs are optimistic about the possibility of selling future output from investment. It is through the effects on expected return on capital that changes in output influence future investment incentives.

CEILINGS AND FLOORS

If an economy's growth rate exceeds the warranted growth rate, what will provide the ultimate check to its growth? It is here that we bring into the analysis the other growth referred to—*growth in the labor force*. The growth in the labor force will ultimately determine the limit of the actual growth in output which an economy will achieve. As the economy increases its actual growth rate, at some point it begins accumulating capital at a faster rate than labor increases. Diminishing returns begin to set in (the law of variable proportions). To the producer, this effect manifests itself as higher wage costs, but for the economy as a whole the problem is a shortage of labor relative to desired output. The individual producer must work his force overtime, with less efficiency and higher wage rates, or employ inefficient workers formerly not in the labor force. The rise in costs reduces the expected return on capital, and entrepreneurs lose the incentive to capital accumulation. The growth rate of investment and income falls, and the economy starts a downward spiral. The growth rate may slow down before reaching the full-employment ceiling as a result of employment shortages in particular industries. This means that immobility of labor may start the downward spiral even while there is some unemployment of labor.

Another possible limiting factor on the growth in demand is of a financial nature. Claims tend to rise along with income, but that does not mean liquid claims rise proportionately. If the government and financial institutions do not convert claims to liquid claims at a rate commensurate with output growth, a shortage of liquid assets or money tends to develop. The transactions demand for liquid assets rises with income, but the supply does not. Interest rates tend to rise, with a resulting drag on investment. This can be expressed in terms of a fall in the desired capital-output ratio, so that despite the rise in output the inducement to invest declines.

Eventually as income continues to rise, the desired savings ratio will likely change in a manner which will limit the growth in output. At higher incomes we can theorize that the public will want to save a larger proportion of income. This increase in desired saving reduces the multiplier effect of investment and thus reduces the incentive to further investment.

One reason the saving propensity may rise is through a shift in income distribution. In a period of rapid expansion, profits are likely to rise relative to wages, particularly if rising prices tend to limit the real income of workers (the purchasing power of their money income). If there is such a wage lag, owners of capital tend to receive a relatively larger share of total output. Large income increases the capacity of corporations to save through retained earnings, with a consequent tendency for saving as a proportion of total income to rise.[2]

There are three main reasons why the actual growth rate cannot indefinitely rise. The ultimate limit is a shortage of labor, but even before full employment, a growing propensity to save or a shortage of liquidity may tend to reduce the growth rate. If the growth rate departs from the warranted growth rate in the downward direction, there are floors to the fall analogous to the ceilings discussed above. As income recedes, consumption as a proportion of income tends to rise. The public attempts to maintain its standard of living despite falling income. Labor costs diminish as the work force rises relative to the capital stock. Money and other liquid assets may remain unchanged despite the fall in income, with a depressing effect on interest rates. Finally, some investment expenditures have little relation to current output and will not respond to the capital-stock adjustment principle. A hydroelectirc dam, for instance, may depend upon demand for electricity for the next half-century. A current period reduction in demand has little effect upon the planning for such investment.

[2] This effect was central to some older underconsumption theories of the business cycle. See W. T. Foster and W. Catchings, *Profits* (Boston: Houghton Mifflin, 1925).

The foregoing offers a possible theory for cyclical fluctuations in output. If there is any divergence between the full employment growth rate and the warranted growth rate, then the actual growth rate is likely to depart from the warranted growth rate. When it does, there is no tendency to self-correction until output hits the floor or ceiling, when it then begins to go in the opposite direction. Suppose, for example, the warranted growth rate is higher than the full-employment growth rate. Income cannot indefinitely move with the warranted growth rate, because of an inadequate labor force. When output begins the downturn, it continues to fall until it hits the floor.

The capital-stock adjustment theory as outlined has omitted at least two important influences. Sales and purchases of goods abroad influence demand, and government consumption and capital formation behave differently from that in the private sector. Later chapters will handle these sectors of the economy separately, but briefly we may say that they inhibit the functioning of the principle. Government demand can act as a stabilizing force. Government has no concern about the flow of output from its capital, and government consumption is not a function of income. Exports (sales abroad) add to demand for a country's output without increasing its capital stock.

SECULAR STAGNATION

Although we have presented equilibrium growth analysis in terms of cyclical movements, the concept is also applied to economic development. The analysis runs in terms of the relation between the natural and the warranted growth. If an economy's warranted growth rate tends chronically to exceed its natural growth rate, it is faced with secular stagnation. The reason is that its desire to save is too high. The desire to save encourages capital formation but discourages the demand necessary to absorb the output of that capital. The economy seldom achieves its warranted growth rate, and capital stock adjustment tends to work in the downward direction.

This concept of secular stagnation is the modern equivalent of an idea which has long haunted students of capitalism—the tendency to overaccumulate capital. Excessive capital accumulation and the consequent falling rate of profit were part of the mechanism which Karl Marx (1818–1883) believed would lead to the downfall of capitalism. Marx believed that labor did not receive the full worth of its output and the surplus accrued to owners of capital. The desire to reap the surpluses of labor stimulates capital accumulation. But there is a deficiency of demand for the output of the rising capital stock because the worker, who would consume, receives only a subsistence, and this deficiency of demand leads to a falling rate of profit.

The stagnation thesis associated with John Maynard Keynes assumes that as income rises, the propensity to save grows larger. At the same time the marginal efficiency of capital falls as the capital stock grows. The result is that the inducement to invest is inadequate to match the saving desired at high income levels. The economy does not generate sufficient demand to absorb the output of which it is capable. Some of the same ideas have appeared in the works of other economists who have stressed oversaving, underconsumption, or over-investment as causes of economic crises.

The warranted-growth concept is a more formal and elegant way of stating the thesis and relating it to population growth. Sir Roy Harrod, who originated the warranted-growth rate concept, stated:

> If the warranted rate is above the natural rate, the actual rate must be below the warranted rate for most of the time, and the centrifugal forces pull it further down, causing frequent periods of unemployment. (This is the dynamised version of the stagnation thesis.)[3]

In its more pessimistic form the stagnation thesis does not appear to exist today. It is a possible explanation for sluggish growth rates that appear from time to time in advanced capitalistic countries, but the term *stagnation* is hardly applicable. This does not mean, however, that the tendency is necessarily absent from the economy. The collective demand for goods expressed through government purchases is such a large share of output in contemporary economies that it may have prevented the emergence of a stagnation drift which otherwise would have occurred.

The warranted-growth concept is equally applicable in analysis of capitalism in its primitive state as represented by underdeveloped countries today. In this case the warranted growth rate is much less than the natural growth rate. The desire to consume is so great that there is underaccumulation of capital. The growing labor force has inadequate capital to work with, and consequently supplies of goods are short. Demand tends to outrun supply, with the economy experiencing a chronic tendency for prices to rise.

INVENTORIES

The operation of the capital-stock adjustment principle is considerably more complex than presented so far because of the role of inventories. Inventories are stocks of goods held by producers for future sale. They consist of stocks of purchased materials, goods in process of production, and finished goods. As soon as man performs

[3] "Domar and Dynamic Economics," *The Economic Journal*, Vol. 69 (September 1959). Reprinted in M. G. Mueller (ed.), *Readings in Macroeconomics* (New York: Holt, 1966), p. 298.

work on any raw materials, such as extraction of coal from the ground, they become economic goods, and until they reach their ultimate use are items of inventory. If producers acquire more goods during a period than they sell, then they have engaged in inventory investment by adding to stocks. A reduction in stocks is *disinvestment.*

The definition of capital includes inventory stocks (circulating capital) as well as fixed capital, and investment includes changes in inventories. The capital-output ratio in growth analysis includes both the ratio of fixed capital to output and the ratio of circulating capital to output, which to the individual producer is the inventory-sales ratio. Presumably the two ratios have something of the same influence on entrepreneurial behavior. In both cases there is some concept of the desired relation of capital to output, and any disturbance to this relationship causes entrepreneurs to attempt to restore it. In the case of fixed capital the unexpected disturbance occurs through changes in output. The amount of fixed capital changes only as a result of entrepreneurs' orders and of depreciation, which they can anticipate. This is not the case with inventory investment. Inventories change as a result of producers' orders and of sales, and sales are unpredictable. If entrepreneurs correctly anticipate sales, any changes in stocks are voluntary inventory investment. Inventory investment resulting from unanticipated sales fluctuations is involuntary, or passive. A change in sales has a two-way effect on the inventory-sales ratio by changing both sales and inventory. This is unlike fixed capital, where a change in sales affects only the denominator of the ratio. Suppose that sales are 300 and stocks are 200. A 5 percent rise in sales will result in a ratio of 185/315. The ratio changes from .67 to .59.

As entrepreneurs attempt to restore the ratio, they increase incomes, and sales rise still further. This frustrates their attempt to build inventory. Attempts to maintain a target inventory level contribute to instability in the same way that the capital-stock adjustment principle works through fixed capital, but the mechanism works slightly differently. Entrepreneurs are not likely to adjust fixed capital rapidly on the basis of short-run changes in sales because, once installed, fixed capital has a life of many years. Entrepreneurs can reduce inventories, and thus they are less hesitant about building inventories in the face of rising demand than they are about building fixed capital, which they cannot reduce. Inventories probably conform more closely to the warranted-growth-rate model than does fixed capital, but inventory investment is quantitatively a much less significant factor in demand than is fixed capital.

On the other hand, changes in inventories absorb the first shocks of changes in demand, and thus slow the fluctuations in net output which ultimately affect the desire to accumulate capital. Net output (and income) consists of total sales of newly produced goods less depreciation and changes in stocks. Suppose that sales after depreciation during a period are 300 and inventories remain at 200 at the beginning of the period and at the end. Then the total sales of 300 are of newly produced goods, since there was no depletion of stocks. Now suppose demand increases to 315. In the short run there is not time to increase output, and inventory depletion accommodates the rising sales. Net output is still 300 [315 - (200 - 185)]. Thus there is no disturbance to the capital-output ratio. Entrepreneurs will eventually order to replace the lost stocks and probably to effect a net rise but, in the short run, changes in inventories have provided the buffer absorbing fluctuations in demand. Inventory investment (positive and negative) could be a stabilizing factor in the economy if entrepreneurs allowed stocks to experience wide swings to offset fluctuations in final demand. It appears, however, that businessmen attempt either to maintain a constant level of inventories or a constant ratio to sales, and in either case inventory investment becomes a destabilizing element in total demand.

THE ACCELERATION PRINCIPLE

The capital-stock adjustment principle as described is closely related to a theoretical process known as the *acceleration principle*. The two principles are essentially the same, though the acceleration principle is somewhat more rigorous in its formulation of entrepreneurial behavior. It assumes that investment in any time period is a constant multiple of output changes in some preceding time periods. The value of this multiple is the accelerator and is the same as the required capital-output ratio. Let us assume three time periods, starting with t_1 and ending with t_3. The change in output between t_1 and t_2 determines investment in t_3.

$$I_{t_3} = \text{Accelerator} \times (Y_{t_2} - Y_{t_1})$$

If the capital-output ratio is 2, then a rise of 10 in income will require investment of 20. Suppose that we start with 400 capital and 200 consumption demand. When consumption rises to 210, capital must rise to 420, which means investment of 20. Suppose that in the next period consumption rises to 215. Capital must then rise to 430, which requires net investment of 10. Investment falls even though consumption demand has continued to rise. The reason is that consumption demand has risen at a slower rate. New capital is needed only for additional output. Capital installed in one period can continue to accommodate output in succeeding periods.

A complete analysis, however, must look at the effects of investment as a component of total output, and in turn the effects of demand for total output, both consumption and investment, on required capital. In other words, investment, too, can stimulate more investment, just like consumption. Obviously it is necessary to assume lagged relationships, since investment cannot be a function of itself in the same period. Also it is necessary to recognize that the investment output will stimulate further income, which in turn increases investment demand. The effect of income on future increases in consumption may also be lagged.

Will the effect of an initial rise continue to cause income to spiral upward, once started, as a result of these multiplier and accelerator effects? The answer depends upon the size of the multiplier and accelerator and the lags assumed, but it is possible that instead of an upward spiral an oscillating path of income movement will be generated. If we start, say, with an assumed rise in investment, this rise will set off further increases in investment and consumption, but these induced changes may not allow income to continue to grow at the rate of increase implied by the initial change. As shown above, once the rate of increase drops, there is an absolute fall in the demand for capital goods, which then reduces income and consumption. If induced changes are very large, say an accelerator of 4, then the rate of increase continues to rise. Very complex models are possible, making various assumptions about the size of the acceleration coefficient, the lag time between changes in output and the effect on investment, the size of the multiplier effect of investment on income, and the lag involved in the multiplier process. Rather than an equilibrium growth rate, the path of output in these multiplier-accelerator models oscillates over time.

The warranted-growth-rate model, on the other hand, is essentially lagless. It assumes that income is a multiple of investment in the same period in which the investment takes place. It assumes that income must grow in the period immediately after installation of new capital by enough to absorb the output of the new capital. It does show that there is a unique growth rate—the warranted growth rate— at which changes in demand and changes in the capital stock will be in equilibrium. It is not necessary for the economy to grow at an increasing rate, but it cannot lapse from the uniquely determined warranted rate, if the economy is to continue to be in equilibrium.

The desired capital-output ratio, and thus the warranted growth rate, should not be thought of as a rigid, autonomous variable. As the discussion of ceilings and floors indicated, as the economy rises toward the full employment ceiling, the incentive to accumulate capital is reduced because of the absence of labor to combine with it. This reduction is a fall in the capital-output ratio, thus bringing the warranted rate closer into line with the actual growth rate and the full-employment (natural) rate. The more quickly the adjustment in desired capital-output ratios, the less significant is the analytical device in separating the warranted and natural growth rates.

SUMMARY

Since the purpose of capital is to accommodate output, producers attempt to maintain an optimum ratio between the capital they employ and their output. Any addition to capital thereby requires an expansion in output to maintain the optimum ratio. As long as capital is a component of output, output must grow in order to maintain equilibrium.

Investment not only adds to capital but also is a component of income. If all consumption is a passive reaction to income, then we can treat income as a multiple of investment, the multiple being determined by the saving ratio. The warranted growth rate is the growth in income which will bring equilibrium between demand and the additional capacity generated by saving. It is given by the saving propensity divided by the desired ratio of capital to output.

If the economy departs from the warranted growth rate, entrepreneurs are in a state of disequilibrium. As they attempt to correct the disequilibrium by changing investment, income responds to the change in investment and the disequilibrium grows worse. If the cumulative forces are pushing upward, the ultimate check is the state of full employment. A labor shortage may then start the economy in the downward direction. A rising consumption propensity, as income earners resist a fall in living standards, provides a check to the fall in the downward direction.

Changes in inventories slow the process, since changes in demand are first met from existing stocks. The sales affect the inventory-sales ratio, and if producers attempt to restore it, they eventually contribute to the instability.

The acceleration principle holds that investment responds to changes in output in preceding periods by a relatively constant multiple, called the accelerator. Multiplier-accelerator models set up at a time sequence of investment effects on income (through the multiplier) and income effects on investment (through the accelerator). The warranted-growth-rate concept is similar to these models, but without the lagged time sequences.

A continuing high warranted growth rate implies secular stagnation. The economy rarely grows at the warranted growth rate because it is higher than the growth in the labor force allows. Such an economy tends toward the downward spiral. A low warranted growth rate implies inadequate growth of supply relative to demand, with the consequence of inflationary tendencies.

SELECTED REFERENCES

American Economic Association, R. A. Gordon and L. R. Klein (eds.), *Readings in Business Cycles*. Homewood, Ill.: Irwin, 1965.

Domar, Evsey, *Essays in the Theory of Economic Growth*. New York: Oxford U.P., 1957.

Duesenberry, James, *Business Cycles and Economic Growth*. New York: McGraw-Hill, 1958.

Harrod, Roy, *Economic Essays*. London: Macmillan, 1952.

Hicks, John R., *A Contribution to the Theory of the Trade Cycle*. New York: Oxford U.P., 1950.

Kaldor, Nicholas, *Essays on Economic Stability and Growth*. New York: Macmillan, 1960.

Phelps, Edmund, *Golden Rules of Economic Growth*. New York: Norton, 1966.

DISCUSSION QUESTIONS

1. Distinguish between dynamic and static equilibrium.

2. Why does investment dictate a need for growth in income if equilibrium is to be maintained?

3. What is the effect on the warranted growth rate of a rise in the desired saving ratio? What is the effect of a fall in the desired capital-output ratio on the warranted growth rate?

4. How are entrepreneurs' investment decisions affected if the actual growth rate falls short of the warranted growth rate?

5. If the actual and warranted growth rates depart, list some factors which may eventually check an upward or downward spiral which results from this departure.

6. How is the warranted-growth-rate concept used to explain secular stagnation?

7. Distinguish between the acceleration principle and the capital-stock adjustment principle.

8. Do fluctuations in inventories tend to aggravate or dampen economic fluctuations? What assumptions do you need to make about entrepreneurs' behavior with respect to inventory investment in order to answer the question?

10

Fiscal Economics

The private market mechanism does not fulfill all of the wants of society. Even Adam Smith in his call for laissez faire recognized the need for state provision of education, public works, and national defense.

In an economy which uses money claims, the government takes its share of national output by a combination of taxes, which transfer money claims to government, and expenditures, which transfer money claims from the government to the economy. The government's employment of taxes and expenditures to meet economic goals is called *fiscal policy*. Though the chief purpose of fiscal policy is to provide for the transfer of output to social uses, its employment produces a number of effects, some intended and some accidental, some obvious and some hidden.

A major reason for the collective as opposed to the private provision of some goods is their indivisibility. In order to provide such goods it is necessary to make them available to all. A quantitatively important good of this nature is the military establishment. Whatever benefits may accrue from military efforts will be available to all members of the economy, and it is not possible to sell these benefits only to those who demand them. Sale of road passage to users only is largely impractical. Protection against crime and commercial fraud is a service to the whole of society, and the fruits of government research benefit all.

Another type of government product provides services which the private market could not offer competitively. Competing postal services would be impractical, and the government chooses to provide the service rather than grant a private monopoly. For similar reasons municipal governments provide water and power services.

Governments assume the responsibility for some services which they feel are desirable for the good of the whole of society, even though a private market is feasible. Partly it is because production of the good is beneficial to nonusers as well as those who buy it. A public library aids the general dissemination of knowledge. Government sponsorship of theaters for the performing arts broadens the possibilities for performances and encourages the creation of new works for the cultural enrichment of society as a whole. Another reason for government support of such efforts is dissatisfaction with the distribution of income. Private companies could sell educational services, but the cost would bear heavily, if they could afford it at all, on the lower-income groups. Free public education helps compensate for inequities in income distribution. All public expenditures, in fact, involve income redistribution to some extent. The benefits of public goods are spread equally, or at least differently from the manner in which the market would allocate an equivalent amount of private goods.

Although government goods normally reduce private goods by an equivalent amount, there are cases in which government purchases may actually raise the economy's real income. Like private goods, government purchases consist of both capital goods and consumption. Government goods which increase the nation's productive capacity are as much investment as are additions to the private stock of capital. Social capital goods, such as irrigation works and roads, serve eventually to increase society's output, though they decrease private product while they are under construction. A government purchase of any kind can raise real income if it results in the utilization of factors of production which would otherwise remain idle. Private product does not fall, and the government purchase is a public good contributing to the real income of all citizens. Real income does not rise, however, if the public good is of no benefit to society, such as an obsolete defense installation maintained by local political pressures.

TAXES

The purpose of taxation at the level of the national government is to reduce private demand for products. The national government makes expenditures by paying with its own liability in the form of money. Since the government is the money creator, it is not necessary for it to take money from the private sector in order to obtain it. Consequently the purpose of taxation is to reduce purchasing power in the private sector so that the combined demand of government and private buyers will not exceed the economy's capacity to produce. This view of taxation is the result of the movement of money creation power to the government. When money consisted of privately created product, the precious metals, governments had to tax to obtain money from the private sector. Today taxation serves to free real resources from the private sector.

Political subdivisions below the national level do not create money liabilities, and therefore their taxation more nearly serves the purpose of obtaining money from the private sector to make expenditures. Regardless of immediate purpose, the real economic effect of taxation is to reduce private demand to avoid the inflation that would result from an excess of demand over supply. The various forms of taxation determine initially where the government will intercept money flows in the economy. Sometimes this initial channel is regarded as the source, or base, of taxation, but the true base is the national output.

The income tax requires money payments to the government in some proportion to the individual's receipt of money income. Basically income is the receipts of the factors of production from the sale of goods and services, and therefore with some adjustments income and output are identical. With a given tax rate (ratio of required tax payments to income) the amount of taxes automatically rises and falls with income. The exactness of the relationship depends upon the lag in tax collection and the closeness of the correspondence between the tax definition of income and current output. Gains from the sale of assets are not a part of current output, but they are a component of income for tax purposes. Such gains vary in the same direction as output, since rising prices accompany rises in demand, though the correspondence is not exact.

A progressive income tax applies higher rates of taxation to higher income levels, and tax revenues rise more than proportionately to income. The purpose of tax progression is redistribution of income. The benefits of government goods accrue to all, and in some cases favor low-income groups, whereas taxation imposes the greatest reduction of purchasing power on high-income groups.

Excise taxes require tax payment in association with the purchase of goods, which means that excise revenues tend to fluctuate with output and sales, the degree of correspondence depending upon the structure of the tax. Deviations from current output occur, for example, if a good is taxed more than once as it moves through the marketplace. In this case shifts in the nature of the production and marketing process may affect the tax. The general practice is to impose the tax only once, though this may be at the retail or the wholesale level. The tax may be at a stated amount per unit of sales, or it may be a proportion of the price, with the latter method relating the tax more closely to national output.

One of the principal objections to the excise tax is that it tends to be "regressive," i.e., the burden of the tax falls relatively more heavily on the low-income groups. All purchasers of a good pay the same tax, regardless of their wealth or income. One proposal to overcome this objection is the imposition of a consumption tax which the consumer pays directly to the government.[1] In this way each individual's total consumption over a period of time determines his tax, and rates of taxation could vary with levels of consumption. The consumption tax could replace the income tax, so that each individual's withdrawals of goods from society, rather than his income, would determine his tax. Saving would not be taxed, with the result that taxation would discourage consumption rather than income.

A value-added tax is imposed directly on current output. The value of any good cumulates as it moves through the production process toward becoming a final product for society's use. At each stage the factors of production add value to the product, which is represented in income to the factors of production. The value-added tax requires each producer to pay a tax in accordance with the value of his production over a period of time. He does not pay tax on the total value of his sales, since that would mean paying tax on the basis of value added by other producers. The tax reduces the income of all the factors of production contributing to value. It is therefore similar to a proportionate income tax levied at the producer level.

The property tax bases tax liability on the ownership of assets. Although not a direct income tax, there is a close relationship, since the ownership of property yields income. The value of property determines the tax, and the income flow from property determines its value. This is true regardless of the nature of the property, though the income from property may not be in a monetary form. Home ownership yields real income in the form of occupancy, and the market valuation of this occupancy determines the value of the property.

With so many types of taxation most persons can expect to pay taxes through more than one type of tax. Often taxpayers complain of "double taxation," but this complaint alone does not offer evidence of inequity. Corporate interests complain that they pay tax on income, and then the remainder of the income distributed as dividends is taxed again. But then payers of property tax also pay tax on income from property; the excise tax is a tax on output, but so is an income tax, since income and output are the same thing. Though a person may justifiably complain of tax inequity, it does not neces-

[1] See Nicholas Kaldor, *An Expenditure Tax* (London: Allen & Unwin, 1955).

sarily arise from the number of taxes paid. Where there are multiple ways of assessing tax liability, the likelihood of inequities is somewhat greater, and this is a strong argument for a single type of tax imposed at a single level of government.

The type of tax and the person making the initial payment does not tell us where the true incidence of the tax lies, and this again complicates the achievement of equity in the tax structure. To know the true incidence of taxation we would need to know what the magnitude and distribution of income would be without the tax and with the tax, but we only know the latter. Analysis indicates that the true incidence is likely to differ greatly from the apparent incidence as initial taxpayers shift the burden.

Let us take the case of a corporation income tax. We cannot say that it is the "corporation" which bears the burden, since ultimately it is people who bear any tax burden. How about the corporate owners, the shareholders? They would bear the burden only if they are unable to shift the burden "forward" by charging higher prices, or "backward" by paying less for purchased factors of production (wages, raw materials, etc.) If the tax applies to all corporations, the inability to shift would mean that the tax had altered the distribution of income between capital and the other factors of production by reducing the after-tax income of corporate capital. It seems more likely that shifting would take place until the distribution of private product approximates the distribution before the tax. The corporate shareholder bears some of the burden, since the government has reduced the private product available for distribution, but it shares the burden with other factors. If we assume forward shifting, then the real private product of those who do not directly bear the tax falls as a result of a rise in prices without a rise in money income. A general tax on all factor incomes would not seem to involve systematic shifting, since the tax leaves relative shares undisturbed. A general excise tax raises prices (including tax) without raising incomes, so that the burden is generally distributed.

A general property tax is similar to a tax on the income of land and capital as factors of production, and generally we can assume shifting to redistribute the burden as in the corporation income tax. Many economists hold, however, that the tax on land is not shifted. The distinction between land and capital in this regard is the following. A tax on the income of capital can be shifted because in the long run any reduction in the income off capital tends to reduce the supply of capital. The reduction in supply raises the return on capital, tending to offset the effects of the tax. With land, however, this is not the case, since the supply of land is fixed. Any return to land is better than nothing to the owner, so that a reduction in return does not decrease the supply. Capital varies in supply because it is a man-made product. By this analysis a tax on land cannot be shifted by the owner, but it is important to distinguish between land proper and the capital which rests on it.

The role of general taxation is to reduce purchasing power in the private sector, whereas the role of selective taxation is more diverse. Selective taxation tends to redistribute real income, but the ultimate redistribution depends upon the true incidence of the tax, which is not known with any degree of precision. We will present a few examples without attempting to generalize on the incidence of selective taxes.

Advocates of some selective taxes, such as cigarette taxes, do so on grounds that they are a "good revenue source." The reasoning is that imposition of the tax will not reduce the purchase of cigarettes appreciably because of the nature of the product. This is known as *inelasticity of price demand.* But this is not really a valid argument for the state, which does not have to exploit demand inelasticity, considering that it can turn to any alternative basis for taxation. If the revenue argument prevails, it really means that the state chooses to tax certain citizens more than others because of their differing tastes. Consumption of alcohol, betting at race tracks, and other activities which do not enjoy full community support are examples of the imposition of such punitive taxes. Taxes on the import of foreign goods (tariffs) are a classic example of such a tax. Their objective (which economic theory does not support) has been to penalize the foreign good to encourage domestic industry.

A selective tax may fall on the consumers of the good taxed or may reduce profits of the industry, but tax policy must consider incidence to avoid unwanted effects. In the case of a regulated monopoly the state limits the monopoly to what it considers a fair return on capital. A tax on the sale of the utility would generally fall on consumers, since requiring the utility to absorb the tax would reduce it below fair return. Utility companies often advertise their contribution to government through taxation, using this contribution as an argument for private ownership. Such a tax is really a tax on utility users, which comprise virtually the whole of the population in technically advanced countries.

A tax on a competitively produced good falls on consumers because companies making such a good earn, by definition, only a return sufficient to induce them to stay in business. If producers had to absorb the tax, products would be withdrawn from the market until firms in the industry were once again earning normal profits. A tax on a monopoly product may, however, reduce monopoly profits if the firm was exploiting its monopolist position. An unregulated monopolist is a firm which exercises sufficient control over output of a good that it can earn abnormal profits, meaning more profits than would be required for it to remain in business.

Selective taxes may serve the purpose of offsetting the social cost of a product in cases in which the market does not require the buyer to bear this cost. This involves a quantification of the difference between the private cost of a good and the social cost and imposing a tax equal to this difference. Such a tax assists the market mechanism in the optimum fulfillment of society's needs. A similar matching of benefit and cost takes place when the state uses tax as a means of private payment for specific public benefits. The outstanding case is the motor fuel tax, with the revenue used for road construction. This type of tax is only applicable where the benefits are specific, which is often not the case with public goods.

Selective taxes by their very nature tend to lead to a reallocation of resources. The tax reduces demand for the taxed products and raises it for others, shifting the factors of production accordingly. This reallocation may in fact be a misallocation if it is not the intended purpose of the tax, since the forced change in the consumption pattern of the community puts it on a lower level of satisfaction.

NATIONAL INCOME EFFECTS

Government expenditures add to demand for product, and taxation, by reducing private purchasing power, decreases demand. Taxes and government expenditures do not have to be equal, however, and the government can use these separate influences on demand to achieve economic goals. In general these goals are to provide for government share of total product in a way that maintains demand at a level that minimizes unemployment and inflation.

The components of output for private domestic use are consumption C and investment I. The public sector also engages in consumption and capital formation, and these two together are designated as government expenditures G. Total output and income Y excluding foreign transactions are $C + I + G$. Private saving is defined as the excess of income over consumption and taxes: $S = Y - C - T$. Substituting for Y,

$$S = C + I + G - C - T$$

$$= I + G - T$$

or

$$S + T = I + G$$

The government does not legislate the amount of taxes it will take from the economy. It legislates the rate of taxation, but the amount of taxes depends upon the base—expenditures, income, or property values. In general, with a given structure of tax rates, tax revenues will change in relation to national output.

The economic effect of taxation is to reduce private income. If consumption is a function of income, then it is related to $Y - T$, not Y. Since taxes themselves are a function of income, we can say that consumption is a function f of $Y - tY$, where t is the proportion of income taken in taxes. If consumption is dependent upon income, then the determinants of total income are investment and government demand.

$$Y = C + I + G$$
$$= f(Y - tY) + I + G$$
$$Y - f(Y - tY) = I + G$$
$$Y(1 - f[1 - t]) = I + G$$
$$Y = \frac{I + G}{1 - f(1 - t)}$$

The larger the tax function the smaller is private income, and therefore consumption. The larger the consumption function the larger is income, with a given level of investment and government demand.

Figure 10-1 shows graphically the equilibrium condition. The saving and tax line shows the combination of the amount that is desired in saving at each income level and the amount that would be taxed, with given tax rates. The actual amount that is saved and taxed must equal the amount of government and investment spending, and the variable that will bring this equivalence is the income level. Why can the income level not be below the point that brings this equivalence, so that investment and government spending exceed taxes and saving? The answer is that these two types of expenditures necessarily result in income in excess of consumption, and this excess can either be saved or taxed. If income is below the equilibrium point, it means that saving is higher than desired at that income level. Spending on consumption will then take place until income reaches the equilibrium point.

The government can employ changes in its own expenditures and in tax rates as means of offsetting fluctuations in private demand and

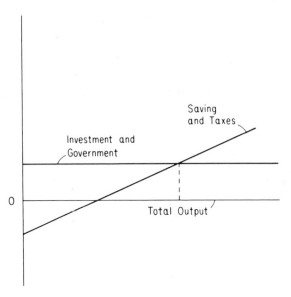

Fig. 10-1

maintaining stable national output levels. If demand is less than the full-employment capacity of the economy, the government may increase its own expenditures. Because of the induced-consumption effect, as the earlier equations show, the government need not increase its demand by the full amount of the gap, allowing the multiplier to make up the difference. If the gap is 20 and the multiplier is 2, then government expenditures need increase by only 10.

The alternative is to lower tax rates and thereby increase the multiplier effect of any autonomous expenditures. The effect of the tax-rate reduction is to raise after-tax income available from autonomous expenditures, and thereby induce more private demand. The effect of government expenditures is an increase in public goods to offset the deficiency in demand of the private sector.

The magnitude of the effect on consumption of any income tax will depend not only on the proportion of income taxed, but also on the structure of the tax. A tax which averages, for example, 10 percent of national income will tend to exert a greater effect in reducing consumer expenditures if it is regressive than if progressive. This differential effect arises because of the greater propensity of lower-income groups to consume out of income. If their income is taxed it will more likely reduce consumption than if the income of the rich is taxed. The rich are more likely to reduce their saving than consumption. The more progressive the tax, then, the larger the proportion of income taxed will have to be in order to achieve a given reduction in

Fiscal Policy for Full Employment

Before government intervention:

Consumption function, $f = 4/5$

Investment, $I = 100$

$$\text{Income, } Y = \frac{I}{1-f}$$

$$Y = \frac{100}{1-4/5} = 500$$

Assumed full employment income = 600.

Balanced budget fiscal policy:

Government spending, $G = 100$

Tax rate, $(t) = 1/6$

$$Y = \frac{I+G}{1-f(1-t)}$$

$$Y = \frac{200}{1-4/5\,(1-1/6)} = \frac{200}{1/3} = 600$$

Taxes, $(T) = 1/6 \times 600 = 100$

$G - T = 100 - 100 = 0$

Deficit fiscal policy for same income level:

$G = 20$

$t = 0$

$$Y = \frac{100+20}{1-4/5} = 600$$

$T = 0 \times 600 = 0$

$G - T = 20 - 0 = 20$ deficit

Surplus fiscal policy for same income level:

$G = 140$

$t = 1/4$

$$Y = \frac{140+100}{1-4/5\,(1-1/4)} = \frac{240}{2/5} = 600$$

$T = 1/4 \times 600 = 150$

$G - T = 140 - 150 = 10$ surplus

consumption. Likewise, if the proportion of income taxed remains stable, consumption can still be affected by an alteration in the tax structure. If taxes are made more progressive, income remaining after tax is redistributed to achieve greater equality, and it is generally assumed that such a redistribution will tend to raise consumption demand.

It seems clear that taxation reduces consumption, but it is difficult to postulate its effects on investment. In the long run the incentive to invest depends upon the demand for final output. Where government expenditures are maintained along with taxation, government demand replaces consumer demand, but capital is required for both types of demand. The two types of demand may have different capital requirements, but aside from this effect, it would appear that public goods are largely a diversion from consumption rather than investment goods. The announcement of tax-rate changes might have a short-term effect on investment incentives, as related to businessmen's outlooks, but this is rather unpredictable for use as a stabilization device.

There are many combinations of changes in tax rates and government spending that will achieve a given objective, but there is at least one that is not so obvious. Increases in both government expenditures and in tax rates will be expansionary, even if tax revenues equal the higher level of expenditures. The reason for this result is that the government is reducing the amount of product that private demand must absorb in order to maintain demand at full-employment supply. Suppose that the government takes one-half of total output, as the United States did in World War II. Then it becomes very unlikely that private demand cannot absorb the remaining one-half, particularly when considering that a portion of private investment must be devoted to production of the public goods. The continuance of strong government demand exercises a stabilizing influence on the economy even if the government does not use short-run changes in its fiscal activities for stabilization purposes. Unlike elements in the private sector, the government does not respond to drops in its income by reducing expenditures. It was the Great Depression of the 1930's and the economic revolution wrought by J. M. Keynes in his analysis of the deficiency of aggregate demand that gave the government this stabilizing role. No longer does economics follow Adam Smith's admonition of 1776: "What is prudence in the conduct of every private family can scarce be folly in that of a great Kingdom."

The government expenditures measure used here does not include transfers of purchasing power from government to private citizens, as when the government makes unemployment compensation payments. Such a transfer payment is not a purchase of output by government. When the private citizen uses the purchasing power to make an expenditure, then it is a part of private product. The effect of transfer payments is to reduce the net withdrawals of purchasing power which the government makes from the private economy through taxation. Consequently our tax measure is gross taxes less transfers.

An increase in transfers has the effect of reducing net taxes, and this is an important way by which governments assist in stabilization —indeed perhaps the most ideal way of relieving deficiency of demand. Short-run alterations in government expenditures for stabilization are somewhat impractical because society does not assign such a low priority to its public goods that they are to be implemented only when private demand falls of its own accord. Public programs are not of such a residual character that they can be turned on and off as an intermission feature in the private market. Alterations in tax rates, if made frequently, would subject the economy to uncertainty which might itself be destabilizing. Alterations in transfer payments to reduce net tax withdrawals offer a means by which the government can return purchasing power to the economy where it is most needed, among the unemployed. One contemporary economist, Milton Friedman, has proposed that transfer payments become a built-in part of the tax system as a negative income tax. Under this plan the government would automatically make payments to persons whose income falls below a given level. In periods of unemployment such payments would automatically rise for the economy as a whole as persons earnings fall. The effect of the plan is that income redistribution activities of the government accelerate as incomes fall. It alleviates some of the distress of economic declines and at the same time promotes recovery.

DEFICITS AND SURPLUSES

Although taxes withdraw purchasing power from the private sector, it is not necessary that the government use the same amount of purchasing power in the same period. It may use less or it may use more. The relation between taxes and government expenditures in a time period is called the government's budget position.

Figure 10-2 shows the factors determining the budget position. The tax line shows the amount of tax revenue that would be forthcoming at every level of national income with given tax rates. With the amount of government expenditures shown, there is only one level of national income that will bring equality between government

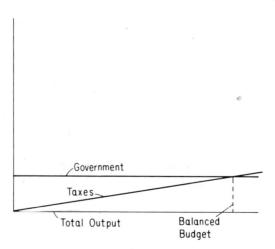

Fig. 10-2

expenditures and tax revenue. At any higher income level, tax revenues will exceed expenditures, and this is called a *government surplus*. Any lower income level will result in a deficit.

When a government runs a deficit, it pays for the goods acquired
in excess of taxation by issuing claims on itself. The total of such
claims outstanding at any one time is called the *government debt*.
One claim which the government may use in financing a deficit is
money, a transferable claim which circulates in the economy as a
medium of exchange of goods and services. When the government
finances a deficit with money claims, there is a net growth in government money claims of the private sector. The source of the claims is
the excess of sales of goods to the government over those required to
be transferred by taxes. Alternatively, the government may issue
claims which bear interest and which do not circulate in the economy as money. In this case the government borrows from the private
sector some of its previously issued money liabilities and then reuses
the money to purchase goods from the private sector. The result of
these transactions is that the private sector's money claims are unchanged, but its interest-bearing claims on the government have risen
by the amount of the deficit.

In the case of a surplus the government collects more of its
previously issued money liabilities than it spends. It may therefore
decrease its monetary liabilities or buy up some of its previously
issued interest-bearing bonds, leaving the money stock unchanged. In
this case the imbalance between government receipts and expenditures leads to a contraction of claims of the private sector on the
government.

The appropriate action with respect to deficits and surpluses, called *debt-management policy*, depends upon economic conditions at the time of the imbalance. If the imbalance occurs as a result of the failure of the economy to reach full-employment levels, and thereby generate budget-balancing revenues, appropriate policy calls for issuance of money or short-term debt to finance the deficit, since these claims will most likely stimulate further spending by the public. A deficit may occur at full-employment output if the tax rate structure is inadequate to generate revenue equal to expenditures. This usually results from government expenditures changing more rapidly than changes in tax rates, which governments tend to change infrequently. If a deficit occurs in these circumstances, the government claims created need to be of a long-term, illiquid nature to minimize the effect of the claim on private spending. The reverse situations apply in the case of a government surplus. At a time of deficient private demand, such a surplus is unlikely, but if it occurs, it should go toward extinguishing long-term bonds rather than money. A surplus at a time when demand is excessive could be used to extinguish money.

In its attempt to stabilize the economy the government will incur deficits and surplus as a by-product of its expenditure and tax policy, but budget imbalance is not a target per se. Various combinations of tax rates and expenditures can achieve a given economic goal, and the budget position will depend upon the combination chosen. A high level of government expenditures may be sufficient to maintain full-employment demand with a tax rate which brings budget balance at full employment. A lower level of government spending will require more private demand, and a tax rate which results in a government deficit may be necessary to stimulate this demand. It is consequently impossible to accept this analysis and at the same time to specify any constraints on the public debt, since this is merely the end result of the application of fiscal policy under different circumstances over a number of time periods. If avoidance of public debt becomes a policy objective, it means either abandonment of economic stabilization as a goal of fiscal policy or reliance upon sufficiently high levels of government expenditures to maintain demand that tax rates can safely be set to match government spending. Generally economists are not persuaded that there are sufficient disadvantages in public debt to forgo fiscal policy that might result in deficits.

Opponents of the public debt often argue that it is inflationary. If we accept that price changes are the result of differential growth rates in demand and supply, then it is only a deficit that results from an unwise fiscal policy that is related to inflation, and this is not necessarily an argument against deficits. The debt might increase demand by its effects on the assets of the public, but tax rates can offset this effect.

Some argue that the public debt is a means of passing the burden of government expenditures to future generations. If there is any burden from government expenditures it is in the private goods that must be forgone at the time that public goods are produced. There is no way of shifting this burden to future time periods. The distribution of available private output is possibly different with the debt than without it, but specifying this redistribution requires many assumptions about what would have happened in the absence of the debt: the size of output, the level of investment, the level of government expenditures, the consumption function, and so on. It is not clear that the debt necessarily results in a distribution of output which is contrary to the public interest.

The public debt could deprive future generations if it is the means of reducing investment in the private economy, since the lower capital stock would reduce future productivity. The debt itself does not necessarily do this, since balanced taxation and government spending could, if sufficiently high, also encroach upon the economy's ability to accumulate capital. Wartime government expenditures often result in debt and in reduced capital formation, but it is the diversion of resources and not the debt which reduces capital. If government expenditures themselves go toward formation of social capital, then the debt is not associated with an activity which deprives future generations of productivity.

SUMMARY

The government acquires a portion of private product to provide society with goods and services whose benefits are diffused. Government products may be indivisible, eliminating them from the market mechanism, or they may be goods which for other reasons society believes the private market would undersupply.

Taxation is a means of releasing resources from the private sector for public use. Most taxes, such as income, property, and excise taxes, are based in some way on the value of current output. The true incidence of the tax is the loss in real income which each person experiences as a result of the tax. This is not necessarily the same as the payer of the tax, since shifting may take place by changes in prices and in redistribution of money income. Selective taxes alter relative prices and therefore change the composition of product demand. Such taxes may be for the purpose of increasing the tax burden to high-income groups, through taxing "luxury" goods. They may attempt to bring the price of a product into closer alignment to total social cost where the market does not reflect all costs.

Taxes reduce consumption, and in general the higher the tax rate the smaller the consumption out of any given income level. Government expenditures have the opposite effect of increasing demand for product. The effects on demand of the two forces are given in the formula

$$\text{Income} = \frac{I + G}{1 - f(1 - t)}$$

where I and G are investment and government expenditures, respectively, f is the desired consumption function, and t is the tax function. Various combinations of tax rates and government expenditures can achieve a given demand level, and the government uses these instruments to minimize unemployment and inflation.

An excess of government spending over taxation, a deficit, results in the private sector acquiring claims on the government, and management of the type of claim issued allows the government to influence the economy's liquidity. Debt creation as a means of accommodating government purchases probably involves a different allocation of private product than would take place with a balanced budget, but the real cost of government goods is the utilization of resources, and the government cannot shift this to the future through borrowing.

SELECTED REFERENCES

American Economic Association, Arthur Smithies and J. Keith Butters (eds.), *Readings in Fiscal Policy*. Homewood, Ill.: Irwin, 1955.

Buchanan, James, *The Demand and Supply of Public Goods*. Chicago: Rand McNally, 1967.

Eckstein, Otto, *Public Finance*, 2d ed. Englewood Cliffs, N.J.: Prentice-Hall, 1967.

Income, Employment and Public Policy: Essays in Honor of Alvin H. Hansen. New York: 1948.

Johansen, Leif, *Public Economics*. Chicago: Rand McNally, 1967.

Lerner, Abba, *Economics of Control*. New York: Macmillan, 1944.

Scherer, J., and J. A. Papke (eds.), *Public Finance and Fiscal Policy*. Boston: Houghton Mifflin, 1966.

DISCUSSION QUESTIONS

1. Whom do you consider bears the burden of corporate income taxes? Excise taxes? Business property taxes? Value added taxes?

2. What are some examples of taxes used to equate private costs with social costs?

3. What are the economic effects of federal income taxes?

4. What are the economic effects of increases in government expenditures, matched by an increase in tax rates which balances the budget?

5. Demonstrate the effects on the national income multiplier of an increase in tax rates.

6. What are the similarities and differences between government transfer payment and taxes? Between transfer payments and government expenditures?

7. What are the possible economic consequences of adoption of a policy against any further increases in the public debt?

11

International Economic Relations

International economic relations consist broadly of the exchange of goods and the creation of claims between nations. These activities arise for the same reasons that they arise within a nation: there are economic advantages to both parties. The effect of international trade is to increase the value of total product available to all parties to the trade. A basis for trade between countries may exist for any or all of the following reasons. Countries differ in their relative endowments of the factors of production. Residents of a country may have a different composition of product demand from those of another country. Production conditions may require a market for a product larger than that of any one country, with the result that countries may benefit from specialization in production, even if their relative factor endowments are the same.

Differing factor endowments is probably the most important motivation for trade. Each country maximizes its production by specializing in the things it does best, and it acquires the goods it does not produce by exchanging with others. Each nation, like an individual, performs the tasks in which it has the greatest comparative, not necessarily absolute, advantage. Even if a man can do all tasks better than another man, it nevertheless is advantageous to employ the less efficient man for at least the tasks which he can perform relatively well. One nation may be more efficient at all production than another nation, but it is still to the mutual advantage of both nations for the inefficient one to produce the goods in which it is relatively most efficient. The effect of specialization and exchange is to increase the goods available to the world, and where the economic welfare of the world is the criterion, there is no valid argument for restricting trade. Restraints on trade—such as tariffs, inhibitory regulations, import quotas, export controls—require a nation to produce goods in which it is relatively inefficient. The diversion of goods to this purpose reduce the total goods available to the country for its use.

The basic reason for differences in factor endowments between nations is factor immobility. Land cannot be moved, but we assume that if economic motivations alone prevailed, labor and capital would distribute itself around the world until there was no geographic difference in the productivity of either capital or labor. But economic conditions do not always dominate, either between nations or within a nation. Legal restrictions and personal desires limit the movement of labor. Legal restrictions, fear of risk, and limited knowledge of alternatives limit the mobility of capital.

Even if factor endowments are the same, production conditions may form a basis for trade. In modern technology economies of scale require a large output to achieve the lowest unit cost. The market in one country may be too small to achieve this output. In the simple case of two industries and two countries, it is advantageous for each industry to produce in only one country and market in both. With no difference in factor endowments, it does not matter which industry locates in which country. Professor Charles Kindleberger has called scale economies "an important explanation of the rise of trade."

> . . .it is known that trade takes place among industrial countries with roughly the same factor proportions, such as Britain, Germany, Japan, and the United States, and that between countries with different factor proportions some trade takes place in like, but not quite identical, goods. Twenty per cent of Britain's imports consist of finished manufactured goods, and 20 per cent of the imports of the United States. This trade is based on specialization which springs from increasing returns.[1]

Even if production does not offer a basis for trade, different desires about the relative proportions of product consumed may do so. With trade each nation can produce the optimum production mix and exchange goods to achieve the optimum consumption mix. In the absence of trade the countries would either have altered production desires, lowering total output, or consumed a less than optimum product mix, lowering consumer welfare.

Efficient resource allocation is the basis for trade, and any impediment to trade involves inefficient resource use. Import controls cause a nation to produce goods which it could acquire with lesser total resources by foreign trade. Export controls prevent the nation from offering goods which would bring it an advantageous exchange.

[1] *International Economics* (Homewood, Ill.: Irwin, 1953), pp. 93-94.

Producers of particular goods may gain as a result of trade restrictions favoring their output, but the gain is necessarily at the expense of others in the nation. Trade restrictions cannot, except under very special assumptions, increase the total goods available to an economy.

NATIONAL INCOME AND FOREIGN TRADE

A nation's total acquisitions consist of the goods it produces and uses domestically plus the goods it acquires from abroad. A country's domestic production exceeds its use of domestic goods by the amount of its exports.

Available goods = Domestic production - Exports + Imports

If exports equal imports, then the goods available are equal to domestic production, but domestic production is higher than it would be without trade because of the more efficient allocation of resources.

Because of external transactions there is a possibility of a divergence between output and income. The two are made equal if income is construed to be not only real goods becoming available during a period but also claims to goods arising from taking of some portion of exports in the form of deferred compensation—claims on foreigners.

If exports exceed imports, then income will exceed the amount of real goods becoming available during the period, with the excess being taken in the form of deferred claims on foreigners.

If imports exceed exports, then true income is less than the total goods becoming available, and a portion of the goods were borrowed from abroad. This concept of income—to include adjustment for foreign claims—makes income and output equal. There is an advantage in a concept of income that equates it to output, but there are also disadvantages. Exports appear to increase real income even if there is no compensation in the form of imports. Imports *in excess of exports* appear to reduce income even though they are real goods available to satisfy the nation's wants. In the domestic economy changes in claims need not enter output calculations because increases in liabilities necessarily match increases in assets. Externally, however, there may be a net increase in claims or liabilities, and these are offset against net trade flows in measuring national income.

An imbalance between purchases abroad and sales abroad is the source of claim destruction or creation. If a nation buys more goods from abroad than it sells, then it must be reducing its previously acquired claims on foreigners or incurring additional liabilities to foreigners. If exports and imports are equal, then there is no change in foreign claims and a nation's real output is equal to the real product becoming available to it.

In terms of their effect on domestic demand, exports tend to increase demand for a country's products and imports tend to reduce demand by diverting it to foreign producers. Export demand can be treated as outside of a country's domestic economy, since foreign conditions determine foreign demand. The total demand facing a country's producers is the demand for consumption C, investment I, government G, and export X goods, less the portion of demand which foreign goods can fill through imports M. Total demand is therefore $C + I + G + X - M$.

Domestic income (including the adjustment for foreign claims) is the principal determinant of a country's import demand. The greater an economy's purchases, the greater the demand for foreign products along with domestic products. Consequently import demand is functionally related m to income. If consumption is also a function f of income, then autonomous investment, government, and foreign demand determines total demand[2] Y.

$$Y = C_d + I + G + X$$
$$= f(Y - mY) + I + G + X$$
$$Y - f(Y - mY) = I + G + X$$
$$Y(1 - f[1 - m]) = I + G + X$$
$$Y = \frac{I + G + X}{1 - f(1 - m)}$$

This equation shows that, given its assumptions, income is a multiple of autonomous government, investment, and foreign demand. A change in autonomous demand will lead to a change in total demand by the multiple, $\dfrac{1}{1 - f(1 - m)}$. Where the initiating change is exports, this is called the *foreign-trade multiplier*. Just as foreign trade affects national income, at the same time it can be seen that changes in national income affect foreign transactions. If domestic autonomous expenditures rise, induced imports rise with income. If

---

[2] For simplicity the exposition assumes that consumption and taxes are separate functions of national income, rather than consumption being a function of income less taxes (private income). Also, C_d is the demand for domestically produced consumption goods only, and all imports are assumed to represent a diversion from domestic consumption demand. This avoids the complication of making some imports a function of autonomous domestic demand and some a function of induced consumption demand.

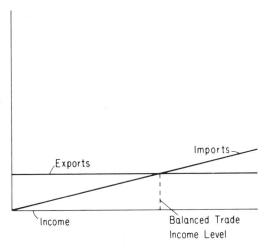

Fig. 11-1

exports are independent of national income, and imports are a function of income, then there is only one level of income that will bring
a balanced-trade position. Figure 11-1 illustrates these relationships.

If a nation's exports exceed its imports, the nation is engaging in
saving, since the excess results in the accumulation of claims on the
outside world. If we allocate all government product between consumption and investment type goods, as private product is classified,
then the total of national saving can be defined as income less consumption, $S = Y - C$. Income is the same thing as the economy's acquisition of consumption and investment goods, both foreign and
domestically produced, plus the excess of exports over imports.
Therefore by substitution we obtain

$$S = C + I + X - M - C$$
$$= I + X - M$$

This equation says that national saving is equal to investment plus
the excess of exports over imports. National saving then consists of
domestic capital formation plus the accumulation of claims on
foreigners.[3] For this reason the foreign balance is sometimes called
net foreign investment. Saving is then the same thing as domestic
plus foreign investment.

Net foreign investment represents foreign claims not offset by
foreign liabilities. A much larger amount of offsetting claims and
liabilities between countries may arise, and these gross credits are
called *capital flows.* Any imbalance between claims and liabilities
necessarily arises from an imbalance in product flows, which we can

call *net foreign investment* or *net capital flows*. Is this the same as a flow of capital as a factor of production? This concept is not easily defined, but it appears that net foreign investment, the trade balance, is the most meaningful approach to defining a true capital flow. It might appear that movements of capital goods only would be a true factor flow, but this is making too fine a distinction between types of goods. For the exporting country it clearly does not matter what type of goods it gives up to acquire the foreign claim. In any event, real resources have been used to acquire a claim on the rest of the world. In the country with the import surplus, investment exceeds national saving, since $X - M$ is negative in the equation $S = I + X - M$. The country can invest more than it saves because it has been able to borrow goods abroad. It does not matter whether these imported goods are of a consumption or capital type. Even if consumption goods, they have released internal real resources which can be devoted to production of capital goods.

It is possible, however, for the export surplus not to result in a true capital transfer. This will be the case if the borrowing country uses the import surplus to increase consumption. The excess of investment over saving then comes about not by a rise in investment but by a fall in saving. In this case what appears to be a capital movement from the standpoint of the lending country is not from the standpoint of the borrowing country. It is for this reason that the concept of capital movement as a factor flow is somewhat elusive.

The motivating force for capital flows is the differential return on capital between two countries. In the absence of restrictions capital will tend to flow from the country with the lower return to that with the higher. The flow allocates factors of production according to their most productive employment, and thereby the flow contributes to maximizing world output. (The point is also applicable to labor flows, but economic arguments are not compelling in this respect.) World output can always rise as long as a factor of production can increase its return by employment in a more productive use.

Since a true capital flow is a special case of a trade flow (an export surplus) the arguments for unrestricted trade flows are also arguments for free capital flows. But free capital flows are an additional requirement for world output maximization, since limita-

[3] Aside from international gifts trade imbalances necessarily give rise to an equal amount of claims. Gifts are conceptually not really a part of international trade. They are domestic products accruing to the giver, often government, and the giver then transfers them abroad. Also, in this analysis gold or any other commodity used for residual settlements is treated as a trade flow like any other commodity. The only form of settlement of net trade imbalances then is changes in claims, which includes but is not limited to money type claims.

tions on the holding of foreign claims will inhibit the initiation of trade, even if trade itself is free to move.

Although capital movements increase world output, it is not clear that both nations necessarily benefit, as is the case with trade. If a country's resources are fully employed, then it is likely that foreign investment will be at the expense of domestic investment, which is what a true capital "flow" implies. The country with the capital outflow loses the productivity benefits of domestic capital formation. Balanced against this loss is the possibility of a flow of goods from abroad as the return on foreign capital accrues to domestic owners. Another effect of the capital flow is an alteration in the relative returns to the factors of production. A capital outflow tends to raise the return to domestic capital, by lessening the increase in capital, thus altering the distribution of output away from labor and toward capital.

The net capital flow—the export surplus—represents the portion of increased claims on foreign countries not offset by increased liabilities. Gross increments in claims and liabilities may take many forms, but there are two primary classifications. Claims may be held as real wealth (including indirect holdings through corporate shares) or as financial claims. Financial claims generally carry a rate of return fixed at the time of the loan, whereas the return on real wealth varies in accord with the productivity of the capital good concerned. The decision to acquire a claim is often though not always independent of any export decision. The equality of net claims and the export surplus comes about in that first claims are acquired by transferring to the foreign country a liability, such as a bank deposit. If the foreign country does not use the bank deposit, then one claim offsets another. If it uses the deposit to buy goods, then the net claims remaining are exactly equal to the export surplus.

Persons in one country may, for example, lend to borrowers in another country by transferring bank deposits to them. An increase in liabilities to foreigners (the *deposit liability*) then matches an increase in claims (the *loan*). If the foreigners use the bank deposit to buy goods in the lending country, then the ownership passes back to someone in the lending country. At this point then imports match the original loan. It is many such transactions as these which make up the total flow of exports and imports, claims and liabilities between countries. If *ex post*, a net capital flow (trade imbalance) results, it is difficult to say which was cause and which was effect. Did credit flows result in a net flow of goods, or did a net flow of goods cause a compensating credit flow? This is analogous to the problem in the domestic economy of whether product imbalances create claims or whether claims lead to product imbalances. It seems reasonable to

assume there are influences running in both directions. The availability of borrowing abroad may certainly induce a country to run an
import surplus, and thus credit can influence trade flows. On the
other hand, an import surplus may arise from the independent import
decisions of many people, and a prior arrangement of credit is not a
necessity; offsetting credit transactions, especially by governments,
may be a largely passive reaction to trade demand.

ADJUSTMENTS TO INTERNATIONAL TRANSACTIONS

Changes in international trade or claims lead to changes in other
economic variables. These induced changes are the way by which a
country adjusts to changes in its external relations. One important
type of adjustment is through the effect of the foreign transaction on
domestic income. Suppose that a country has an increase in its
exports, starting from a position of equality between its imports and
exports. This rise implies an export surplus matched by an equal
amount of increased claims on foreigners. The increased exports will,
however, in turn pull up imports as the foreign-trade multiplier is
increasing income in the exporting country. At the same time further
rises in incomes are being checked in the foreign country by the
depressing effect of the imports on demand. Thus the gap between
imports and exports is closing. This income effect is a means by
which a country tends to adjust its imports to its exports. The adjust-

---

Income Adjustment Mechanism
to Foreign Trade

Assumptions:

Derived consumption = 70% of income

Imports   = 10% of income

Exports and imports are initially in balance, and exports rise by 10.

$$\text{Change in income} = \frac{\text{Change in exports}}{1 - \text{consumption function } (1 - \text{import function})}$$

$$= \frac{10}{1 - .70\,(1 - .10)} = \frac{10}{1 - .63} = 27$$

Rise in imports = $.10 \times 27$ = 2.7

Export surplus = $10 - 2.7$ = 7.3

ment is not complete, however, because the propensity to save is also limiting income fluctuations. Income changes continue until saving and imports equal exports and investment, and thus imports do not necessarily equal exports.

Another way by which an economy tends to adjust to foreign-trade swings is through interest rates. As exports rise, the resulting adjustment in interest rates may cause residents of the exporting country to want to hold more claims on the importing country. This will be the case if interest rates rise in the importing country and fall in the exporting country. If the original export rise was at the initiative of foreign countries, as assumed, then they had to give up highly liquid claims to acquire the goods—perhaps previously held bank balances on the exporting country (transferring them to residents of the exporting country) or deposits on their own banks (increasing their liquid liabilities to foreigners). This increase in liquid assets in the exporting country tends to lower its interest rates, in turn improving the relative attractiveness of foreign-held claims. Opposite results are happening in the importing country.

These interest effects are, however, highly uncertain. For one thing, at the same time the supply of liquid claims is changing, the demand for liquid claims is also changing. Increased exports increase national money income, and this may increase the demand for liquidity. Another complicating factor is the possibility of offsetting changes in liquidity initiated by government. This is particularly likely in the country with the import surplus if rising interest rates are not desired. Finally there is the matter of expectations of return on capital. If the exporting country's demand is rising, this may lead to expectations of increased total return on capital, tending to pull up interest. This effect lessens the desire to hold foreign claims and increases the desire of foreigners to hold claims on the exporting country.

A third possible mechanism of adjustment is through the price system. As exports stimulate demand, the relative strengths of price pressures become greater in the exporting than in the importing country. Price differentials may develop which reduce the attractiveness of the goods of the exporting country. If they work at all, price effects are a relatively slow means of adjustment.

If the economy does not adjust through income, interest rates or prices, governments may provide compensating capital flows to maintain economic equilibrium. Government intervention will in fact normally be among the first measures to adjust capital flows to trade imbalances. Governments provide automatic facilities by which intergovernmental credits make up the difference between private credit flows and the trade imbalance. If citizens of a country want more goods from foreigners than they are able to trade and borrow, then they may draw foreign claims from their government to make up the difference. To do so they exchange with their government domestic money claims which they hold on the government. The government may arrange an intergovernmental loan to acquire the foreign claims, in which case intergovernmental lending provides the residual which private lending has been unable to accommodate. The government may hold some previously acquired claims on foreigners which it may use for the residual, in which case a reduction in government claims on foreigners provides the mechanism of accommodation. These governmental methods of offsetting imbalances cannot continue indefinitely, and when a country is employing them, it is in a "deficit" position with respect to its international transactions.

If a government is unable or unwilling to arrange for residual claims, then the private market will be unable to acquire larger import surpluses than foreigners are willing to lend. Though this is clearly true in the aggregate, it is sometimes difficult to visualize when applied to individual cases. Residents of a country initially receive their income in the form of claims (money), and what is to prevent them from employing these claims for the purchase of foreign goods, even if their desires exceed the country's exports? The answer is that these are claims on domestic institutions (banks or government) and foreigners are unwilling to accept them. If the government will not convert them into usable foreign claims, then they are useful only for the purchase of domestic goods.

There is still another possibility for the holders of these claims, and that is to offer them to foreigners at a reduced value, assuming no legal prohibition against such a sale. The claims are obviously not of a money nature internationally if they are not accepted for goods on the international markets, even though they may be of a money nature domestically. The money claims of one nation may then be sold at varying rates for the money claims of another nation. It does not matter whether the units of account of the claims have the same or different names. It is the fact that they are usable for the output of different countries that establishes their differential character.

The residents of a country desiring more imports may offer claims on their products in exchange for claims on the products of another country. The rate of exchange between the two claims then affects equilibrium between exports and imports and credit flows. The country selling claims must offer more and more of its own unit of account to acquire claims of a given unit of account in the foreign country. This means that it must offer more and more of its own goods for a given amount of foreign goods. The market may not reach equilibrium until the value of imports equals the value of exports, expressed in either unit of account. Or, foreigners may be persuaded to hold some of the claims of the selling country, thus accommodating an import surplus. This might be the case if foreigners thought the value of the import surplus country's claims would rise in the future.

In view of the complexities of matching international trade and credit flows, one may wonder why similar problems do not arise between regions within a country. There are many explanations, but perhaps the principal one is the existence of a common claim—money claims on the government—which can always be shifted between regions. The transfer of this asset is clearly the first way by which a regions settles a trade deficit. Since a money claim is usable in all parts of the country, there is never the necessity of selling the claim at a depreciated rate of exchange. As long as residents of one region possess money claims, they can always run an import surplus with other regions. Secondly, each region also holds other types of claims which are national in scope, though perhaps not international, and can easily transfer these to another region to run an adverse trade balance. Thirdly, residents of a region can more easily borrow from other regions than from other countries. But even within a country

---

Effects of Exchange Rate Change on the
Terms of Trade

Yenland produces fruit which sells for 20 yen a bushel. Pesoland produces copper at 30 pesos a pound.

Exchange rate: 1 yen = 2 pesos
Terms of trade: 1 bushel of fruit = $1^1/_3$ pounds of copper
New exchange rate: 1 yen = 3 pesos
Terms of trade: 1 bushel of fruit = 2 pounds of copper

If Yenland exports 1,000 bushels of fruit, trade is balanced if she imports 2,000 pounds of copper.

---

an adverse trade balance cannot continue indefinitely, and eventually the residents must reduce their purchases from other regions when borrowing power is limited and existing claims are used.

In summary, governmental policy with respect to exchanging

foreign claims for its own money liabilities determines the short-run manner in which a country is able to balance trade flows with credit flows. If the government provides residual financing to close any emerging gap, then the country's money unit of account can remain at a fixed relation to other countries' units of account. This is the fixed-exchange rate system. If the government does not maintain fixed exchange rates, then fluctuations in the rate of exchange can bring equilibrium in foreign transactions.

Any government's intervention ultimately is limited either by its holdings of foreign claims (international reserves) or its ability to borrow them through intergovernmental credits. If it exhausts these possibilities the government may then have to turn to alterations in exchange rates as a means of reaching equilibrium. It may do this either by setting a new rate of exchange between its own and other units of account or by letting the exchange rate finds its own level in a free market. In either case the effect is to alter the relative prices of foreign and domestically traded goods so that imports are discouraged and exports encouraged. Just as there is always a price that will clear domestic commodity markets, there is always an exchange rate that will equalize exports and imports (assuming no net credit flows).

The effect of a change in the exchange rate is to alter the terms of trade—the quantity of exports a country must give up for a given quantity of imports. As the terms of trade deteriorate, the desirability of imports diminishes while other countries increase their demand for its exports. If one country's monetary unit becomes worth 10 percent less of another country's unit, the effect is the same as a 10 percent rise in prices of exports of the country whose monetary unit has become more costly.

When the government sets an exchange rate at which it will provide foreign claims, it does not expect that equilibrium will always prevail at that rate. The government provides residual claims when this is necessary for temporary periods, perhaps a matter of years. If imbalance in foreign transactions is chronic, the government may set a new rate, called a *revaluation*, which will bring equality in foreign transactions.

SUMMARY

The effect of international trade is to raise world output. Nations stand to gain from trade because of differing factor endowments, differences in product demand, or the need for large markets to achieve economies of scale.

Exports increase demand for a country's product and imports decrease demand for domestic output. If a nation exports more than it imports, it takes a portion of its proceeds from current production in the form of claims on foreigners, a form of national saving. Any change in exports will have a magnified effect on demand through induced consumption. The larger the consumption function and the smaller the import function, the greater will be this multiplier effect.

The difference between exports and imports is the measure of net capital flows from a country. This difference is the source of net changes in claims between countries. Net capital flows can occur when there are differences in rates of return between countries.

Changes in a country's foreign-trade position cause further changes in a country's economic situation. A rise in exports increases domestic demand by a multiple, which in turn increases imports through the import function. Changes in exports tend to cause changes in interest rates which are conducive to a net capital flow from the country with the export surplus.

The immediate effect of a change in trade will depend upon governmental policy. Governmental capital flows are used to accommodate imbalances which may arise in private transactions if the government wishes to maintain a fixed rate between its own and other monetary units of account. Otherwise rates of exchange between monetary units will change until exports, imports, and private capital flows are brought into balance.

SELECTED REFERENCES

American Economic Association, Richard Caves and Harry Johnson (eds.), *Readings in International Economics*. Homewood, Ill.: Irwin, 1967.
Ellsworth, P. T., *The International Economy*. New York: Macmillan, 1964.
Haberler, Gottfried, *A Survey of International Trade Theory*. Princeton: Princeton U. P., 1961.
Kindleberger, Charles, *International Economics*, 4th ed. Homewood, Ill.: Irwin, 1968.
Meade, James, *The Balance of Payments*. New York: Oxford U. P., 1951.

DISCUSSION QUESTIONS

1. Explain the difference between absolute and comparative advantage.
2. How does a change in exports tend to affect imports?
3. How does a change in income tend to affect imports?
4. How does a change in the marginal propensity to import tend to affect income?

5. Why are governments motivated to provide residual financing to accommodate imbalances between a country's exports and imports?

6. What are the differences and similarities between international payments and interregional payments within a country?

7. How are international capital movements defined? Why are they not defined according to movements of real capital between countries?

12

Welfare Economics

The purpose of the economic system is to provide for man's material welfare. All production must be measured by this criterion. The branch of economic inquiry known as *welfare economics* concentrates on evaluating the satisfaction which the economic system yields—not just its size—and the implications for welfare of alternative economic policies. In a sense, all economics is welfare economics, but the main stream of economic analysis assumes that maximum output, measured in market prices, is the means of maximizing welfare. Welfare economics is more concerned about the distribution of output, recognizing that additional goods have different satisfactions to different people. It is concerned about nonmarket aspects of the economy, recognizing that economic activity may also reduce satisfaction, or that it may yield satisfaction not reflected in the market. And it is concerned about the allocation of product to current consumption and capital accumulation and the effects of this allocation on welfare.

The philosophical justification for capitalism offered by Adam Smith (1723-1790) is an argument in welfare economics. Smith tried to show how the unfettered workings of the market mechanism maximized economic welfare without the necessity of intervention by government. This was a considerable achievement—to rationalize the individual efforts of thousands of people making and buying things, each trying to serve his own self-interest. It was not by their benevolence that sellers produce the goods that buyers want, and charge what they cost to produce, but by a force outside the producers' control—competition. If a producer turns out the wrong good, he will not be able to sell it. The prices of goods that are in demand will rise, and resources will shift to the production of these goods. If any producer attempts to charge more than the cost of production of his good (including a normal profit), his excess profit will attract other producers to that good. The increased supply will bring down the price to the cost of production.

More rigorous theories have since been developed to judge the
ability of the economy to utilize resources—its given factors of production—to produce the selection of goods that will yield the most
satisfaction. Let us frame the explanation of these theories in terms
of the problem that the economy must solve: What amounts of each
possible good will be produced, given the fact that there are limits to
the total production possibilities as determined by the availability of
the factors of production? To consider all possible combinations of
goods would be impossibly complicated, but we can demonstrate the
essence of the solution by considering the choice between two alternative goods. One can then visualize that the same process is occurring among all goods. Mathematically we can say that the economy
reaches general equilibrium in a system of simultaneous equations.

To consider only two goods we shall have to assume that the
production of all other goods has been decided, and we still have
resources left which we can allocate as we like between the production of, say, gallons of milk and bushels of wheat. To use small
figures for simplicity, if we devoted all resources to producing milk,
we could get 50 gallons a month. If we used these factors of production for wheat, we could get 50 bushels a month. There are also
various combinations which could be produced, such as 48 gallons of
milk and 6 bushels of wheat. All of these combinations are called the
production possibilities. We can say that the opportunity cost of
producing one good is the amount of the other that must be forgone.
We need not dwell on the conditions likely to determine the various
possible combinations, except to note that they are technologically
determined. There is, given available knowledge and resources, a
given amount of one good that the factors of production can produce when released from production of another good. The ratio of
these two amounts is called the *marginal rate of transformation.*

Which of the various combinations of milk and wheat will the
economy produce? We cannot determine the combination from production possibilities alone and must bring in an additional consideration—the relative satisfactions which the society will achieve from
consumption of the two goods. We cannot measure satisfaction absolutely, but we can indicate relative satisfactions by posing the question: How many units of one good will yield the same satisfaction as
one unit of the other good? The answer, we assume, will depend
upon the number of units of each already possessed. If a society has
a lot of milk and no wheat, then we assume it would take a great deal
of additional milk to yield the same satisfaction as one unit of wheat.
The trade-off between goods at which satisfaction levels are equal is
called the *marginal rate of substitution.*

Two conditions must be fulfilled for the economy to achieve its optimum allocation of resources in producing the two goods, milk and wheat.

1. No point of production must be chosen which does not fully utilize resources. In our earlier example the economy must not produce 46 gallons of milk and 6 bushels of wheat, because it is possible to increase the production of milk without reducing the production of wheat.
2. The marginal rates of substitution and of transformation must be equal. This is because the ratios at which goods are capable of transformation must satisfy consumers in the ratios at which they are willing to acquire goods on the market. Otherwise the economy could shift its production and increase satisfaction.

In general, there is only one combination of the two goods that will satisfy these conditions. There are many possibilities for the marginal rates of substitution and transformation to be equal, but they will generally be either beyond the production capability of the economy or below the maximum production level. There is only one point of both equality of the two rates and maximization of the production level.

Figure 12-1 illustrates the possibilities. The curve represents the various combinations of milk and wheat which are possible. At any

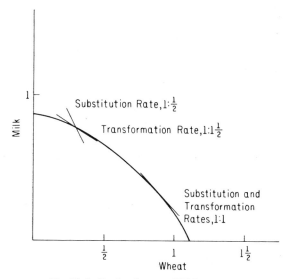

Fig. 12-1. Production-possibilities curve.

point on the curve there is a unique marginal rate of transformation between milk and wheat determined by technological conditions. At point *E* (equilibrium) it is 1 milk: 1 wheat; at point *D* (isequilibrium), 1 milk: 1½ wheat. Also shown at two points is the marginal rate of substitution between the two goods as determined by the society's satisfactions. The substitution rate will differ at each point along the production-possibilities curve. At point *D* the society would be willing to give up 1 milk for only ½ wheat because it has so much more milk than wheat. But that rate of substitution is not the same as the transformation rate (1:1½). Point *E* is the only ratio of production of milk and wheat that is compatible with our defined optimum.

How does the production level get to this ratio? Under the market system discrepancies between the amounts produced and the amounts purchased will alter production until it equals the amounts that will maximize society's satisfactions. At point *D* consumers receive the same satisfaction from acquiring 1 additional milk or ½ additional wheat, because they already have a relatively large amount of milk. Consequently if they would exchange 1 milk for any amount more than ½ wheat, they would be able to increase their economic satisfaction. Producers at this point can acquire 1½ additional wheat by giving up 1 milk, while consumers would be willing to give up 1 milk for anything more than ½ wheat. There is thus an obvious incentive to shift production toward wheat, since its value in exchange is greater than its cost of production in terms of milk. The following option open to producers demonstrates this incentive:

1. They can shift production of 1 milk to 1½ wheat.
2. They can offer wheat on the market for, say ¾ wheat for 1 milk, a clear advantage to consumers.
3. Since they made 1½ wheat, they get 2 milk from the exchange, a net gain of 1 milk.

The above process of market trading shifts production away from milk and toward wheat. As the shift takes place:

1. Transformation rates gradually shift as the amount of wheat which can be produced by forfeiting milk production diminishes.
2. The marginal significance (rate of substitution) of wheat gradually diminishes as consumers acquire more of it relative to milk.
3. There is no further incentive to shift production when both rates are the same, 1:1.

This example shows how the market must act if it is to guide the economy to the optimum production level. The example is framed in terms of a barter economy to emphasize that the basic decision the economy makes is the determination of the goods which its factors of production will make. The economy's choice is not between money and goods. Its real choice is between alternative goods. Under a monetary economy it is money prices that will lead the system to the optimum level if it is functioning properly. If the economy is overproducing milk, the money price of milk will fall and the money price of wheat will rise because of consumer preferences. This change in relative prices will cause producers, in their attempt to maximize the money value of their output, to shift production. In equilibrium the ratio of the money price of the two goods will correspond to the marginal rates of substitution and transformation, which are equal.

This system describes the determination of the relative values of goods which directly satisfy consumer satisfactions. The values of the factors of production are then derived from the values of the goods they produce. In equilibrium, the value of the factors used to produce one unit of a good can be defined in terms of that good. The land, labor, and capital necessary to produce one gallon of milk have a value of one gallon of milk or, which is the same, one bushel of wheat. It is the output of the factors that determines their value, not the value of factors that determines the value of their output.

The theory of resource allocation under the market system was developed on the assumption of a capitalistic economy, but it has since been recognized that it is also a feasible allocative system under socialism. Although under socialism capital and land are owned by the state, the managers of producing enterprises can be given the same kind of goals to follow as private producers under capitalism. As shortages and surpluses develop under one set of outputs, they are instructed to change prices to clear the markets. At the same time, in response to higher prices, they shift production in the indicated direction. Rate of return on capital can be used as targets for the socialistic enterprises' success to assure that each enterprise is in fact conforming to market directions and to assure that comparisons of alternative production possibilities adequately consider utilization of capital in the production process. In short, public or private ownership of capital is not necessarily a factor in judging the efficiency of the market mechanism.

DEPARTURES FROM OPTIMUM CONDITIONS

The theory outlined in the preceding section is designed to show how a market system can reach an optimum output. To determine the extent to which an actual market system can meet this test, we must consider the conditions necessary for its fulfillment. For one thing, consumers must have full knowledge of products and prices in order to effect the trade-offs that will maximize their satisfaction. All units of production of each good must be of the same quality, or else the purchaser may inadvertently lower satisfaction. Advertising plays no role in such a system, since advertising attempts to persuade the buyer that the advertised products are superior. If all products are homogeneous, and consumers are aware of the fact, no advertising message could get through. The massive presence of advertising in present markets is itself evidence that the economy is not conforming to the optimum model.

An essential requisite of market efficiency is complete freedom of all factors of production to shift toward the composition of output indicated by market signals. In practice, restrictions on entry into particular lines of production are common. Advertising is one means of restriction, since it gives producers an entrenched position in the market and convinces buyers that new products are inferior. Complex production processes often involve large start-up costs, inhibiting the entry of new firms. Preventing access to knowledge of production technique, through secrecy or patent protection, inhibits production by other firms. Trade-union agreements contribute to labor immobility. In our example, if the economy is to reach its optimum, producers of milk must be free to become producers of wheat. There must be no way that producers can over the long run charge prices which do not correspond to rates of transformation.

The market system is also weakened by economic forces which lie outside of market considerations. If the market mechanism does not reflect all costs and benefits of a particular production, then it may cause the good to be over- or under-produced from the standpoint of the society's economic welfare. Costs or benefits external to the market are called "externalities."

An external cost is a reduction in economic welfare not reflected in the market that the society must bear as a result of a particular production. Examples abound in contemporary societies: polluted air and water, noise, increased congestion. Either society as a whole bears the external cost or it falls to some other market. Pollution of the waterways by petroleum reduces the fish catch, increasing the cost of fish. The economy could increase its economic welfare if it reduced the production of petroleum and increased the fish catch, but the unfettered market has no way of so directing the allocation of resources. The price of guns may reflect the resource cost of producing guns, but it does not reflect the loss of life and limb by man and animal occasioned by their use.

In the case of external economies the market underestimates the value of the good to society as a whole or to other markets. An urban transit system is valuable not only to its riders but to those who breathe more easily and walk more safely from reduced auto congestion. A theater provides enjoyment beyond its immediate audience by fostering the creation and perfection of works of the performing arts.

Where externalities exist, there is no way that trade can increase or decrease production of the affected good. The individual may feel that society's total consumption of a good involves cost, such as air pollution, but there is no way he can express this on the market.

INCOME DISTRIBUTION

Another welfare consideration which the market system ignores is the distribution of income. The conditions for an optimum economic system are compatible with any number of income distributions. The competitive system does not tend to any particular pattern of income distribution. This is so because the distribution of income will affect the price of goods, and ultimately the "value" of factor services which go into making these goods. A society with heavy concentrations of income may place a great value on diamonds and devote much resources to their mining and cutting. A society with income equality might place a higher value on transistor radios because of the more widespread distribution of available purchasing power for luxuries. Both societies could be regarded as operating at an optimum of economic allocative efficiency.

Another influence of income distribution is on the allocation of total product between consumption goods and capital goods. Each individual is assumed to balance current satisfaction from goods against anticipated future satisfaction through saving. The saving of all individuals is the same as society's capital accumulation. The proportion of total income which each person wants to save is presumed to increase with his income. The greater is inequality in income distribution, the greater will be aggregate saving. Consequently the "value" which society places on capital goods, as opposed to consumption goods, is determined by its income distribution. The wealthy value capital goods highly because they can afford to; they can save and still have enough purchasing power left over for a high level of consumption.

Because of the income-distribution problem, maximization of output cannot be regarded as the goal per se. The ultimate goal is total welfare, and output is only a means to that end. It is because of the difficulty of measuring welfare that output so often serves as its proxy. If output is taken as the goal, it could lead to serious departures from the welfare of the community. "Goals" are by definition value judgments, but welfare economics cannot avoid value judgments—that is what it is all about.

Suppose a way is found to increase output slightly by consolidation of farms and to achieve the consolidation the government forces small farms to sell out to large ones. A few farmers get rich, output is increased slightly, and many farmers become poorer. Should such a move be undertaken simply because it raises output, with distributional effects ignored? Most would probably say the policy is unwise, unless some way were devised to overcome the redistributional effects.

A positive move toward redistribution of income can be a way of increasing total welfare even if total output is not raised. We assume that an incremental dollar of purchasing power means more to a poor man than to a rich man. Consequently a shift of income from the rich to the poor will increase the satisfaction of the poor more than it will decrease that of the rich. Redistributional effects may come from price changes even if income is unaffected. A policy that raises the price of some good, say apartment rentals, relative to others, say home ownership, involves a shift in real income away from apartment occupants, if their money income remains the same.

If it could be done without decreasing the total amount of product available, complete equality in distribution would bring the highest level of welfare. Complete equality would seem impossible, however, in a capitalist economy, since it eliminates any incentive to risk taking. Redistribution of income toward more equality raises welfare as long as it does not reduce the total output available.

CRITERIA FOR INTERVENTION

Advertising, monopoly, externalities, income distribution criteria—all have weakened Adam Smith's "invisible hand" of the market. In its place has risen the theory of second-best. This theory says we should recognize the departures of the market system from optimum and devise market intervention consistent with these departures, rather than attempting to remove them. For example, a tax on a particular good tends to distort consumer allocation. But if the good bears external diseconomies, the tax may compensate. If most firms in an economy are monopolistic, matters are not helped by a policy which fosters competition in a few places. Equal degrees of monopoly do less to distort consumption patterns than do mixed monopoly-competitive markets. The theory of a second-best is essentially a frame of reference, which says that solutions should be consistent with conditions as they exist, not with an idealized model.

A test which will unambiguously establish a case for market intervention comes from the work of Vilfredo Pareto (1848-1923). "Pareto optimality" is a situation in which it is not possible to make anyone better off without making someone worse off. The perfectly functioning market system as described earlier is a Pareto optimum. If an economy is not at Pareto optimum, intervention will improve it. In a very strict interpretation almost any change will likely leave someone worse off, but there are some cases in which the rule seems applicable. Measures to decrease unemployment would seem to come close. If there is increased government demand in the face of unemployment, total output can be raised. In this situation government spending may take place without the imposition of additional taxes, so that the action is largely a gain without significant adverse impact. Another example is a shift of resources to more productive employment. Suppose it could be found that a given number of doctors could handle twice the number of patients by associating in a clinic and specializing. Here the total availability of medical services is increased, or alternatively the doctors can handle the same patient load with increased leisure time.

Another example is the imposition and enforcement of contract law. Everyone benefits from fulfillment of contracts, assuming that other parties too will abide by the contract. Policing of contract by the state bestows an unambiguous benefit on all.

The Pareto test is a form of piecemeal planning. It does not define a universal optimum because there is a Pareto optimum consistent with each income distribution. It merely says that for a given income distribution there is no way of moving to a higher level of satisfaction without altering that distribution. A demonstration that a given situation is not Pareto optimum is a sufficient but not a necessary condition for intervention.

Most situations are not so clear-cut. There are possibilities that involve gains to some but losses to others. In weighing the benefits and losses we run up against the formidable problem of interpersonal utility comparisons. We need in some way to compare the gains and losses of different individuals to decide if there is a net gain or loss to society as a whole from a given action. This was the problem in the farm example above. We assumed that the loss of utility by the small farmers outweighed the gain of utility by the rich farmers. The result was that net total satisfaction for the community as a whole dropped, despite the fact that output rose. But this assumption was purely a judgment. There seems no way to measure differences in utility to different persons.

A classic example of interpersonal utility effects is the tariff. The

imposition of a tariff will likely benefit those involved in the production of the protected good; it will likely harm those who purchase
the imported good or close substitutes. A weighing of these gains and
benefits is a part of the tariff decision. Minimum wage laws are
intended to benefit the low wage earner, but they increase the cost
of those who buy their services. Most any government expenditure
involves such considerations. Some enjoy the government good more
than others; some have higher tax burdens than others as a result of
the government demand.

In certain cases the distribution of costs and benefits may be
quite obscure, in addition to the difficulties of measurement. If the
government guarantees loans to home owners, this class of borrowers
surely benefits, but who pays? It is whoever does *not* get a loan
because of the guarantee. The granting of patents and copyrights
benefit the holder, and it is not clear whether there is a loss somewhere else in the economy or whether this is a case of achieving
Pareto optimality. The resulting monopoly encourages price-fixing,
to the possible harm of the buyer, but in the absence of the monopoly the product might never have become available.

How then shall we decide a given policy if it involves gains for
some and losses for others? Generally economists seek to determine
if there are net gains in aggregate product from the move. If there
are, it is taken to be a wise move, because the redistribution effects
can be offset if desired, and there will still be a net gain for someone.
But a concept of net gain itself is not easy, because remember that
we cannot measure output by pounds or other objective scales; we
measure it by market prices. Any change in supply or in distribution
will affect market prices, and thus "before" and "after" measures at
prevailing market prices may not show a real gain. Suppose that a
scarcity of water makes agricultural products very high in a locality,
and an irrigation project will increase produce and lower their prices.
How do we measure net gain?

The index number approach to this problem compares "before"
and "after" quantities with fixed prices, which we shall call Period I
and Period II. The expenditures (income) of Period I are the sum of
Σ prices paid in the period times quantities bought at those prices
$\Sigma P_1 Q_1$. In Period II we measure expenditures in Period I prices to
see if there is a net gain. If the sum of Period II quantities times
Period I prices is greater than the expenditures of Period I, then the
policy is probably desirable, assuming no distribution effects or assuming the distribution effects are in the desired direction. If undesired distribution effects take place, a redistribution can be effected
which will still allow each individual to increase his total purchases,
valued at Period I prices.

The measurement of quantities in the new situation times prices in the old is a measure of gain because the goods of Period II could not have been bought in Period I. Another test is to apply prices of the "after" situation to the quantities of the two periods. Gain is indicated if the sum of Period II prices times Period II quantities exceeds Period II prices times quantities in Period I, or $\Sigma P_2 Q_2 > P_2 Q_1$. This is the better of the two tests, because it reflects prices that arise from the income distribution that would prevail after the change, which is the relevant one.

Another criterion for welfare intervention is known as the *compensation principle*. If those who benefit from a given change could compensate the losers and still have something left, then the change is a net social benefit. Losers could be compensated and everyone would be better off. The test only requires that compensation *can* be paid. The fact that it can be paid does not necessarily mean that it should since the income distribution before the change is not necessarily the optimum one. There are, however, some bases for favoring compensation. One reason is that a change which involves redistribution is more likely to be opposed than one which is neutral with respect to distribution. Another is that a loss of income involves, presumably, a considerable drop in welfare for the one suffering the loss. A man who loses $100 in income is in a worse position than one who never had the $100 in the first place. The prevailing bias toward income maintenance is often revealed in policy measures, such as disaster relief. Persons who lose their homes in natural disasters are assisted in acquiring new ones, though a large segment of the population never had a home in the first place. The courts decide compensation for personal injury on the basis of the income lost by the sufferer.

Though it is an approach toward measuring net gain, the compensation principle does not solve the problem of interpersonal utility comparison. To compare gains and losses is to assume that a dollar gained by one party has the same utility as a dollar lost by another party. Where compensation is not actually made, the gains made by some may be much less than the losses suffered by others, even though the money magnitudes might indicate otherwise. A given amount of money has a different utility to different individuals.

The index number test and the compensation test are usually impossible to apply precisely, but the concepts are useful in policy decisions. If it can be established that there is a net gain for society as a whole for a given policy proposal, there is a strong presumption for its application. Who gets the gain and who bears the loss is a separate matter which can be handled by distribution policy. As long as there is a net gain, there is a possibility of everyone being better off. Removal of a tariff on wool, for example, may harm sheep owners, but if it results in a larger total national income, the sheep owners can be more than compensated for the loss. A technological innovation may cause unemployment, but if the result is a net gain the unemployed can be more than compensated for their losses.

The cost-benefit analysis of social projects is an application of welfare criteria similar to the compensation test, though its scope still does not embrace all of the concepts involved in welfare economics. The cost-benefit approach tries to balance all of the gains of a proposed expenditure against its cost to determine if the project is desirable. A program of public vaccination against disease, for example, involves costs in material and personnel. The benefits are equal to the medical costs of treating disease that would be expected to arise in the absence of inoculation. The costs of public training of unskilled workers is measured against the expected rise in productivity of the workers as a result of the training. This kind of cost-benefit analysis differs from the market concept because it looks at aggregate, rather than individual cost and utility, and it can take into account externalities. In the program of public inoculations, those paying the cost are not necessarily the same ones receiving the benefit. A principal limitation of the analysis is that it is limited to those things which are measurable in money terms. The grief of deaths from diseases are not measured—only the money costs of caring for those who survive. The increased happiness of workers who are trained is not entered as a benefit—only the value of their production. Cost-benefit analysis is a necessary first step in the ordering of social projects, but nonmoney factors must be considered in making the final decision.

IMPORTANCE OF WELFARE CRITERIA

All decisions of government in pursuit of economic goals have significant welfare implications, and often these are unrecognized. As one author has written:

> It does not seem to be realized how *detailed* the agreement on ends must be if a consistent theory of welfare economics is to be erected. There are an infinite number of policy combinations capable (in theory) of securing full employment. No two will have precisely similar effects on all the variables which influence welfare.[1]

A movement to full employment may not be a case of achieving a Pareto optimum if the movement disturbs economic welfare. Economic welfare may be reduced by the policies chosen if total product

[1] J. deV. Graaf, *Theoretical Welfare Economics* (London: Cambridge U.P., 1967, originally pub. in 1957), p. 168.

is reduced, even though every one is employed; if resource use is shifted so that satisfaction from output is reduced, even though product is maximized; and if income may be redistributed in such a way as to cause a negative effect on total satisfaction.

All government economic policy affects the allocation of resources even if total output, rather than allocation, is the goal. Governments largely employ fiscal and monetary policy for their effects on total product demand, attempting to achieve a product demand which maximizes output and minimizes price movements. Where a number of combinations of policies can achieve that purpose, the combination should be chosen which either interferes least with resource allocation, or interferes in a way that compensates for inefficiencies in the market, in accordance with the theory of second best.

One important effect of the policy mix chosen is on the allocation of product between capital and consumption goods. This allocation is a fundamental decision which the economy must make, since all capital accumulation involves a sacrifice of directly usable goods available in the immediate time period. For the individual this allocation takes the form of the decision to save out of income, though the saving may not be directly in the form of capital. At the margin an amount of money income saved or spent on consumption yields the same satisfaction. With a given income distribution the total desired saving out of full-employment income can be considered the community's desired capital formation. The many savers in the economy are not, however, the same persons who make the investment decision. Whether actual capital formation will equal the desired saving depends upon the expected return on capital and the rate of interest.

One school of thought holds that the proper monetary policy is the one which will effect an interest rate that will make investment equal desired saving at the full-employment level. If the rate of interest is higher than this optimum, it means there are some who would like to be lenders and others who would like to be borrowers, if rates were lowered. A lower interest rate will move toward a Pareto optimum by making both lenders and borrowers better off, provided it does not go below the point at which true lending (i.e., an excess of income over consumption) equals borrowing. Application of this rule for the welfare optimum does not require that desired saving be unchanging at the full-employment level. Suppose, for example, that the economy reduces its purchases of automobiles, leading to a deficiency of aggregate consumer demand. Monetary policy can then seek lower interest rates to stimulate investment to absorb the reduced consumption (rise in savings desires). The rule is also applicable whether or not changes in interest rates themselves affect desired saving. If saving is sensitive to interest rates, then a smaller change in interest rates will be required for a given effect on demand. Any lowering of interest rates will simultaneously reduce desired saving and increase investment, both going in the right direction toward closing the gap between full-employment output and demand.

Application of monetary policy as described does not yield an unambiguous separation of monetary and fiscal policy. Taxes directly affect saving by reducing disposable income out of which consumption-saving decisions can be made, and thus the saving function cannot be taken as given independently of tax policy. Income tax rates affect the after-tax distribution of income, and income distribution affects desired saving.

Government expenditures, too, are a form of collective consumption or capital formation, depending upon the type of expenditure. Through spending and taxation the government can direct the allocation of resources toward social capital formation. Fiscal policy may also affect private investment decisions by its influence on the expected rate of return on capital after taxes. It does not appear, then, that the decision with respect to capital formation is a result of market decisions in the private economy. It is a decision made through the political process, and it is necessary for this decision to be correctly made if the market process is to arrive at an optimum allocation of resources.

From a welfare standpoint a clear advantage of fiscal policy over monetary policy is that the incidence of fiscal policy is more precisely determined, and amenable to control, than is the incidence of interest rates. It is somewhat easier, say, to pinpoint the burden of income taxes than of higher interest rates. Interest rates probably affect expenditures directly made on credit more than cash expenditures, and interest itself involves transfers of income from interest payers to interest receivers, but the ultimate recipients and payers and their income status is not known.

Although at any one time both a monetary and a fiscal policy are necessary (as long as the government has a role in the economy), it is not necessary that both be varied in accord with stabilization needs. Monetary policy could be aimed at some stable goal—interest rate stability or stable growth in the money stock—and fiscal policy be varied to accomplish short-run stabilization goals. The effects of stabilization policy then can be more accurately determined, and maximization of welfare, along with maximization of output, can be a more direct goal of stabilization policy.

Another government policy with widespread welfare effects is the rate of exchange between a country's monetary unit and that of other countries. The government may stabilize the rate of exchange or leave it to the free markets. Since the positive action is one of fixing the rates, we consider then the welfare effects of choosing this alternative over free market rates. Only a general sketch is possible.

First, how will the move affect total output? Will it be larger if rates are fixed, using common prices in the two situations? The movement to fixed rates could increase income by providing a stable environment for international trade, encouraging international specialization and exchange. It could reduce real income if the government finds it necessary to take restrictive fiscal and monetary measures to protect its international reserves in order to allow it to continue defending the rate. Differing views on these possibilities are a part of the explanation of differences in views on the desirability of fixed vs. free-exchange rates.

If fixed rates are maintained, who will be the gainers? If we assume that fixed rates encourage foreign trade, then the gainers would appear to be those engaged in exporting and those who purchase imports. The losers are those who will bear the brunt of balance-of-payments adjustment to protect the reserve position. Who these are will depend upon the type of policy the government will follow in maintaining balance of payments equilibrium. If monetary policy is the principal instrument, those who purchase with borrowed funds are most affected. If fiscal policy is the instrument, the type of taxation will determine who bears the incidence.

In all cases, both gainers and losers, the incidence is quite diffused. Almost everyone purchases some imports. Almost everyone is affected by tax-rate changes. The entire problem is so complex that welfare economics clearly does not provide a definitive answer. It does, however, provide something of a systematic approach to making the decision and introduces criteria for evaluation that are not readily evident upon first examination of a policy instrument.

Because of such problems as externalities and income distribution, which the market system cannot handle, maximization of economic welfare inevitably requires some direction of the economy arising from outside the system itself. The rules determined outside the system are sometimes called the *social-welfare function*. What this means is that some value judgments must be made through the political rather than the economic process, whether this political process be a dictator or a pure democracy. The society must decide in some way, for example, whether it wants income equality or income concentration. Unassisted the market process will not arrive at any particular income distribution, since the ownership of the factors of production is socially determined. The society must decide on the amount of capital it wants relative to consumption; individual decisions will not necessarily arrive at the amount of capital the society wishes to pass on to future generations.

In the more advanced economies welfare economics is likely to assume increasing importance. As the economy's absolute output levels rise, questions of distribution become increasingly relevant. As the system becomes more complex and more interrelated, externalities assume increasing importance. When a society is at a very low level of economic production, it is rather clear that an increase in goods will increase welfare. In an affluent society it becomes reasonable to question whether straining the last ounce of output is perhaps less important than directing attention to the distribution of available goods and the quality of the social environment.

Welfare economics is not fully developed, and it inherently suffers from operating as a system of value judgments. Positive, measurable economics is more appealing to many practicing economists. Inevitably, welfare judgments must be made, and it is likely that the science of economics will devote increasing attention to developing a logical structure for decision making.

SUMMARY

Welfare economics is concerned about the ability of the economic system to produce and distribute goods in the manner that will lead to the highest level of satisfaction. A perfectly functioning market system serves economic welfare by assuring that resources are employed in a manner that will maximize the output of the factors of production in making goods that will maximize the satisfaction of the buyers. Between any two goods the optimum position requires that resources be fully used in production and that the following two ratios are equal.

(a) The marginal rate of substitution, which is the amount of one good which would have to be increased to just balance the loss of satisfaction from losing one unit of another good.

(b) The marginal rate of transformation, which is the amount of one good which can be produced from resources released from production of one unit of another good.

The market optimum is not achieved if there are restrictions on movement of the factors of production among alternative outputs or if there are costs and benefits from production which are external to the market system. The market system also does not necessarily lead to the income distribution that would maximize welfare.

The theory of second-best holds that external intervention in the market system may be justified by its imperfections, but intervention should not take the form of attempting to restore the ideal wherever possible. It should recognize imperfections and form policy consistent with them. The achievement of Pareto optimum is one test for justifying intervention. An economy is in Pareto optimum only if it is not possible to make anyone better off without making someone else worse off. The index number criterion says that a given policy will raise welfare if it raises output, where output comparisons are made at a constant price level, i.e., prices prevailing before or after the change. The compensation principle holds that a change is desirable if, as a result, those who gain can compensate those who lose and still have something left over.

SELECTED REFERENCES

Baumol, William, *Welfare Economics and the Theory of the State*, 2d ed. Cambridge, Mass.: Harvard U.P., 1965.

Bergson, Abram, *Essays in Normative Economics*. Cambridge, Mass.: Harvard U.P., 1966.

Graaff, J. deV., *Theoretical Welfare Economics*, paperback ed. London: Cambridge U.P., 1967; first published in 1957.

Little, I. M. D., *A Critique of Welfare Economics*, 3d ed. New York: Oxford U.P., 1957.

Meade, J. E., *Principles of Political Economy*, 2 vols. Chicago: Aldine Publishing, 1965-68.

Mishan, E. J., "A Survey of Welfare Economics, 1939-59," *Surveys of Economic Theory*, Vol. I. New York: St. Martin's, 1966.

Myint, Hla, *Theories of Welfare Economics*. London: Longmans, 1948.

Pigou, A. C., *The Economics of Welfare*, 4th ed. London: Macmillan, 1932.

Scitovsky, Tibor, *Welfare and Competition*. Homewood, Ill.: Irwin, 1957.

DISCUSSION QUESTIONS

1. What is meant by the "opportunity cost" of producing a good?

2. Why under optimum conditions must the marginal rates of transformation and of substitution be equal?

3. Why under optimum conditions must production always be on the production possibilities curve?

4. How do externalities interfere with achievement of the welfare optimum through the market mechanism?

5. How does a change in income distribution influence a society's allocation of resources?

6. Define "Pareto optimum" and cite examples of situations which would violate the Pareto optimum.

7. What are the difficulties involved in determining whether a given policy change increases total output? How does the index number approach attempt to solve these problems?

8. What is meant by the "compensation test?"

9. What are the welfare considerations involved in government interest rate policy (aside from its role in stabilizing total output)?

PART II
DESCRIPTIVE ECONOMICS

13

Social Accounting: National Output

Since the production of goods and services is the means by which the economic system serves man's welfare, a measure of a nation's output is a rather indispensable tool for analyzing its performance. Neither the concept of total output nor the process of measuring is especially simple. Perhaps more important than an absolutely correct measurement is consistency—consistency over time and consistency between nations. To an increasing extent nations are adopting uniform methods of national accounting, and such multilateral organizations as the United Nations, the International Monetary Fund, and the European Economic Community are facilitating this movement toward uniformity. The United Nations annually publishes national account statistics for nations submitting them, and the discussion in this chapter largely employs the United Nations format. A few of the more developed countries issue data on a quarterly basis.

The first problem to consider in output accounting is a unit of measurement. The standard used is the price at which the goods or services change hands in the marketplace, expressed in terms of the national monetary unit. Since most goods do exchange in the marketplace, data are available for their evaluation. There are some exceptions in goods which their producer consumes without sale, and for these goods values are imputed. Market prices of similar transactions are the basis for the imputation. The principal imputations in this regard are food products produced and consumed on the farm and the rental value of homes occupied by their owner. Neither of these sources of consumer satisfaction passes through the market place and the nation's product would be understated if they were not included. It would be inconsistent to include similar items which were sold and exclude these which were not.

The acceptance of market value assumes that this price properly represents the value of a product to society as a whole. There are many reasons why this assumption is questionable. The price may not represent the total social cost, as in the case of resulting air or water pollution, and the price overstates the social benefit of the good. Where monopoly exists, prices may not conform to the conditions which would equate private benefit to the buyer and cost to the seller, with the result that monopoly prices may overstate benefits. Another problem concerns income distribution. The goods which a society produces will conform to the desires of those with ability to purchase—not necessarily to the desires of society as a whole. The value of a yacht may be great for a tycoon yet negligible for an itinerant bean-picker, but the market will value the yacht at the tycoon's ability to pay. Despite these problems governments have devised no alternative to the market valuation of products, and this is what they use in official statistics.

METHODS OF PRODUCT MEASURE

Using market prices, national accounting measures product (1) according to its end use, (2) according to industrial classification of its producers, and (3) according to its distribution among the factors of production.

The industrial classification approach to measuring output is to gather data from each producing unit (largely business enterprises) concerning the value of its output over a period of time. For each producing unit, its contribution to value represents the total value of goods which it sells or accumulates in stock, less the value of goods which it purchases from other producing units. This measurement is then called the *value-added* method of output calculation, recognizing that most producing units create only a portion of the value of output they sell. The summation of value-added for all producing units is the total value of production for the nation.

Each firm's value-added is the contribution of its factors of production to product. The firm's purchases which are excluded from its value-added therefore do not refer to its factor payments—wages, interest, dividend, rent.

The more widely used output measure classifies goods according to end use and gathers data at the point where goods are sold for end use. The value of this output measure is its greater simplicity of collection and greater usefulness as an economic tool. The end-use classification corresponds to aggregate demand for a society's output, and the classifications are in accord with the theory of demand.

The economy's production consists of consumption goods,

fixed-capital formation, exports, and changes in stocks of inventories. Foreign purchasers take exports, and the other three classifications go to private and government purchasers, with government including both central and provincial governments. The sum of fixed-capital formation and changes in stocks are domestic investment (or domestic capital formation).

In principle, consumption goods are those that yield direct and immediate satisfaction to their user. Fixed-capital goods are those that, through time, will yield an output of goods and services. The output may be of either consumer goods or of other capital goods. Stocks represent goods of all types held by producing units (and in some cases government) for later use.

The economy's output of goods for any period is measured by sales of goods to their final users. All of an economy's economic transactions are not included in the measurement. Used goods are not a purchase of current output because they were a part of output in previous years, and were so counted when sold. Land purchases are not included because they are not a part of output; they are merely transfers of assets between holders. Tax payments are not a purchase; they are merely transfers of claims to output from the private to the public sector. The classifications of purchasers are (1) households and nonprofit institutions, (2) enterprises (business), (3) government, and (4) foreign. Households are individuals and families in their capacity as the ultimate users of production. Nonprofit institutions purchase goods which in turn satisfy consumer wants, so that their end use is in the same conceptual framework as households. All purchases of current output by this sector are consumer goods with the exception of residential construction and construction of buildings used by institutions, both of which are a part of capital formation. Consumer purchases include such items as food, clothing, shelter (direct and imputed rent), refrigerators, personal automobiles, and so on. The inclusion of these highly durable goods, such as automobiles, illustrates the necessarily arbitrary division between capital and consumer goods. It would be possible to consider an automobile a capital good, and its service of transportation a consumer good, in the same manner as the separate treatment of housing and rents. Interest payments on loans for the purchase of consumer goods are not a part of output. They are merely transfers of claims to product from borrower to lender, and are not a compensation for current production.

Business enterprises are individuals or organizations which produce goods for sale. In addition to private businesses the term includes public enterprises such as the postal service, which provide goods or services for others. By definition, an enterprise cannot buy consumer goods. The only purchases of a business for its own use is capital. All other goods which the enterprise purchases are necessarily acquisitions associated with goods it sells. Raw materials purchases, for example, are not a part of product because they are included in product later sold by the firm. Other types of purchases are not so obvious, but the principle still holds. A firm's purchase of legal counsel is not product for the nation; it is a part of the cost of other product which is sold. The same applies to advertising and similar outlays.

The same principle could apply to purchases of capital goods, but then the economy would be treating only its output of consumer goods as its national product. Fluctuations in the composition of output between capital and consumer goods would influence the total size of output if it included only consumer goods. Capital goods consist of the enterprises' addition to plant (buildings), machinery, trucks, and other equipment with a life of at least one year.

Government purchases offer considerably more difficulty in delineating between capital and consumption. Payments to government employees are clearly consumption services, since the purchase is not a good which will carry over to future periods. In the computation the service of the employee is valued at his wages. At the other extreme a government office building will yield to the government (or someone else if the building is sold) the services of occupancy for years to come. The greatest problem concerns military procurement and related activities, where the good does not yield economic output in the conventional sense of the term, and the good has only limited possibilities for civilian application. In general, countries treat military goods as consumption rather than capital formation, although the dividing line between military and civilian is itself subject to somewhat arbitrary determination.

As with the private sector, the accounts are concerned only with purchases of current output of goods and services, not with the purchase of land or other assets. Government transfers of purchasing power to the private sector are not included because they are not purchases of output. Transfers, such as retirement benefits and unemployment compensation, are means by which the government surrenders to elements in the private sector a certain portion of claim to current production. Transfer expenditures are therefore not a part of expenditures on output, but they may give rise to such expenditures when their recipients exercise the claim which they have received from government. Government interest payments also are not a part of output purchases and are treated as a transfer.

Sales of products abroad, as exports, represent the final outlet for domestically produced goods and services. Exports include all transfers of goods and services to foreigners for which compensation is received, and all gifts of goods and services from residents of the exporting country. The only exception is military goods transferred abroad by government, which are entered as government purchases rather than exports.

Each of the categories of expenditures represents an overstatement of domestic production because some of the purchases were of imported goods. To eliminate the overstatement it is necessary to subtract imports from the total of expenditures, since it is impractical to subtract imports separately from the sales to each sector.

Expenditures of final users net of imports are almost the total of current output, but there is one additional possibility: changes in inventories of stocks on hand. At all times producing units hold some stocks. They hold materials which they have purchased for further employment in manufacture. They have goods which have been partially manufactured but are still going through the process of production. They have finished goods in stores or warehouses awaiting sale. During any period of time flows out of and into inventory are roughly in balance, but if they are not, it means that sales to final users either overstated or understated output during the period. Consequently changes in stocks, either positive or negative, must form a part of output measurement. Changes in government stockpiles of materials are also in this category. If the valuation of the economy's stocks are higher at the end of the period than at the beginning, it means that production exceeded purchases for end use, and the increment to stock becomes a part of output. If the value of inven-

TABLE 13-1
Gross National Product, United Kingdom and United States
Expenditures at Current Prices, 1967

	U.K. (millions of pounds sterling)	U.S. (billions of dollars)
Private consumption	25,135	494.3
Government consumption	7,105	166.8
Gross domestic fixed-capital formation	7,111	133.4
Increase in stocks	126	4.7
Exports of goods and services	7,048	39.5
Less imports	7,614	39.3
Expenditures on gross domestic product	38,911	799.3
Net factor income from abroad	412	4.6
Gross national product	39,323	803.9

Source: United Nations, *Monthly Statistical Bulletin*, November 1968.

tories falls, it means that sales were in excess of current production. It is necessary to use the same price levels in measuring beginning and ending inventories in order to measure changes in physical stock rather changes in prices.

One final step in computing a country's output is to consider output of its factors of production in foreign countries. The principal item here is income from foreign investment—assets held in foreign countries. Some countries, including the United States, treat such earnings as exports. If not, then it is necessary to add the item, net factor income from abroad (recognizing two-way flows), to derive the total of gross national product. The measure before addition of this item is called *gross domestic product*.

<h2 style="text-align:center">FACTOR INCOME</h2>

All output must give rise to an equivalent amount of claims to output distributed to the factors of production employed. This receipt of income from the sale of current output is consequently another way of approaching the measurement of output. In general such income consists of the return to property (land and capital) and the return to labor in the form of wages and salaries.

The measurement of factor returns must be consistent with the measure of sales of output. Sales of existing assets are excluded, and thus gains from the sales of assets are not a part of product. Changes in stocks must be measured in constant prices in computing business income. Receipts in the nature of transfers, such as receipt of consumer interest, must be excluded.

Taxation represents a way in which current output, or income is distributed. Total income may be measured after direct taxation (in which case a separate income entry is necessary), or before taxation. The United Nations system treats all income accruing to individuals on a before-tax basis. This consists of wage and salary income and of property income, such as rent, interest, and dividends from corporations. Some income does not accrue to persons, and this is the income retained by corporations. This retained income represents the claims on current production accruing to the corporation after it has paid its dividends and its taxes. This entry is called *corporate saving*. Finally, we must include taxes paid by corporations as income, since corporate saving treats income net of taxation. It would have been possible to lump the corporate saving and taxation together as undistributed corporate profits, but the United Nations prefers the former treatment. Note that taxes paid by the noncorporate sector are not shown separately, and therefore its income is on a before tax basis.

TABLE 13-2
Distribution of United States National Income, 1967
(Billions of dollars)

Compensation of employees		469.7
Income of unincorporated enterprise		58.4
Income from property:		89.4
Rent	20.1	
Interest	46.5	
Dividends	22.8	
Corporate transfer payments		2.8
Savings of private corporations		23.5
Direct taxes on corporations		33.2
Less interest on the public debt		10.7
Less interest on consumer debt		13.4
National income		652.9

Source: Compiled from data in *Federal Reserve Bulletin*, Vol. 54 (May 1968).

The sum of income is less than the sum of gross national product for two principal reasons. One reason is that gross national product makes no allowance for the fact that some capital is used up in the course of making current product. To this extent the total of purchases of goods overstates the net product available for distribution, since some of the purchase price represents compensation for depreciation of capital. The producer measures his net return by the rise in the value of his assets (less liabilities), and depreciation allowances recognize that the value of existing capital declines as it is used. Consequently these depreciation allowances must be subtracted from gross national product to arrive at income to the factors of production. Gross national product less depreciation is the same thing as net national product at market prices.

Another reason that gross national product exceeds national income is indirect taxes. These are taxes which are assumed to be a part of the purchase price of goods. They include such items as sales taxes, taxes on property (including land) of both business and households. The seller of a good is essentially acting as a collection agent for government. Taxes on residences are reflected in rent, actual or imputed. Since gross national product measures purchases-inclusive of these taxes, it overstates income from the factors of production.[1] It is logical to argue that these indirect taxes should be subtracted from measured expenditures in computing gross national product, in which case they would not give rise to a discrepancy between income and expenditures on product. The reason for not making this adjust-

[1] It is the excess of indirect taxes over subsidies that is subtracted from national product to arrive at income. Subsidies are government payments to business in the nature of transfers. They give rise to factor income not matched by an equivalent expenditure.

ment at the expenditures level is to maintain a national product measure which most closely resembles the economy's demand for output. The purchaser looks upon the price to be paid inclusive of taxes in allocating demand, and netting out indirect taxes would impair the analysis of aggregate demand and its allocation among different products.

> . . . it is reasonable to suppose that indirect taxes influence relative market prices rather than factor incomes. This, indeed, is the object of making the distinction between indirect taxes and subsidies on the one hand and direct taxes and transfer payments on the other.[2]

Although interest payments by government and consumers do not give rise to current income, interest payments by business are a source of factor income. Business interest payments are not a part of output measurement because no business purchase, other than capital formation, is final product. But interest payments are a means by which business allocates the total return on capital. Enterprise interest payments, like wages, are a component of income, not expenditures. They are a form of allocation of product.

FINANCE OF CAPITAL FORMATION

The basic income and product accounts give rise to an account which shows the relationship between saving and investment and imbalances in receipts and expenditure in the foreign and government sectors. This essentially derives from the national income identity that saving is equal to investment plus the government deficit (excess of government spending over taxes) plus the excess of exports over imports.

Domestic capital formation (investment) is the sum of gross expenditures on fixed capital and changes in stocks.

Private producing units consider a portion of their receipts as compensation for deterioration of existing capital rather than a return on capital. These depreciation allowances are a part of the economy's gross saving. In the government sector, depreciation allowances apply only to public buildings. Such allowances mean that a portion of taxation is applied against the government consumption of capital. The accounts also allow for depreciation of private housing though many owners make no explicit allowances.

Any net capital formation (i.e., in excess of offsets to capital consumption) must then come from net saving. The major form of such saving is the excess of household income over consumption

2 United Nations, *A System of National Accounts and Supporting Tables,* Studies in Methods, Series F, No. 2, Rev. 2 (New York, 1964), p. 8.

TABLE 13-3
Finance of Gross Domestic Capital Formation in Canada, 1964
(Millions of Canadian dollars)

Provision for consumption of fixed capital		5,575
Private enterprise	4,998	
Government enterprise	577	
Saving		5,318
Government	1,668	
Private corporations	1,252	
Households and non-profit institutions	2,398	
Deficit on current account.		428
Adjustment for stock valuation		-121
Residual error		- 89
Gross domestic capital formation		11,111

Source: United Nations, *Yearbook of National Accounts Statistics, 1965*, p. 56.

spending and taxes and the undistributed income of corporations. The remaining forms of financing capital formation are an excess of taxes over government spending (a type of forced saving for the private sector) and the excess of imports over exports (a form of saving for foreigners). The following shows the derivation of this account from national income identities:

$$\underset{\text{Investment}}{I} + \underset{\text{Government}}{G} + \underset{\text{Exports}}{X} = \underset{\text{Saving}}{S} + \underset{\text{Taxes}}{T} + \underset{\text{Imports}}{M}$$

$$\underset{\text{Domestic capital formation}}{I} = S + (T - G) + (M - X)$$

ADJUSTMENT FOR PRICE CHANGES

All measurements in income and product accounts start with the evaluation of product in terms of prices prevailing at the time. This means that between any two time periods, the total value of output may change as a result of changes in the physical volume of goods and services, a change in the prices at which goods and services exchange, or some combination of the two. For comparisons over time it is necessary to attempt to separate these movements in prices and real output. A conceivable approach to this problem is to value output at two price levels—the one prevailing and some other price level in a time period used as standard. For example, if 1965 is the standard price level, then for output in 1970 each product carries the value at which it exchanges in 1970 and the value at which it would have exchanged in 1965. Any growth in output on the latter basis represents growth in real output. Any growth in output measured at current prices represents changes in both output and prices. The change in prices is obtained by dividing the change in total expenditures by the change in real output. (Actually all values are expressed as ratios of the standard year.)

In practice it is not feasible to price each product exchanged at two different price levels, since product actually exchanges only at current price levels. A shortcut is to measure independently movements in prices (based on sample prices) and in total expenditures (which is always the product of real output times the price at which it exchanges):

$$\text{Price} \times \text{Output} = \text{Expenditures}$$

$$\text{Output} = \frac{\text{Expenditures}}{\text{Price}}$$

Derivation of Change in Real Product
(Hypothetical Example)

	Year 1	Year 2
Output	700	800
Price index	1.00	1.06

Output in year 2 expressed in year 1 prices:

$$\frac{800}{1.06} = 755$$

Growth in output in constant prices:

$$\frac{755 - 700}{700} = 7.9\%$$

A single price index for all goods may be used, or separate price indices may be used to adjust components of national product separately. An index for residential construction prices is used for residential construction expenditures, an export price index for export purchases, and so on. Expenditures are expressed in terms of monetary units. Prices are expressed in terms of a ratio to the standard, or base, year. The resulting real output is also in monetary units, and represents an approximation of the value of output if it were repriced in terms of the base year. This figure by itself is not very meaningful, but it provides a basis for comparisons over time when converted into a percent change in terms of the base year.

Growth in real output results from the combination of growth in the labor force (derived from population growth) and growth in productivity (defined as output per man-hour worked). The ability of an economy to increase its material satisfaction is measured by the growth in real output per capita. This is also the most relevant comparison of economic performance between countries. There is the additional complication of finding a common unit in which to express product value, since each country's prices are in terms of its own monetary unit. The monetary unit of one country is the common unit, and other monetary units are converted to it at the prevailing ratios of exchange.

SUMMARY

National output can be measured by expenditures on a nation's current production of goods and services valued at market prices. To eliminate intermediary transactions and avoid double counting, only expenditures by the final user of products is included, and then net changes in stocks of inventories are added. Households are the final users of consumer goods, and in addition they purchase capital goods through residential construction.

Capital-goods purchases of enterprises, and changes in their inventories, are their only purchases included in output measurement. Governments also purchase consumer and capital goods. The net of exports over imports is added to the total of domestic purchases.

Income measures total product according to distributive shares of the factors of production. Depreciation of capital and indirect taxes are included in the expenditures measure of output, and must be subtracted in deriving national income. Income is usually measured before deduction of direct taxes. Domestic capital formation is equal to after-tax income in excess of consumption, plus the excess of taxes over government expenditures, plus the excess of imports over exports.

National product valued in terms of some previous price level, called the *base period*, is measured by output at current prices divided by the price index. The index is the ratio of prices in the current year to prices in the base year. Changes in national product adjusted for price changes is a means of measuring growth in real product.

SELECTED REFERENCES

Miernyk, William H., *The Elements of Input-Output Analysis.* New York: Random House, 1965.

Ruggles, Richard, and Nancy Ruggles, *National Income Accounts and Income Analysis*, 2d ed. New York: McGraw-Hill, 1956.

United Nations, *A System of National Accounts and Supporting Tables*, Studies in Methods, Series F, No. 2, Rev. 2. New York, 1964.

Usher, Dan, *The Price Mechanism and the Meaning of National Income Statistics*. New York: Oxford U.P., 1967.

DISCUSSION QUESTIONS

1. What are the objections to the use of market prices to measure total output?

2. In the final sales method of output calculation, what purchases of businesses are included as end use, and why?

3. The value-added method of output measurement classifies goods according to industry of origin. Why is this classification considered less useful than the classification yielded by the final sales method?

4. How is a decrease in inventories accounted for in the final sales method of output measurement?

5. If domestic capital formation is less than private saving, in what form is the remainder of private saving taken?

6. How does a rise in salaries of government employees affect national output? National income?

14

Social Accounting: Financial Flows

Economic transactions between persons and groups can be divided into two fundamental categories: goods and credit. Credit, or financial flows, involve changes in assets and liabilities. Transactions in goods usually involve also a credit flow.

Social accounting has so far concentrated largely on goods, since these are the ultimate objective of the economic society. But financial flows are a significant feature of the capitalist economic system, and undoubtedly influence production and sale of goods. There is a growing interest in the measurement of financial flows, as evidenced by this United Nations statement:

> It is envisaged that, at some future date, the United Nations System of National Accounts will be extended to include flow of funds and input-output tables, in the first instance, and national balance sheets as a longer term objective. Many national statistical offices have made progress with, or are at present examining the possibility of, extending their national accounts in these directions and it seems likely that, sooner or later, it will become necessary to establish international standards in regard to them.[1]

The United States has made the greatest advance in aggregate financial accounting, and this chapter describes in a general way its "flow of funds" accounts. The treatment omits many details and employs simplifications in order to place major stress on the basic objective of the accounts.[2]

The flow of funds accounts are a complete measure of all economic transactions between designated sectors of the economy. They

---

[1] *A System of National Accounts and Supporting Tables,* Studies in Methods, Series F, No. 2, Rev. 2 (New York, 1964), p. vii.

[2] For a more detailed exposition, see the following publications of the Board of Governors of the Federal Reserve System, *Federal Reserve Bulletin,* Vol. 45 (August 1959) and Vol. 51 (November 1965), and *Flow of Funds/Savings Accounts, 1946-1960 Supplement 5* (1961).

include, but are not limited to, the flows involved in national output accounting.

Transactions between economic units can be as detailed or as aggregative as desired. There are transactions between individual units in the economy, or individuals can be aggregated into groups, considering transactions of the group as a whole. A broad grouping, corresponding to the grouping of national output accounts, consists of (1) households, (2) business enterprises (nonfinancial), (3) business enterprises (financial), (4) government, and (5) foreign. Financial enterprises are separated from nonfinancial because the purpose of the accounts is to illuminate the nature of financial flows in the economy. There is no need to separate these types of institutions in output accounting because financial institutions' contribution to output is rather small. But consolidating them with other businesses in the financial accounts would net out transactions of economic interest.

Each sector has over a specified period of time (a year or a quarter) transactions which are "sources of funds" for the sector and transactions which are "uses of funds." Sources can be considered as transactions tending to increase the sector's claims to current output. Uses are transactions which employ claims to output in the time period. By the nature of the definitions the sources of each sector must equal the uses. This overall equivalence has its origin in double entries for single transactions. Let us take the case of an individual's purchase of goods from a corporation, using a check on his demand deposit for payment. The accounts show:

Source	Use
Individual	
Reduction in deposit claims	Current purchase
Corporation	
Receipt from current sale	Increase in deposit claims
Bank	
Increase in liabilities to corporation	
Decrease in liabilities to individual	

With respect to national output, income from current output is a source and expenditures on current output a use. An additional source is borrowing, or increases in liabilities. An additional use is lending, or increases in financial assets, including money. A decrease

---

Sectors in U.S. Flow of Funds Accounts

Consumer and Nonprofit Organizations

Business
    Farm business
    Noncorporate nonfinancial business
    Corporate nonfinancial business

Government
    Federal government
    State government
    Local government

Financial Institutions
    Commercial banks
    Monetary authorities
    Mutual savings banks
    Savings and loan associations
    Credit unions
    Life insurance companies
    Noninsured pension plans
    Other insurance companies
    Finance companies
    Security brokers and dealers
    Open-end investment companies
    Agencies of foreign banks
    Banks in U. S. possessions

Rest of the world

---

in liabilities is a negative source. For financial business, the biggest components of sources and uses are changes in financial assets and liabilities. For the other sectors transactions associated with current output are the largest components of sources and uses.

Output transactions are valued at current prices, as in national output accounting. Financial transactions are valued at current market prices of the asset in question, and this valuation introduces problems in the accounts which destroy some of its symmetry. For one thing, this valuation technique allows a sector to have a net increase in claims which does not arise from saving of current output. The increase may come from a rise in the market valuation of its existing claims. Another complication of this measure is that the increase in value of claims of one sector may differ from the change in value of the same instruments held as liabilities by another sector. The net worth of a corporation is its assets less its fixed price liabilities. The claims of shareholders on this net worth may have an entirely different value, depending upon market prices of common stock. Despite these complications market value still seems the most meaningful, since this is the way that each sector views its own position.

HOUSEHOLD SECTOR

The household sector starts with income from current output as a source of funds. This is essentially national output less taxes and corporate withdrawals from income in the form of capital consumption allowances and undistributed profits. Households use funds for consumption, and the remainder is household saving.

Household saving is now matched with other sources and uses of funds. The additional sources are net increases in liabilities, i.e., the algebraic sum of increases and decreases. Saving and net borrowing then are equal to net increases in assets (except for changes in market values). These assets are real (capital formation) and financial.[3] Another way of stating this relation is that gross saving (net saving plus capital consumption allowances) is equal to gross investment (capital expenditures plus net growth in claims on other sectors). Since income and output are on a gross basis, a portion of saving is capital consumption allowances.

For this sector the greatest financial source of funds is mortgages, with the sector's net change in financial liabilities largely to financial enterprises. Mortgages are a natural source of borrowing for the sector, since much of its capital formation is in residences. The greatest financial uses of this sector are acquisition of deposit type claims on financial institutions.

BUSINESS ENTERPRISES

The sources of funds for business enterprises from current output are their capital consumption allowances and undistributed income remaining after taxes. Income distributed as dividends accrues to other sectors, largely households. Corporate saving occurs largely in nonfinancial enterprises rather than financial, and the principal additional sources of funds for these businesses are flotations of bonds and bank loans. The principal uses of funds are in capital formation.

By their nature financial institutions acquire most of their funds from borrowing and use their funds largely for lending. This sector

[3] The United States treats production of household durables as capital formation rather than consumption.

TABLE 14-1
Financial Sectors in the Flow of Funds 1967, Fourth Quarter
(Billions of dollars at annual rates)

	Transaction Category	Uses	Sources
1	Gross saving		3.0
2	Capital consumption		1.1
3	Net saving (1 − 2)		1.9
4	Gross investment (5 + 10)	2.7	
5	Private capital expenditures, net	.9	
6	Consumer durables		
7	Residential construction		
8	Plant and equipment	.9	
9	Inventory change		
10	Net financial Investment (11 − 12)	1.8	
11	Financial uses, net	83.2	
12	Financial sources		81.4
13	Gold and official U.S. foreign exchange	−.5	
14	Treasury currency	.5	
15	Demand deposits and currency		14.7
16	Private domestic	.7	12.7
17	U.S. government		1.2
18	Foreign		.8
19	Time and savings accounts	.4	40.8
20	At commercial banks		23.8
21	At savings institutions	.4	17.0
22	Life insurance reserves		4.6
23	Pension fund reserves		8.5
24	Consolidated bank items	1.6	1.6
25	Credit market instruments	73.1	2.2
26	U.S. government securities	13.6	
27	State and local obligations	9.9	
28	Corporate and foreign bonds	8.9	.9
29	Corporate stocks	8.4	2.9
30	1- to 4-family mortgages	10.4	1.0
31	Other mortgages	8.5	
32	Consumer credit	3.1	
33	Bank loans not elsewhere classified	6.5	−2.4
34	Other loans	3.9	−.2
35	Open-market paper	2.9	2.4
36	Federal loans		−2.5
37	Security credit	4.3	2.1
38	To brokers and dealers	.9	2.1
39	To others	3.5	
40	Taxes payable		−.5
41	Trade credit	.3	
42	Equity in noncorporate business		
43	Miscellaneous financial transactions	2.7	7.2
44	Sector discrepancies (1 − 4)	.3	

Source: *Federal Reserve Bulletin*, Vol. 54 (May 1968), p. A-66.

includes such intermediaries as commercial banks, savings and loan associations, savings banks, insurance companies, finance companies, securities dealers, and the monetary authorities of the federal government. They issue a wide variety of liabilities tailored to the types of assets that the economy wants to hold. Important among them are deposit-type liabilities and obligations to purchasers of insurance for compensation under contengencies specified by the insurance contract. The principal uses of funds are in acquisitions of mortgages, stocks and bonds, consumer and business loans, and government securities.

GOVERNMENT

The government includes all public bodies—federal, state, local, and various public authorities. The principal income from current output is taxation and the principal use of funds is for purchases of current output. The accounts do not distinguish between capital formation and consumption, and therefore the only asset acquisitions are financial. Some financial assets are acquired under special programs, such as pension funds of government employees and loans to the private sector for specialized purposes. The major financial source of funds is the issuance of various types of bonds. Often this sector's increase in liabilities exceeds its increase in assets.

FOREIGN

To complete the accounts it is necessary to include a sector for the transactions of the rest of the world with the United States. This sector acquires claims on U.S. output from its exports (U.S. imports) and uses claims for its imports (U.S. exports). An additional source of funds for the sector is increases in its liabilities to the United States; an additional use is increases in claims on the United States. The Balance of Payments section in this chapter treats the foreign sector in more detail.

ASSETS AND LIABILITIES

The flow of funds measures increments to assets and liabilities. At any one time each sector also has a stock of assets and liabilities accumulated from the past. The United States statement of assets and liabilities includes only those of a financial nature. Problems of measurement and data gathering have not yet allowed regular compilation of real assets and liabilities.

TABLE 14-2
United States Financial Assets and Liabilities, December 31, 1967
(Billions of dollars)

No.	Transaction Category	HH A	HH L	Bus A	Bus L	S&L A	S&L L	Total A	Total L	USG A	USG L	Fin A	Fin L	RoW A	RoW L	All A	All L	Disc
		Households		Business		State and Local Governments		Total		U.S. Government		Financial Sectors		Rest of the World		All Sectors		
1	Total financial assets	1617.9		357.0		103.0		2077.8		99.7		1103.5		93.9		3375.0		
2	Total liabilities		385.7		546.7		166.7		1099.0		334.7		1018.9		108.2		2560.9	
3	Gold stock																	
4	Official U.S. foreign exchange									.1		12.0		29.5	2.3	41.6	2.3	
5	IMF position									.7	2.9	1.6			.4		.4	
6	Treasury currency									3.4	4.6	6.6	.1			6.6	4.6	-2.0
7	Demand deposits and currency	100.9		45.6		12.1		158.6				14.2	200.4			184.6	200.4	
8	Private domestic												188.8			172.8	188.8	16.0
9	U.S. government									8.0			7.8			8.0	7.8	-.2
10	Foreign												3.8	3.8			3.8	
11	Time and savings accounts	329.7		22.7		15.9		368.3				.9	379.0			379.0	379.0	
12	At commercial banks	134.5						173.1				.2	183.1			183.1	183.1	
13	At savings institutions	195.2						195.2				.7	195.9	9.5		195.9	195.9	
14	Life insurance reserves	115.7						115.7			7.3		108.4			115.7	115.7	
15	Pension fund reserves	182.2					41.4	182.2	41.4		22.3		118.5			182.2	182.2	
16	Consolidated bank items											29.6	29.6			29.6	29.6	
17	Credit Market instruments	867.0		50.6	341.5	72.8	122.1	990.4	830.4	64.5	291.4	991.4	93.2	33.5	41.6	2079.7	1256.6	
18	U.S. govt. securities	83.8		12.4		27.8		124.0		10.7	291.4	154.4		12.9			291.4	
19	State and local obligations	40.8		5.1		4.1	117.5	49.9	117.5			67.5					117.5	
20	Corporate and foreign bonds	6.3			123.0	35.7		42.0	123.0			107.7	19.5	2.3	9.5		152.0	
21	Corporate stocks	726.8						726.8				124.0	44.8	16.2	7.0	867.0	44.8	
22	1-4 family mortgages	9.3	226.3		7.6	5.2		14.5	233.8	7.7		210.9					236.1	
23	Other mortgages		15.8		89.1				104.9			97.2	2.3				104.9	
24	Consumer credit		99.2	22.8				22.8	99.2			76.5				93.2	99.2	
25	Bank loans n.e.c.		13.4		89.9				103.2			118.5	8.2	2.1	25.1		118.5	
26	Other loans		12.2		31.9		4.7		48.7	46.0		34.7	18.4	2.1	3.0		92.3	-.9
27	Open market paper				12.8				18.8				14.1				21.4	
28	Federal loans		1.3		4.3		4.7			45.3		26.8	4.4		22.1		45.3	
29	Security credit	2.7	12.3					2.7				20.1	10.6				23.2	
30	To brokers and dealers	2.7						2.7				7.6		.3			10.6	
31	To others		12.3									12.6	10.6		.3		12.6	
32	Taxes payable				16.8	2.2		2.2	16.8	15.9						18.1	18.1	
33	Trade credit		2.6	163.6	122.9		3.1	163.6	128.6	5.8		3.2	1.3		.3	172.6	133.7	-39.0
34	Miscellaneous financial transactions	19.7	4.0	74.4	65.5			94.1	69.5	4.0	4.1	24.0	78.0	17.2	63.5	139.3	215.1	75.8

Source: Federal Reserve Bulletin, Vol. 54 (May 1968), p. A-77.9.

Approximate U.S., Flow of Funds, 1966*
(Billions of U.S. dollars)

Sources		Uses		Surplus or Deficit (−) on Income and Product Account = Net Change in Claims on Other Sectors

Households

Income	520	Consumption	409	
		Investment†	93 §	18
Increase in financial liabilities‡		Increase in financial assets‡		Net increase in claims on other sectors
	25	—	43 =	18

Nonfinancial Business

Income (capital consumption and retained earnings)	74	Capital expenditures	93	−19
Increase in financial liabilities		Increase in financial assets		Net increase in liabilities to other sectors
	40	—	21 =	19

Financial Business

Income (capital consumption and retained earnings)	4	Capital expenditures	1	3
Increase in financial liabilities		Increase in financial assets		Net increase in claims on other sectors
	53	—	56 =	3

Government

Tax income	153	Expenditures	153	0
Increase in financial liabilities		Increase in financial assets		
	10	—	10 =	0

Foreign

Income (U.S. imports)	41	Expenditures (U.S. exports)	43	−2
Increase in financial liabilities		Increase in financial assets		Net increase in liabilities to other sectors
	6	—	4 =	2

Total of deficits and surpluses 0

*The figures are only approximations to 1966 data. Exact data were not used in order to preserve the internal consistency of the accounts and their basic concept, as well as to avoid numerous statistical references.

†Unlike investment in the U.S. national product accounts, investment in the flow of funds accounts includes consumer durables. Accordingly, consumption allowances on them are a part of household gross saving.

‡The increase in liabilities within each sector is the algebraic sum of increases and decreases in liabilities. A similar observation holds for each sector's increase in assets.

§All underlined figures are components of domestic investment of the private economy. By the nature of the accounts they are equal to household saving (520 − 409 = 111) plus corporate saving (74 + 4) plus the government surplus (0) plus the excess of imports over exports (41 − 43 = −2). The sum of these is 187, which is the same as domestic private investment.

Source: Data from which these approximations were derived are from *Federal Reserve Bulletin,* Vol. 53 (May 1967), pp. 850–861.

There are also some differences in measurement of financial claims between the flow of funds accounts and the national financial balance sheet. A principal difference is in the treatment of corporate shares. In the flow of funds accounts proceeds from the sale of new stock shares is a source of funds for corporations. In the balance sheet, there is no entry for liabilities attributable to capital stock because of the absence of a meaningful way to measure this liability. Holdings of capital stock are measured at market value. Because of this discrepancy, and because real assets are excluded, the total of assets for all sectors greatly exceeds the total of liabilities.

For the household sector and financial enterprises, financial assets exceed financial liabilities. For the other sectors, liabilities exceed assets.

BALANCE OF PAYMENTS

A country's international balance of payments is in principle the same thing as the foreign sector of a flow of funds account. Both are complete statements of economic transactions of a country with the rest of the world over a time period. The balance of payments was computed long before development of the flow of funds concept, and in part the flow of funds is the extension to domestic sectors of the treatment long accorded the foreign sector. All countries compile balance-of-payments accounts, whereas national financial accounting is in the experimental stage in only a few countries.

Because of the more widespread use of balance-of-payments accounts, this section will consider the foreign sector from that standpoint. It largely uses the procedures of the International Monetary Fund, which compiles balance-of-payment data submitted by the individual countries of the world.[4] The flow of funds looks at the rest of the world in terms of its income from the country in question. The balance of payments reverses this perspective. It views the rest of the world with respect to income received from it and payments made to it. The signs are reversed between the balance of payments and the flow of funds, but otherwise there is little difference.

For international comparisons, nations' balance-of-payments accounts are presented in terms of U.S. dollars. Transactions conducted in other monetary units are converted to the dollar at the prevailing rate of exchange. For a country other than the United States the balance of payments can be looked upon as the total of transactions

[4] See International Monetary Fund, *Balance of Payments Manual*, 3d ed. (Washington, D.C., 1961).

which cause the country to receive dollar claims on the United States and the total of transactions which cause it to lose dollar claims. For the United States the accounts measure transactions causing it to increase its dollar liabilities and transactions causing it to decrease its dollar liabilities.

The reason for this difference in concept is that the U.S. dollar is a money used as a payments media around the world. Countries hold dollar claims because they can be used for transactions with all countries, not just the United States. Conversely, the United States does not need to hold the money claims of other countries because it can use its own liabilities in international transactions. The subject of international valuation is much more complex than this, but the approach is of some use in understanding the measurement of international flows. Regardless of measurement, a source of funds can still be considered as an increase in claims to world output and a use of funds as the employment within the time period of claims to world output.

The transactions in current output which give rise to sources of funds, or receipts, for a country are its exports. These are goods sold and shipped to foreigners, and services performed for foreigners, such as insurance, shipping, and tourist expenditures in the host country. Shipments of monetary gold do not enter as an export. Monetary gold is that held by governments for its value as a claim on the world, and is therefore among the capital items considered below. Shipments of military goods as grants are excluded from exports, partly because no payment is involved and the goods do not give rise to receipts. Parallel concepts are employed with respect to imports, which are a use of foreign funds.

Current receipts also include income from services of a country's factors of production working abroad, such as foreign earned wages and income from foreign investments, and payments to foreign factors are a use of funds. Since these are in separate entries, they are therefore not a part of exports and imports. The final item of current receipts and expenditures is gifts from and to foreigners. These transfer payments are made by both government and private payers.

The difference between current sources and current uses is the surplus of the nation on current account. If positive, it is a type of saving for the nation.

Additional sources and uses of funds come from changes in assets and liabilities, called the *capital account*. A net rise in foreign assets (increases less decreases) is a use of funds. It is a means by which the nation takes compensation for its receipts. A net rise in liabilities is a source of funds. The principal items in the capital account (recognizing the possibility of two-way flows in each case) are as follows.

Direct Investment. The acquisition of real capital in a foreign country is a claim on the country. The acquisition differs from an import in that the goods remain in the foreign country, but otherwise the effects on the balance of payments are the same. Direct investment is also defined to include acquisition of corporate shares in cases in which the buyer effectively controls the foreign corporation.

Financial Claims. These are various types of claims designated in money terms, irrespective of the monetary unit employed. It is the international separation of the claimant and obligor that creates a balance of payments entry, not the monetary unit employed. Included are short- and long-term loans, bonds, mortgages, and corporate shares where the buyer has a minority interest. In this category also are money claims—currency and demand deposits—and other deposit-type claims.

Monetary Gold. Gold is a physical asset, but governments consider it as an international claim. An outward shipment of gold is therefore a decrease in foreign assets, and as such, a source of funds. An inflow of gold is a use of funds.

If there is any imbalance in current account, there will necessarily be an imbalance in capital account. The equivalent of total sources and uses is true for individual transactions as well as the sector as a whole, as explained in flow of funds accounting. If a nation has a surplus on current account, then its net increase in foreign assets will exceed its net increase in foreign liabilities. This is its net lending to the rest of the world. This net increase may be in any form, including gold or monetary-type claims on foreigners, or any highly illiquid claims, such as direct investment. If the nation has a deficit on current account, it is a net borrower from the rest of the world, irrespective of the type of liability incurred.

Nations employ the concept of "deficit" and "surplus" in the balance of payments to refer to specifically selected capital transactions. A true deficit or surplus can occur only in the current account, and therefore the concept as applied to the overall accounts has a special definition.

For most nations a deficit or surplus takes the form of a net change in foreign assets of a highly liquid nature, without regard to changes in the composition or size of other foreign assets and liabilities. The assets considered consist of government holdings of gold and short-term or demand claims on foreign financial institutions and governments, including the International Monetary Fund. (Claims on the International Monetary Fund are largely the equivalent of gold which the nations have deposited in the Fund.) In some cases similar claims held by the nation's banks enter the computation. Most foreign financial assets included in the computation are dollar claims on U.S. obligors, principally the U.S. government and banks. If the algebraic sum of changes in all assets included in the computation is positive, the nation has a surplus in its balance of payments. If negative, there is a deficit.

Gold and net claims on the International Monetary Fund are virtually the only foreign asset which the United States employs in measuring a balance-of-payments position, but the United States also considers changes in its liquid liabilities (largely deposit liabilities and U.S. government securities) to foreign governments. Increases in such liabilities contribute to a deficit, decreases to a surplus. It is the net result of changes in these liabilities and in the designated assets that measures the overall balance-of-payments position.

TABLE 14-3
Canada's Balance of Payments, 1967
(Millions of U.S. dollars)

Exports	10,635
Imports..	10,087
Trade balance	548
Net receipts from investment income, services, and transfer payments	-941
Total	-393
Long-term capital outflows	737
Long-term capital inflows	2,019
Net inflow	1,282
Net short-term capital outflow, including errors and omissions...	-872
International Monetary Fund accounts	15
Gold and foreign exchange (increase -)	-32
Net official monetary movements	-17

Source: *Annual Report, 1968*, International Monetary Fund, p. 114.

The reason for the concepts of deficit and surplus lies in the purpose for which nations hold the assets included. Nations hold them as reserves for financing external transactions which the private economy cannot accommodate. A loss of such reserves (or, in the case of the United States, increases in claims upon them) impairs the future ability of the nation to provide such residual financing.

SUMMARY

The flow of funds accounts measure economic transactions, financial and real, between sectors of the economy. Each sector has a source of funds from other sectors through income from current output and through borrowing (net increases in liabilities). Each sector uses funds for purchases of current output and acquisitions of financial assets (net lending). The total of each sector's sources of funds is equal to uses. The national balance sheet is limited to statements of financial assets and liabilities held by each sector.

The major sectors of the economy are households, businesses (separated between financial and nonfinancial), government, and the rest of the world. There are further subdivisions of these sectors.

The rest of the world sector is similar to the balance of payments, which measures for a country its total receipts and expenditures from the rest of the world. The balance on current account consists largely of the difference between exports and imports. The capital account measures changes in assets and liabilities between countries, including monetary gold. Any surplus in the current account is necessarily matched by net lending to the rest of the world, and any deficit by net borrowing. *Deficit* and *surplus* in the total balance of payments refer to decreases and increases, respectively, in selected foreign assets, including gold.

SELECTED REFERENCES

The Flow of Funds Approach to Social Accounting, Vol. 26 of *Studies in Income and Wealth.* Princeton, N.J.: Princeton U.P., 1962.

Flow of Funds in the United States, 1939-53. Washington, D.C.: Board of Governors of the Federal Reserve System, 1955.

Powelson, John, *National Income and Flow of Funds Analysis.* New York: McGraw-Hill, 1960.

Revell, Jack, *The Wealth of the Nation.* New York: Cambridge U.P., 1967.

Yanovsky, M., *Social Accounting Systems.* Chicago: Aldine Publishing, 1966.

DISCUSSION QUESTIONS

1. Define "sources" and "uses" of funds as used in flow of funds accounting.

2. Explain why valuation of financial assets at current market prices introduces internal inconsistencies in the flow of funds accounts.

3. Why are the total of corporate profits not a source of funds for business enterprises?

4. Why don't the total of assets and liabilities match in the national balance sheet of the United States?

5. What considerations are involved in distinguishing between financial (portfolio) investment and direct investment in international capital flows?

6. How are international transfer payments treated in balance-of-payments accounting? How are international interest payments treated?

15

The Economy and the State

The desirable role of government in the economy has remained a central theme of economic debate since the beginning of capitalism some five centuries ago. The development of a working alternative to capitalism—communism—and the wide divergence of the governmental function between the two systems have intensified this debate in the twentieth century.

Capitalism is a system in which the major production decisions are made by private owners of capital and land. The resulting output accrues to the owners of these instruments of production and to the class of free laborers whom they employ. Along with this structural definition is an underlying philosophy which sanctions the individual's acquisition of material wealth as a socially beneficial pursuit. A characteristic of capitalism is a social surplus—a continued excess of production over current consumption. The resulting accumulation of capital leads to continued growth in output, endowing capitalism with an inherently dynamic nature. Another source of continuing change is the flow of innovations from the socially sanctioned entrepreneurial quest for profit.

Although economic growth has accompanied capitalism, growth is not the inevitable outcome of a goods-making society. It appears that society has experienced sustained growth in only the last two centuries. Sumner Slichter arrived at this conclusion by taking the earliest known measured output data and projecting backward. Starting with an estimated output of $1,100 (1955 prices) per worker per year in the United States in the 1870's, and assuming European output to be about the same, a backward projection of a growth rate as small as 1 percent per annum would have indicated output of only $7.80 at the time Columbus sailed. The implausibility of such result indicated to Slichter that "the conclusion is inescapable that during most of human history productivity was not increasing at all."[1] The immediate predecessor to capitalism was *feudalism*, a system dominated by the church and the military. The producing unit was the manor, ruled by its lord from an hereditary land grant and worked by an unfree class of serfs. There was no strong central government under feudalism, the degree of political unification at any one time depending upon the strengths of allegiances between lords. It was around 1500 that the merchant class of Venice, Florence, and other cities gave birth to *capitalism* and the capitalist spirit. Capitalism and the strength of monarchies grew together, and the alliance between the two was called *mercantilism*, an interval of about three centuries between feudalism and unfettered capitalism.

In the mercantilist stage of capitalism, state regulation of business was widespread and complex. The crown granted monopolies (exclusive commercial rights) for both domestic industry and foreign trade, an example of the latter being the famous British East India Company. Subsidies were granted. Import and export restrictions were imposed. Motives for trade restriction were diverse, such as manipulating foreign trade to accumulate gold and prohibiting the export of nonmanufactured materials to promote domestic industry. The literary spokesmen for mercantilism were chiefly pamphleteers interested in current policy issues, such as Thomas Mun (1571-1641), a director of the East India Company.

ADAM SMITH (1723-1790)

Adam Smith's *Wealth of Nations* (1776) was a critical attack on mercantilist thought. It also gave birth to "classical economics," a system of economic thought which prevailed for at least a century and which is still influential in many lines of economic inquiry. It was in this debate over government intervention that economics as a separate discipline began.

Smith attempted to show how a system of private production and trade, largely unregulated, resulted in the maximum public good—an assumption necessary in some degree if capitalism is to be defended in principle. In his own famous phrase Smith described "the invisible hand" of the market as the ultimate enforcer of the public good. The producer of a good must ultimately charge no more than the value of that good to society. If he charges more, competitors

[1] *Economic Growth in the United States* (New York: Free Press, 1961), p. 55.

will emerge and drive the price down. Furthermore, through competition producers will make exactly those goods which society wants. If they do not, they will be unable to recoup the cost of production. Rising prices for goods which the public does want at first raise the rate of profit, attracting production to them until their prices are equal to costs.

> As every individual, therefore, endeavors as much as he can both to employ his capital in the support of domestic industry that its produce may be of the greatest value; every individual necessarily labours to render the annual revenue of the society as great as he can.[2]

Smith made a virtue of thrift—the willingness to forego consumption for capital accumulation—as the source of economic growth. It is private effort "in spite both of the extravagance of government, and the greatest errors of administration" which "maintain the natural progress of things towards improvement . . . ."

State monopolies are contrary to public interest because they distort the allocation of capital toward the protected enterprise, especially colonial trade. "Every derangement of the natural distribution of stock is necessarily hurtful to the society in which it takes place." (p. 597)

Writing in the early stages of the Industrial Revolution and in the land of its origin, Smith helped free capitalism from its mercantilist grip and wrote a treatise which became the classical statement of the capitalist philosophy.

KARL MARX (1818-1883)

Rather than Smith's "system of natural liberty," Karl Marx saw capitalism as a fierce class struggle which would culminate in the establishment of a socialist state by the working class. He felt that the state under capitalism had become the servant of the "bourgeoisie," the owners of the means of production.

> The executive of the modern state is but a committee for managing the common affairs of the whole bourgeoisie. . . .
> The bourgeoisie, wherever it has got the upper hand, has put an end to all feudal, patriarchal, idyllic relations. It has pitilessly torn asunder the motley feudal ties that bound man to his "natural superiors," and has left remaining no other nexus between man and man than naked self-interest, than callous "cash payment." It has drowned the most heavenly ecstasies of religious fervor, of chivalrous enthusiasm, of philistine sentimentalism, in the icy water of egotistical calculation. It has resolved personal worth into exchange value, and in place of the

[2] *Wealth of Nations*, Modern Library ed. (New York: Random House, 1937), p. 423.

numberless indefeasible chartered freedoms, has set up that single un-conscionable freedom—Free Trade. In one word, for exploitation, veiled by religious and political illusions, it has substituted naked, shameless, direct, brutal exploitation.[3]

Marx was more concerned with the distribution of output than with society's total production. Workers, being at the mercy of the owners of capital for their employment, are paid only enough to maintain their existence, but their production exceeds this amount. This "surplus value" of labor accrues to the owners of capital. The history of capitalism is the history of class struggle between the bourgeoisie and the proletariat, the class of laborers. He believed that capital which utilized employed labor was inevitably a social product and should not be subject to private ownership.

Marx saw capitalism as a phase in the evolution of economic society. In their quest for surplus value the capitalists would tend to increase the accumulation of capital, continually displacing labor and maintaining a "reserve army" of the unemployed. The eventual out-come of capitalism was to be collective ownership and operation of capital, resulting from the conflict between the bourgeoisie and the proletariat. Each capitalist would attempt to build his stock of capi-tal to gain surplus value. Each capitalist's gain is only temporary, however, and as competitors add to capital also, the rate of profit on capital tends to fall. The class struggle intensifies as employers at-tempt to recoup their losses by increasing the work day, working labor harder, and employing lower wage women and children.

Marx was not explicit about the organization of society under the leadership of the proletariat. He felt that the political state as it existed in his time was an instrument for the subjugation of one class by another. Marx's followers in the Soviet Union, which has adopted his ideology, believe the state will wither away and organizations of the people, such as trade unions and cooperatives, will manage the economy.

Capital is a collective product, and only by the united action of many members, nay, in the last resort, only by the united action of all members of society, can it be set in motion.

Capital is therefore not a personal, it is a social power.

When, therefore, capital is converted into common property, into the property of all members of society, personal property is not thereby transformed into social property. It is only the social character of the property that is changed. It loses its class character.[4]

Socialism is a system of collective ownership and management of the means of production. Marx was not the first socialist, but he was

[3] Karl Marx, *The Communist Manifesto*, Gateway ed. (Chicago: Regnery, 1954), pp. 18-19. First published in 1848.
[4] *Ibid.*, pp. 42-43.

the first to provide what he called a "scientific" analysis of the weakness of capitalism. His immediate forerunners were the French utopians, who advocated the creation of a rationally determined socialistic society. It was Marx's distinction that he provided a critical analysis of capitalism and refuted its earlier apologists. His major work, *Das Capital*, was published in 1867.

JOHN MAYNARD KEYNES (1883-1946)

It was J. M. Keynes who introduced to economics the concept of deficiency of aggregate demand. He reasoned that the amount the public wishes to save is a function of their income. Unless the desire for capital accumulation is adequate to absorb saving that would be generated at the full employment output level, demand will be deficient and unemployment will result.

Keynes' solution to the problem, now widely adopted in capitalist economies, was government intervention to stimulate demand through tax policy and the substitution where necessary of direct, government demand for products to make up the gap between private demand and the economy's output potential.

Like Marx, Keynes foresaw a tendency for the rate of profit to decline over the long run, and he expected that it would lead to the need for increasing government intervention.

> I conceive, therefore, that a somewhat comprehensive socialisation of investment will piove the only means of securing an approximation to full employment; though this need not exclude all manner of compromises and devices by which public authority will cooperate with private initiative. But beyond this no obvious case is made out for a system of state socialism which would embrace most of the economic life of the community.
>
> It is not the ownership of the instruments of production which it is important for the state to assume. If the state is able to determine the aggregate amount of resources devoted to augmenting the instruments and the basic rate of reward to those who own them, it will have accomplished all that is necessary. Moreover, the necessary measures of socialisation can be introduced gradually and without a break of the general tradition of society.[5]

Unlike Marx, Keynes was not concerned about the distribution of output or class struggle. His interest in the socialization of investment was to ensure adequate demand for output, and he was concerned that the state go only as far as necessary to achieve this purpose. His advocacy of state intervention was to ensure some perpetuation of the system rather than its overthrow. Paul Sweezy, a

[5] *The General Theory of Employment, Interest and Money* (New York: Harcourt, 1936).

student of Marxism, has pointed out Keynes' contrast with Marx as follows:

Keynes ignores technological change and technological unemployment, problems which figure as an integral part of the Marxian theoretical structure. Keynes treats unemployment as a symptom of a technical fault in the capitalist mechanism, while Marx regards it as the indispensable means by which capitalists maintain their control over the labor market .... A socialist can only blink his eyes in astonishment when he reads that there is "no reason to suppose that the existing system seriously misemploys the factors of production which are in use ...." But perhaps most striking of all is Keynes's habit of treating the state as a *deus ex machina* to be invoked whenever his human actors, behaving according to the rules of the capitalist game, get themselves into a dilemma from which there is apparently no escape.[6]

EOCNOMIC SYSTEMS[7]

With respect to state control the economies of the world can be divided into capitalist, communist, democratic socialist, and to a minor extent, fascist.

In communist countries, such as the Soviet Union and mainland China, the state owns and operates the means of production. The state employs workers and pays them with state-created money. Workers return the money to the state when they purchase goods from the state. Wage rates in the Soviet Union are according to the value which the state places on the services of the worker, and there are wide differences in earnings. Occupations requiring long training, such as those of teachers and scientists, earn more than factory workers, and there is a wide differential between skilled and unskilled factory work. Industrial managers are relatively well paid, but their standing is not as high as in capitalist countries.

Operating on the periphery of the state-owned enterprises are the cooperatives and a minor amount of private enterprise. Producer and consumer cooperatives are owned by worker-members who share in their profits. Collective farms are a similar organization in the agricultural sector. Private enterprise consists of individuals who sell goods or services, but who, in accordance with Marxist doctrine, cannot hire laborers. Among the more important of these are cultivators of private household garden plots.

The state controls most prices in the Soviet Union, the main exceptions being the output of small, private farm plots, but even

---

[6] Robert Lekachman (ed.), *Keynes and the Classics* (Boston: Heath, 1964), pp. 34-35. (Originally published in *Science and Society*, October 1946.)

[7] Much of the information in this section is from Allan Gruchy, *Comparative Economic Systems* (Boston: Houghton Mifflin, 1966).

these cannot drift far from prices available in state stores. The basic objective of Soviet pricing is to bring equality between wages paid and available goods and to distribute resources in accord with the economy's demands. Increases in real purchasing power are to come about through stable prices with increased wages.

As in capitalistic economies the price mechanism serves as a means for channeling production in accord with the public's demand, though the price system has less autonomy in this regard in communist countries. Some Eastern European countries have been more inclined to rely on the price mechanism than has the Soviet Union. The starting point for the determination of relative prices is the costs of the products sold. However, prices of some essential goods, such as bread, do not fully recover costs, and prices of some luxury goods, such as cameras, more than cover costs to discourage their purchase. Relative costs have largely been set on the basis of wage payments, which in turn reflect relative scarcity of labor skills needed. Critics of the Soviet market process believe that the costs of capital have not been adequately included. In any market system prices are a means of allocating scarce resources. If any costs are omitted in a particular product, the market will direct more resources to the production of the product than it should, given the overall limitation of resources. If relative prices do not adequately reflect capital costs, then there will be a tendency to waste capital. Inadequate consideration of capital arose from the method of capital provision in establishing state-owned enterprises. Rather than buying capital, firms received capital appropriations, without setting up a procedure for depreciating it and charging this depreciation in pricing output. For some years the Soviet Union has been revising its system of capital provision.

In the Soviet Union workers are free to shift their employment among various state-owned enterprises, but the relatively better paid university graduates may be placed by the state. Consumers get less than one-half of the output of the Soviet Union, with the state appropriating the remainder through various ways for collective use. Income taxes are relatively unimportant. There is no need to exact taxes according to income, as is done through the progressive income tax of capitalistic countries, since incomes in the first instance are a matter of state policy. The state's share of output comes mainly through taxes on consumer goods and disguised taxation in the form of surpluses of state enterprises. Any enterprise that charges more for its products than it pays to laborers or other state enterprises incurs a surplus. For the economy as a whole the state surpluses are the output of workers in excess of what they have received. They are thereby working part of the time for capital formation and other collective goods administered by the state. Most of the nation's saving is state capital formation. The principal means that workers have of saving is the retention of a portion of their money holdings, the purchase of government bonds, and the construction of owner-occupied housing.

Standing between capitalism and communism, but closer to capitalism, are the democratic socialist countries, such as Norway and Sweden, operating largely in a private market system. The state has nationalized only certain strategic industries, such as transportation. Gruchy has pointed out the distinction between these systems and capitalism.

> As long as private industry and agriculture perform satisfactorily, no move is made to nationalize the economy on a wide front. But the government has a more positive role under democratic partial socialism than it does under controlled or regulated capitalism . . . . Economic activities are carried on within the framework of annual and longer-term national economic plans. These plans set forth broad annual economic goals in terms of production, employment, and investment, but no specific targets are established for individual private enterprise.[8]

In implementing national economic plans socialist countries employ more extensive controls than capitalist countries, such as controls over prices and investment controls in the form of quotas, licensure, and tax incentives. Social welfare systems occupy a more prominent role in these countries than under capitalism.

Fascist countries, such as Spain, operate within a private capitalistic framework, but the central direction, with extensive controls, comes from the nondemocratic state. Since fascist defeats in World War II, fascism has not been an important force in the world economy.

THE STATE IN CONTEMPORARY CAPITALISM

Although the majority of economic decisions under capitalism are private, the capitalism of today is far from the laissez-faire system which Adam Smith advocated. In a wide variety of ways the governments of capitalist countries participate in the economy.

Governments act through their taxing, spending, and monetary powers to maintain and stabilize aggregate demand in general accordance with Keynes' analysis of the causes of the deficiency of aggregate demand. The most important economic influence of capitalist governments is the proportion of national output which government takes for collective purposes. In the United States about one-fifth of

[8] *Ibid.*, p. 19.

product goes to the federal government and political subdivisions, about the same proportion as in countries under socialist governments.

In addition to this direct allocation of product to the public sector the government provides purchasing power to private citizens for their own expenditures, equivalent to about 7 percent of national product. These are called *transfer payments* in that the government takes income from one sector of the economy and transfers it to another. These transfer payments are in such programs as unemployment compensation and retirement benefits.

Generally in the United States government hires labor directly for the service elements of its activities but purchases from private enterprise the goods which it uses. For example, direct government employes provide postal service, but their equipment, such as delivery trucks and buildings, comes from private firms. In a similar way, government employes using goods from private enterprise provide education, police protection, road supervision (but not construction), and military protection. In socialist countries goods-producing enterprises, such as steel, are government-owned, but this is generally not the case in the United States. As a result, government directly employs only 13 percent of the civilian labor forces.

The contrast between "public" and "private" enterprise is overdrawn, as noted by John Kenneth Galbraith:

> Were it not so celebrated in ideology, it would long since have been agreed that the line that now divides public from so-called private organization in military procurement, space exploration and atomic energy is so indistinct as to be nearly imperceptible.[9]

There is increasing concern in the United States over the economic power of such enterprises in a web called the "military-industrial complex." Galbraith suggested that the intensity of the cold war has been maintained because it serves the needs of the industrial system. In a farewell message when he left the Presidency, the late Dwight Eisenhower warned of the dangers of the "... conjunction of an immense military establishment and a large arms industry . . . ." He stated:

> In the councils of government we must guard against the acquisition of unwarranted influence, whether sought or unsought, by the military-industrial complex. The potential for the disastrous rise of misplaced power exists and will persist.[10]

Capitalist theory depends upon competition to regulate private enterprise in the public interest. The highly technical and secret na-

[9] *The New Industrial State* (Boston: Houghton Mifflin; 1967), p. 392.
[10] From excerpts in the Los Angeles *Times*, September 28, 1967. The speech was delivered January 17, 1961.

ture of government undertaking—space exploration and complex weapons systems—and the gigantic cost of single projects tend to insulate these purchases from the ordinary market mechanism. Firms serving government, such as highway contractors, are not new, but the increasing importance and complexity of government purchases and the dependence of some firms on them bring to the fore the question of whether the government should produce directly those goods for which government is the sole buyer.

Public utilities in the United States are largely under private ownership, but the conditions of their operations give them a public character. The government grants utility monopolies in the form of exclusive territorial rights, since duplicating facilities in these enterprises would be socially costly and competition would probably be unworkable. The government directly regulates the prices of these firms, which means that it indirectly regulates their rate of return on capital. Socialization of such enterprises would not involve an extreme alteration of the role of government. Shareholders with a near guaranteed rate of return would become government bondholders. The principal effect of such a transition would be the assumption by government of decisions over capital investment in the industries.

The transport industry—rails, airlines, buses, trucks—is also regulated with respect to rates and territorial rights, and city governments own directly some urban transport systems. Regulation of the transport industry is not quite as tight as public utilities, but it is clear that they too are imbued with a public character.

The government also exercises regulatory influence over essentially private activity. It protects labor organization and provides a mechanism for labor election of bargaining representation. It sets minimum wages and otherwise intervenes in conditions of employment. It regulates the safety of food and drugs. It sets and enforces standards of fair trade, including minimal regulation over advertising claims. It grants charters to banks and other financial institutions and regulates them for safety. It makes rules for the sale of corporate shares.

Subsidies, direct and indirect, are a means by which the government influences the allocation of resources among competing needs. Taxes levied on the basis of income or spending can discriminate by taxing certain types of activity more heavily than others. The provision of such facilities as air terminals and traffic control at less than cost to the airlines tends to understate to the user of air services the true cost. Government loan guaranties channel resources to the affected activities by lessening risk.

The role which capitalist theory assigns to competition in enforcing the public interest leads to special legal safeguards to minimize monopolistic elements in the economy. The law cannot ensure a competitive economy, but it does prevent overt acts which may tend to promote monopoly. Conspiracies among firms to fix prices are illegal, and corporate mergers can be blocked if they tend to restrain competition, but these negative acts are not sufficient to prevent the emergence over time of large firms which dominate an industry.

Galbraith looks upon antimonopoly laws as a façade to avoid more fundamental reforms by promulgating the idea that competition is being maintained to guard the public. The most vigorous advocates of such laws, and of strengthening them, are the defenders of laissez-faire economics. They believe the government's responsibility is to assure an economy regulated through a competitive market and that this type of governmental intervention will on the whole result in greater economic freedom. Henry Simons (1899-1946) wrote:

> There must be outright dismantling of our gigantic corporations and persistent prosecution of producers who organize, by whatever methods, for price maintenance and output limitation . . . . Legislation must prohibit and administration effectively prevent, the acquisition by any private firm, or group of firms of substantial monopoly power, regardless of how reasonably that power may appear to be exercised.[11]

He favored an absolute limitation on both the amount of property a single corporation may own and on the amount of its advertising.

Another purpose of government intervention is to make private industry bear the full social cost of its activities. An example of unborne cost in the absence of intervention is the chemical factory which spreads noxious fumes into the atmosphere. State intervention can alleviate the worst of such imbalances between private and social cost, but a full-scale assault on the problem would probably be inconsistent with the private market. The state can transform social cost into private cost, as when it requires industrial plants which pollute rivers to develop alternative waste-disposal methods, but all cases of unborne costs are not amenable to such solutions.

SUMMARY

In the first phase of capitalism, which began about five centuries ago, monarchs granted trading monopolies and imposed restrictive regulations on commerce. Adam Smith attacked this system, called *mercantilism*, in 1776 and argued that the unregulated market mech-

[11] *Economic Policy for a Free Society* (Chicago: U. of Chicago Press, 1948).

anism was the most efficient means of increasing national wealth. In the next century (nineteenth) Karl Marx characterized capitalism as a system of class warfare between labor and capitalists, which would eventually fall to a socialist society. John Maynard Keynes, writing in this century, believed that private capitalism will not necessarily sustain an output level that employs the total labor force.

Following Marx, communist countries today do not allow the private employment of labor, and the state owns most of the capital. The state employs labor, pays money wages according to the laborer's skill, and sets money prices for state goods according to their cost of production. Democratic socialist countries allow private markets and employment but own more capital and provide the economy with more direction than do capitalist governments.

Following Keynes, capitalist countries intervene in the economy to maintain an output level that will employ all labor. Capitalist governments utilize a large portion of national output for collective purposes. Governments restrain some monopolist elements because of the deviation of relative prices of products from their true costs if monopolistic pricing occurs. Some government intervention is designed to reduce the social costs of pursuits which result in costs which the producers would not have to bear on the private markets.

SELECTED REFERENCES

Feiwel, George R. (ed.), *New Currents in Soviet-Type Economies: A Reader.* Scranton, Pa.: International Textbook, 1968.
Galbraith, John Kenneth, *The New Industrial State.* Boston: Houghton Mifflin, 1967.
Gruchy, Allan, *Comparative Economic Systems.* Boston: Houghton Mifflin, 1966.
McKean, Roland, *Public Spending.* New York: McGraw-Hill, Co., 1968.
Shonfield, Andrew, *Modern Capitalism.* New York: Oxford U.P., 1965.
Solo, Robert A., *Economic Organization and Social Systems.* Indianapolis, Ind.: Bobbs-Merrill, 1967.

DISCUSSION QUESTIONS

1. How do you believe Karl Marx and Adam Smith would change their views of the economic system if they lived today?
2. What did Keynes mean by the "socialization of investment?" Has this socialization been effected in the advanced capitalistic countries?
3. Contrast the role of the price system in communist and in capitalist countries.
4. Do you agree with the statement in the text that democratic socialist

countries (such as Norway and Sweden) stand closer to capitalism than to communism?

5. What are the arguments for direct government ownership of the firms from which government acquires goods?

6. What is the justification for granting monopoly rights to public utilities?

7. What problems are involved in vigorous enforcement of laws designed to curtail monopolistic elements in the economy?

16

Government Financial Policy

The government influences the size and composition of total output by influencing creation of assets and liabilities, both its own and that of the private economy. The creation of assets facilitates sectoral imbalances—production in excess of use by one group matched by use in excess of production in another group—and such imbalances leave as their residual a claim of the surplus group on the deficit group. The more easily such claims come into existence, the more easily can a producer dispose of his output.

The government itself may run an imbalance between taxes and expenditures, and the size of this imbalance is the result of its fiscal policy. The private sector holds the assets resulting from this imbalance, and the composition of these claims is a part of the government's financial policy. In addition to determining the composition and size of claims on itself, the government also prescribes regulations with respect to the use of these claims by the private economy as it specifies the amount which banks must hold in relation to their deposit liabilities. Governments also influence the creation of claims within the private economy by prescribing the terms which such claims may bear, such as length of maturity or maximum interest rate payable.

GOVERNMENT MONEY

The government is the only issuer of money which carries legal-tender status, meaning that the holder of any asset so designated can use it to settle any obligation expressed in money terms. Government legal tender is in two forms. Liabilities of the government issued in note or metallic form, called *currency* and *coin*, are claims of the bearer and circulate from hand to hand as the economy's payments

215

medium. Governments also issue claims to individual holders as a deposit type of money. Normally banks are the private holders of these claims. The government agency responsible for both of these money type claims is the central bank, such as the Bank of France, Bank of England, or the United States Federal Reserve.

Government money comes into being as the government uses money liabilities to finance a deficit or as it exchanges one type of obligation for the other. At any one time the government has outstanding from past deficits claims of both a money and a nonmoney nature, and the relative amounts of the two can be changed by market exchanges.

Let us start with the issuance of money claims. If the government acquires more goods from the private economy than it takes through taxation, it issues a deposit claim on itself to the supplier of the goods. The supplier deposits the check in a bank, and the bank in turn deposits it in the central bank. The public thereby holds an additional amount of money equal to the excess of government purchases over tax receipts.

Now suppose that the government wishes to reduce the amount of money in the private economy. The government may then sell interest-bearing securities, say a five-year bond. The purchaser of the bond pays for it by writing a check on his deposit account at a bank. The purchaser's deposits have decreased and his bondholdings have increased by an equal amount. The government then uses the check received to reduce its deposit liability to the bank where the purchaser held his deposit, and at the same time the bank reduces its deposit liability to the purchaser. This process of substitution between money and nonmoney liabilities of the government is termed *open-market operations*, being conducted through market transactions in government securities with the public. The central bank is responsible for these operations under a broad government mandate.

Whether open-market operations change the public's holdings of currency (and coin) or of government deposits is purely a matter of public preference. Deposits and currency are always interconvertible, and the government can determine the total but not the composition. When the public holds currency, it holds direct money claims on the government. When it holds deposits, the public holds claims on the banks and banks hold claims on the government. (Banks do not hold government money equal to their deposit liabilities, and regulation of this relationship, as discussed below, is another aspect of government financial policy.)

If the government wishes to expand money, it exchanges money for securities. If it wishes to contract money, it sells securities for money. One must not conclude, however, that all securities sales and purchases have this effect, for the net effect will depend upon the relation between government spending and taxes at the time. If the government sells securities equal to its government deficit (excess of spending over taxes) then there is no net money effect. The government withdraws money from the security sale, but then returns it to the economy through its expenditure deficit. The net change in the public's holdings of government claims in any time period is a result of open-market transactions and the government's net expenditure position.

In addition to purchasing their own securities governments also designate certain other purchases that they pay for by the issuance of money claims. The most important of these is assets associated with the international value of a government's money issue. A government buys money issues of foreign countries in exchange for its own money issue. The government then holds as an asset the foreign claim, and it issues its own money liability in an equivalent amount. These transactions occur at the initiative of holders of foreign money rather than the initiative of the government making the purchase. The government must also sell foreign money for its own money liability when requested, in which case it then loses the foreign asset and extinguishes an equivalent amount of its domestic money liability. The United States buys and sells gold under arrangements similar to those in which other countries buy and sell foreign money, and these transactions have the same types of domestic money effects.

Some countries also buy certain domestic assets by direct money creation. These might include export loans, loans to developing industries, or any type of loan singled out for direct financing through the government's money system. Generally such monetization of private assets is through a private bank which acquires the asset and then sells it to the central bank, a process called *rediscounting*. Private banks may also borrow directly from the central bank. Such operations involve a swap of assets and liabilities between the bank and the government, and the borrowing bank can in turn lend out the money claim borrowed.

These special money-creating purchases need not have a net effect if the government balances them with offsetting transactions in its own securities. The United States terms such offset operations "defensive" open-market policy. Defensive policy is difficult to operate if the initiating change is large relative to the stock of government securities which the domestic economy holds or can absorb. In particular, government sale and purchase of foreign money results from swings in the country's foreign-trade position. Where a country's external transactions are large relative to domestic product, these swings may result in substantial changes in domestically held money.

Domestic money-creating programs, such as advances to banks, offer less of a problem because they are under domestic control. If they result in excessive money creation, the solution may be to change the program itself.

In addition to determining the proportion of money to non-money debt, the government also determines the type of nonmoney debt which it will issue. The principal difference in such debt is its maturity, which ranges from perpetuities (no fixed date of maturity) to short-term bills of perhaps 90-days maturity. The maturity specifies the time at which the government will convert the security to money, usually a fixed amount according to the terms of the security. In addition to this fixed maturity date securities may also provide for a fixed periodic payment in the interval. A perpetuity provides for the fixed periodic payment as long as the bond is held, and the government can redeem it only by buying it from a holder.

Generally the shorter the maturity the more easily can the holder convert the claim to real goods. Consequently a shift of the composition of the government debt to shorter maturities tends to increase the demand for current output. Such shifts in maturity are termed *debt-management policy*. The government may effect such a shift by buying securities of one maturity and selling those of another, by replacing maturing issues with those of different maturities, and by fixing maturities on net new issues.

Economic stabilization calls for a shift of government debt away from money debt and short-term securities, and toward long-term securities, when there is a need to curb excess demand. The opposite policy should be employed in periods of unemployment and deficient demand. This stabilization goal often runs in conflict with another government objective, which is to minimize the interest cost on the government debt. If the government issues long-term debt in periods of economic expansion, it will generally pay relatively high interest rates on this debt because of competing demands for borrowing. In an economic slump, when interest rates are low, the government must forgo taking advantage of the rate and at that time issue its money debt or its short-term debt. These conflicts often result in the failure of governments fully to employ their debt policy for stabilization purposes. The conflict becomes especially sharp during wartime when government deficits may run very large and inflationary pressures are strong.

BANK RESERVES

The portion of government money which banks hold constitutes bank reserves. The recipients of government money may exchange it for deposit claims on banks when they prefer deposits to currency. The holder of the deposit can use it to make economic transactions by transferring it to others through a check, an order to a bank to make payment to another party. If the transfer is to another depositor in the bank, then the bank merely shifts the ownership of its claim from one depositor to another, and its assets are unaffected. If the transfer is to a depositor in another bank, the bank losing deposits must transfer reserves to the bank receiving deposits. One bank gains deposits equal to deposits lost by another bank. A simple method of effecting the reserve transfer is to shift reserve deposits at the central bank. As the public's deposits move from one bank to another, then the banks' deposits with the government central bank also move from one bank to another.

Since the public holds and uses deposits without having to transfer them into currency, it is possible for the banks to create deposits in addition to those which they receive through deposit of government money. Bank deposits can exceed the banks' holding of currency because the public is content to use deposits and does not demand currency conversion. The relation between the reserves they hold and the deposits they can create is determined either by legal restraints or banking custom.

Let us presume that banks prefer to hold 10 percent of deposits in reserves, and that a customer deposits £100 million from the sale of securities to the government. The bank receiving the deposit then has £100 million of reserves. If it keeps 10 percent on reserve, then it can lend out, or purchase securities equal to £90, in which case its balance sheet will show the following net changes:

Assets	Liabilities
Increase in loans.........£90	Increase in deposits £100
Increased reserves........£10	

If the receiver of the proceeds from the bank loan or security purchase takes currency, then the result is that the bank has had a net addition of reserves of £10 and of deposits of £100. Since deposits are usable as a medium of exchange, they too are money, and the net increase in money is £190 (£100 of deposits and £90 of currency).

Suppose that the loan is in the form of a deposit entry, as it is likely to be, and the deposit continues to be used in the banking system. Immediately after making the loan the bank's balance sheet will have changed as follows:

Assets	Liabilities
Increase in loans....... £90	Increase in deposits...... £190
Increased reserves....... £100	

As the newly created deposits flow through the economy, the issuing bank will likely transfer deposits and reserves to other banks, and the balance sheet will then return to a net increase of £10 in reserves and £100 in deposits. Other banks will show an increase in reserves and deposits of £90 as a result of the transfer from the first bank. These banks may then lend out £81 and retain £9. As the proceeds of this loan flow to other banks, they too may loan out 9/10 and keep 1/10. If we take as given an increment of £100 for the banking system, then the system can expand until:

$$\text{Reserve ratio} \times \text{Deposits} = \text{Reserves}$$
$$1/10 \text{ Deposits} = £100$$
$$\text{Deposits} = \frac{£100}{1/10}$$
$$\text{Deposits} = £1000$$

More generally, with a given level of reserves, the maximum deposits will equal reserves divided by the ratio of reserves to deposits. In the earlier example, in which £10 remained as reserves, deposits expanded to £100. The amount of loans and securities which the banks acquire during expansion will equal deposits less reserves.

Just the reverse situation happens if the banking system loses reserves. Suppose that the government sells securities of £100 in order to reduce outstanding government money.

(a) The government decreases money liabilities and increases bond liabilities.

(b) A bank depositor loses his deposit, used to buy securities, and increases securities holdings.

(c) The depositor's bank loses £100 of deposits and £100 of reserves.

(d) The Bank is deficient in reserves because it held only £10 behind the deposits.

(e) The bank sells £90 of securities to make up the deficiency.

(f) The buyer of these securities uses his bank deposit, presumed to be held on another bank, losing bank deposits and gaining securities.

(g) The bank on which this check was drawn loses £90 of deposits and £90 of reserves, but only held £9 of reserves. This bank too must sell securities.

(h) The process continues until total deposits have decreased by £1,000 as a result of the original £100 withdrawal.

If the government sets the reserve to deposit ratio, then the legal reserve requirement determines the limits of deposit expansion. If we

---

Determinants of Money Stock

Assumption: Government issues 50 billion sol in money claims, convertible between currency and deposit liabilities to banks.

Public prefers 1/3 of money as currency.

Reserve requirement against bank deposits is 10%

$$\text{Money stock} = \text{Government money} \times \frac{\dfrac{\text{Deposits}}{\text{Reserve}}\left(1 + \dfrac{\text{Deposits}}{\text{Currency}}\right)}{\dfrac{\text{Deposits}}{\text{Reserve}} + \dfrac{\text{Deposits}}{\text{Currency}}}$$

$$\text{Money stock} = \frac{50 \times 10\,(1 + 2)}{10 + 2} = \frac{1500}{12} = 125$$

Money stock = 125 billion sol

Currency = 41 2/3 billion

Deposits = 83 1/3 billion

Reserves = 8 1/3 billion

---

take as given the total of government money (currency held by the public and bank reserves) then an additional variable determining the money stock is the proportion of government money held by the banks. The public determines this as it works out its desired ratio of deposits to currency in its total money stock. The ultimate money stock depends upon the ratio of deposits to reserves D/R, and the ratio of deposits to currency D/C, determined by public preferences:

$$\text{Maximum money} = \text{Reserves and currency} \times \frac{D/R\,(1 + D/C)}{D/R + D/C}$$

The maximum money stock may not come about if the banks do not use their reserves to expand to the limit, in which case they hold some excess reserves.

There are then two ways by which the government can change the potential money stock. It may change government money, largely through open-market operations, or it may change reserve requirements. Reserve requirement changes are also a way by which unwanted changes in government money can be neutralized. If for-

Alternative Money Supply Routes

20% Reserve requirement:

Reserves = 30

$$\text{Demand deposits} = \frac{30}{1/5} = 150$$

Bank holdings of
   loans and securities = 150 - 30 = 120

10% Reserve requirement:

Reserves = 15

$$\text{Demand deposits} = \frac{15}{.10} = 150$$

Bank holdings of
   loans and securities = 150 - 15 = 135

eign trade causes an increase in reserves through foreign-money in-flows, then an increase in reserve requirements can prevent the inflow from causing a money expansion. Countries which experience wide swings in foreign trade relative to the size of the domestic economy tend to use variable reserve requirements more often than do other countries. Open-market operations tend to predominate in those countries where a large volume of government securities is actively traded. In these circumstances the government may buy and sell its own securities for money-control purposes without account-ing for an unduly large portion of transactions in these securities. The United States, Great Britain, and Canada use open-market trans-actions as the most frequent instrument of monetary change. The chief advantage of open-market operations is their flexibility. The government can initiate change quickly and in small amounts with-out any necessity of public announcement. Reserve requirement changes require advance notification to the banks.

A number of governments also impose *liquidity ratios* on banks and other financial institutions. These specify a required ratio of certain selected assets to the institution's deposit-type liabilities. The most common asset required is short-term government securities, but any asset which the central bank may rediscount is sometimes in-cluded in the liquid-asset category. Liquidity ratios strengthen the central bank's ability to control the bank's holdings of currency and deposit reserves. The reason for this is that the liquidity requirement prevents the banks from attempting to obtain reserves by the sale of liquid assets or the discounting of these assets with the central bank in return for reserves. In the case of government securities an attempt by banks to sell them would tend to force down their price if many banks were trying to sell simultaneously. The government might feel compelled to buy the securities through the central bank to maintain the price, and this would make available more reserves to the banking system at a time when the increase in reserves might not be desirable. Liquidity ratios arose in the postwar years because of the large volume of government securities which the banking system bought during World War II. The ratios served to lock in these securities holdings and prevent the banks from attempting to convert them to reserves.

Liquidity ratios do not provide a limit to deposit expansion as long as there are adequate amounts of the specified assets in the economy. When this is the case, the ratios serve more to affect the distribution of bank lending than the total. In the case of government security requirements the ratios assist the government in flotation of its securities by insuring a bank market for them. As an alternative the government could issue more direct-money liabilities and neutralize the expansionary effect with higher reserve requirements. Such a move involves a reduction in the role of the private banking system, and the security reserve is a way of meeting the government's needs with a minimum alteration in the adjustments of the private banking system.

DISCOUNT RATES

In addition to receipt of deposits of government money banks may also obtain reserves by borrowing from the central bank. The banks may then use the borrowed reserves as the basis for multiple loan and deposit expansion. Setting the regulations for borrowing and the rate of discount applied is a means of influencing the amount of reserves and the terms of bank lending. The central bank may lend directly to a private bank, or it may purchase from the bank loans which the bank has made to others.

Discounting practices vary widely among countries. In some countries with limited open-market operations discounting is an important means of providing reserves. In some cases the volume of discounts outstanding may even exceed bank reserves, as banks have borrowed from the central bank and then loaned out the proceeds in the form of currency to the public. Some governments use discounting as a means of influencing the types of lending in the economy by favoring the purchase of some types of loans over others.

In the United States, discounting is quantitatively unimportant because of the predominance of open-market operations in providing reserves and the resulting restrictive regulations to limit bank borrowing. The chief importance of the discount rate is in the reaction of financial markets to the central bank's discount rate.

A rise in the discount rate is an indication of the central bank's desire for more restrictive lending conditions throughout the economy. As a result of such a rise, lenders may come to expect higher interest rates to prevail in the future. The possibility of higher future rates discourages lending because, if interest rates rise, the market value of financial assets falls. If a reduction in lending takes place, this itself causes the rise in interest rates sought by the central bank. From the standpoint of money supply and demand, a rise in the discount rate increases the demand for money to hold. The public prefers to hold money idle rather than lend it out because of the anticipated rise in interest rates.

The difficulty with employing this instrument of policy is its unpredictability. The relation between the discount rate and other rates of interest vary from country to country and from time to time. At times the market may react more strongly than the central bank would like, and at other times more weakly. The importance of the discount rate lies in its being in most cases the sole rate of interest actually set by the government's monetary authorities. The government does not fix the rate on government securities, since there might be no willing buyers at an unrealistic rate. The government can only set the rate on its lending, not its borrowing, and the discount rate is the lending rate of the monetary authorities.

Another way by which banks borrow reserves from the government is through government deposits with private banks. Such deposits offer a way by which the government can engage in transactions in its securities without causing a bank reserve effect. If the government is selling securities for the purpose of later purchases of goods from the economy (incurring a deficit), it may leave the proceeds of the sale on deposit in the banking system so that reserves do not fluctuate with the transactions. In effect, the government loans to the banking system reserves it acquired through the securities sale.

Central-bank discounting is not the only means by which governments lend to the private sector of the economy. The discounting procedure results in government money creation along with the lending, but governments also influence economic activity by loans which do not arise from money creation. Governments make development

Government Deposits and Reserves

Commercial Banks

A	L
Loans and 160	200 Private deposits
securities	
Reserves 40	

Government sells 10 of securities and neutralizes the reserve effect:

A	L
Loans and 160	190 Private deposits
securities	
Reserves 40	10 Government
	deposits

Government purchases goods from proceeds of security sales:

A	L
Loans and 160	200 Private deposits
securities	
Reserves 40	

loans to strategically important industries. They lend to agriculture, to home owners, to utilities, to veterans, to students, and so on. In these loan operations the economic role of the government is to serve as intermediary between those with surpluses on current output account and those with deficits. In the absence of money creation the source of such lending is either taxation or government borrowing. If taxation is the route, then the government takes the surplus through taxes and lends it to the deficit unit. The public in general, through government, holds a claim on the borrower, but the claim is not specifically matched by claims of surplus units. If borrowing is the route, then the surplus units hold bond claims on the government, and the government holds loan claims on the deficit units. In general, the effect of such programs is to increase product demand by enabling sectors of the economy to run deficits when they otherwise could not finance them.

SAVINGS DEPOSITS

There is a greater variety of practices among countries with respect to control of savings deposits than control of demand deposits. Many, though not all, countries require reserves against savings de-

---

Effect of Saving Deposit Reserve
Requirement on Demand Deposit

Assumption:

Demand deposit reserve requirement = 15%

Saving deposit reserve requirement = 5%

Beginning balance sheet for all commercial banks (including only deposit liabilities and related assets):

	A		L	
Loans and securities	127.5		150	Demand deposits
Reserves	22.5			

Customers convert 20 of demand deposits to saving deposits. With reserves given, the banks' balance sheet will be, after all adjustments:

	A		L	
Loans and securities	140.8		143.3	Demand deposits
Reserves*	22.5		20	Savings deposits

*21.5 applies against demand deposits; 1 applies against savings deposits.

The savings deposits reduce demand deposit by 6 2/3:

$$-1 \text{ reserves} \div .15$$

---

posits, and in some the requirement is the same as that against demand deposits. Whether demand deposits alone, or the total of demand and savings deposits, is the object of control is a matter of individual national policy. In the United States, banks must maintain reserves against savings deposits in the same form (currency or central-bank deposits) but at a lower ratio than demand deposits. Generally analysts do not consider that this reserve requirement absolutely limits the amount of savings deposits. The reason is that there are always reserves held against demand deposits which the banks can shift to use against savings deposits. Such a shift reduces potential demand deposits, but the Federal Reserve can, and likely will, provide reserves to meet such a loss. Institutions which are not commercial banks, i.e., do not maintain demand deposits, do not have these reserve requirements.

Because of the existence of savings deposits and many other forms of liquid assets, government money control does not mean control of liquidity. In some ways money control may itself give rise to other types of claims. The more stringent the money control the greater is the incentive for the private economy to develop substitutes.

Control of the interest rate which financial institutions can pay on deposits offers a means by which the government can extend its influence to private claims without necessarily controlling the absolute amount of such claims. Deposit-rate control is also applicable to demand deposits, but is less important as an instrument of stabilization in current practice. Some countries do not allow demand-deposit interest, as in the United States, or banks do not pay it as a matter of business practice, as in the United Kingdom. Where a government does control a deposit rate, in general the effect of such control is to limit the ability of the institutions to offer attractive liabilities to savers, and therefore to limit the economy's liquid assets. A lowering of the deposit ceiling is consequently a restrictive measure in that it reduces the ability of the institutions to serve as intermediaries, forcing more borrowers to issue primary securities directly to lenders. A rise in the ceiling allows financial institutions to pay rates more consistent with market conditions, but does not necessarily obligate them to pay the higher rate.

The effect of a change in the deposit-rate ceiling differs from the effect of a discount-rate change because in the latter case the government offers loans at the rate set. In contrast, the deposit-rate ceiling prohibits the creation of a private claim that the economy might otherwise choose. With both rates the principal significance lies in their relation to other rates of interest. The lower the discount rate in relation to other rates of interest, the more expansionary it is— because the effect is to reduce the cost of borrowing from the government in comparison to the return from lending. The lower the deposit-rate ceiling in comparison to other rates, the less attractive are the institutions' deposits. A simultaneous rise in both the discount rate and in deposit-rate ceilings will likely have a net restrictive effect. A rise in the discount rate tends to raise market rates of interest through the effect on speculative money holdings. The rise in deposit-rate ceilings may do no more than allow banks to maintain the same relation between their rates and market rates of interest. A rise in deposit rates alone could have a restrictive effect if the market took it as a signal of central-bank intent to pursue a generally restrictive monetary policy. This restrictive market effect might more than offset the expansionary effect resulting from the banks' increased ability to intermediate by offering more attractive deposit terms.

SELECTIVE CONTROLS

Although the previous section treated deposit-rate regulation as an adjunct to monetary control, it might alternatively be considered as a variety of "selective controls"—regulation of the terms of private lending differentiated according to type of asset. In addition to interest-rate ceilings, such controls have included minimum down payments, as in consumer borrowing or home mortgages; maximum maturity, or length of contract; and ceilings on the amount of loans of particular types which a single financial institution may issue.

The more a government relies on these selective, direct controls, the less is its need for general monetary controls. In Norway, for example, control of the money stock is less important than in many other countries because of more direct government influence in the allocation of resources. Financial institutions and the government agree annually on the maximum amount of mortgage and commercial credit lenders will extend. This credit agreement specifies interest rates to be charged and a rough distribution of credit by industry.

The advantage of selective controls is their ability to impose restraints on some parts of the economy without the necessity of controlling others. Money-stock control is a general type of regulation. It limits the amount of money in the economy but leaves it to the private market to work out the allocation of available resources. In the resulting contest for borrowing, those who are the economically strongest will emerge as the winners, but this result may not be in accord with the government's economic objectives in imposing controls. Those who favor selective controls believe that it is the government's function to influence the allocation of product as well as the size of aggregate demand. A major target in such distribution is the allocation between capital and consumer goods. Capital goods might feel the impact of general policy more than consumer goods, with the result that the economy's productivity in future periods is less than it otherwise would be. With selective controls, general monetary conditions can remain expansionary with consumer credit controls reducing borrowing for consumption. The same principle is applicable for more refined classifications of borrowers. Controls may favor export industry loans over loans to retailing, equipment loans over construction loans, loans to provincial governments over loans to industry, and so on. In all cases the rationale for selectivity is the economy's relative need for the favored product, in accord with the government's overall economic plan.

Advocates of controlling the terms of lending—such as down payment requirements—believe that these offer a more tangible and direct influence on lending than does general monetary policy. They make this argument especially with respect to consumer credit. The size of the required initial down payment may be a greater deterrent to consumer borrowing than a rise in interest rates, since the latter is spread over many payments. Borrowing for construction is for both residential and commercial uses, and the allowable length of the loan may exert a considerable influence over the size of required periodic payments under the terms of the loan.

Opponents of selective controls oppose government intervention in the allocation of private product. They believe that the market system will more nearly achieve society's optimum output without government intervention. Government attempts to stabilize the output of individual product lines interferes with fundamental adjustments which are continually taking place in product demand.

INDICATORS OF FINANCIAL POLICY

Considering the variety of government financial policy measures, there is clearly no one measure of such policy. Money-type controls are presumably the more important measures, and these give some indication of whether the government's overall policy is to stimulate or to contain aggregate demand.

Observers widely use countries' discount rates for international comparisons, perhaps because of the simplicity of such comparisons. The term *interest rate* has the same meaning in all countries, and differences in discount rates are an indicator of differences in monetary policy. Aside from simplicity, the discount rate has little else to offer as a measure of monetary policy. Unless the government changes the discount rate often, it is not sensitive to changes in monetary conditions which are taking place. The use of discounting varies widely between countries, and the importance of the rate will partially depend upon the government's policy with respect to the availability of lending at the official rate. The importance of the discount rate in influencing other rates of interest also varies with the banking institutions of different countries.

Another possibility for measuring a country's monetary policy is to observe changes in its money stock. The rate of growth of the economy's output over the long run provides a basis for comparison. If the money stock is growing at a greater rate than output potential, it is considered evidence of an expansionary monetary policy. A similar approach is to observe the ratio of money to national output. A rise in the ratio may come from either a fall in output or a rise in money, and the latter would be more indicative of an intentionally expansionary monetary policy. The ratio is not useful for short-term analysis because data on national output are available only with a considerable lag and cover a time span no shorter than three months.

The money stock is the result not only of government policy but also of bank actions, and the existing money stock may not be exactly in accord with the government's policy objectives. More direct investigation of government intentions requires analysis concerning the source of money growth or the relation between the potential money stock, which government determines, and the actual money stock, which depends upon bank and public reactions to government policy. One way of focusing more directly on government is to observe changes in government money as opposed to total money. It is possible that total reserves and currency could grow but that banks fail to utilize their reserve potential. In this case, observation of government money changes would come more closely to measuring government policy than would observation of the money stock. Observation of reserve changes must also consider any changes in reserve requirements. A fall in reserves might appear contractionary, but not if a fall in reserve requirements more than offset it.

Another measure of monetary policy, looking at its effects, is interest rates, assuming that these reflect the supply of money in relation to demand. For this purpose it is necessary to choose one or more interest rates which are representative of the general spectrum of interest rates in a country. Generally the rate of interest on government securities is the most likely candidate. Any private securities may reflect changes in risks on the particular security, whereas government securities bear no risk of default on money payments as stated in the contract.

ALTERNATIVE SYSTEMS

Through their creation of deposit liabilities, banks share with government the determination of the size of the money stock. The government can determine the maximum size of deposits through reserve requirement policy, but it cannot determine the amount banks will actually create. If banks do not utilize all of their reserve availability, they hold *excess reserves*, and total deposits are less than the maximum possible.

Advocates of "100 percent reserves" do not believe that banks should share money creation with the government. The 100 percent reserve plan means that a bank would have to hold currency or deposits with the government equal to its deposit liabilities. The effect of this would be that the public would actually hold deposits on the government, with banks serving merely as intermediaries. Since the government would be the issuer of all money liabilities, a change to such a plan would require the government to increase its money liabilities if the total money stock were not to fall. With government the sole money issuer, the government would be able to more easily determine the size of the money stock of the country, and open market operations and discounting would become the sole means of money creation. The government might also eliminate discounting if it did not wish to lend to the private sector through the banking system.

Implementation of 100% Reserve Plan

Before implementation:

Commercial Banks

A		L
Loans	60	100 Deposits
Securities	25	
Reserves	15	

Reserve requirement = 15%

Government imposes 100% reserve requirement and buys assets from banks to provide reserves:

Government increases holdings of private assets: 85
Government increases liabilities to commercial banks: 85

A		L
Reserves	100	100 Deposits

Government money liabilities	Public money assets
100 deposits	100 deposits

In addition to more precise money control, the 100 percent plan would increase the safety of money assets by making them all government direct liabilities. If the value of a private bank's assets falls below its deposit liabilities, the bank may "fail," and depositors may lose their deposit holdings. To varying extents governments insure depositors against such failure, but insurance is not complete. In the United States the Federal Deposit Insurance Corporation will insure each deposit in a bank only to $15,000. A depositor holding more than this amount may lose the excess if the bank fails. The 100 percent plan would more directly make deposits the responsibility of the government.

Opponents of the plan point out that it would drastically change the nature of banking. Banks now in existence would have to continue their operations in the same way as other financial institutions —borrowing through such means as bonds, savings type deposits, and the issuance of capital stock. Their demand-deposit activity would cease to be a means of lending, though the banks might continue to maintain the deposits as a service to their loan customers. Such changes involve a cost to those affected—such as bank management and bank borrowers—a cost which any assessment of the 100 percent plan must consider.

The plan makes a rather sharp distinction between assets considered as money and other assets. Some of these other assets also have money characteristics, and in time it might also appear desirable for government to assume these liabilities. Present practice with respect to reserve requirements also distinguishes sharply between money and other assets, but the 100 percent reserve plan involves more serious consequences for this distinction.

Accounting in Bank Failure

Bank Before Failure

	A	L	
Loans and securities	21.5	23	Deposits
Reserves	3.5	2	Capital*

*Asset less liabilities to others.

Loans default in amount of 3:

	A	L	
Loans and securities	18.5	23	Deposits
Reserves	3.5		

Assets do not equal deposit liabilities because capital was inadequate to compensate for losses.

At the opposite extreme, some have proposed complete abolition of mandatory reserve requirements where they exist. (British banks maintain them by convention rather than by law.) Banks would then be free to hold whatever amount of reserves relative to deposits which they felt prudent. The government would continue to issue money as direct liabilities—transferable between deposits and currency—and banks, like others, would be users of government money. The government would exercise precise control over its own money liabilities, but would not attempt to control or differentiate sharply between private liabilities of a money or nonmoney nature. The continuance of government deposit insurance would not be in conflict with such a policy, since it already applies to nonmoney types of liabilities issued by financial institutions.

OBJECTIVES OF FINANCIAL POLICY

The primary objective of government financial policy is to stabilize demand for a country's product at a level that approximates the potential output of the country. If demand is below this level, the country does not achieve its maximum output. If it is above, real supply cannot match demand, and inflation threatens. Influencing asset creation is an indirect way of influencing product demand, and for this reason is somewhat less precise than measures such as fiscal policy. The first impact of financial policy falls on the financial markets, which determine interest rates in the course of trading in assets. Changes in government financial policy, particularly in money, may come very quickly. Open-market operations may change reserves within a day. It is unreasonable to expect that commodity demand will change as rapidly, but the economy can reach an equilibrium through changes in interest rates.

How quickly do changes in financial markets result in changes in commodity markets? Some observers believe the lag may be very long, and the existence of this lag argues against the employment of monetary policy for short-run stabilization purposes. To illustrate the lag, let us assume an expansionary open-market operation that results in a lowering of the rate of interest. Time is required for potential borrowers to become aware of the easier availability of lending. When they do decide to increase their borrowing, more time is required to plan expenditures, especially construction projects. Once construction begins the economic impact may spread over many months. As a result of these lags, the major impact of a change in monetary policy may come long after other factors have obviated the need for its effects. In some cases the lagged effects of a prior monetary policy may be reinforcing rather than counteracting undesired economic conditions.

Aside from these lags in the transmission of policy actions to the economy, there are also lags in the recognition of need for change by the authorities. Data available inevitably cover past rather than present conditions. Different data rarely all point in the same direction, and interpretation of a change in the direction of the economy may await receipt of confirmatory evidence.

There is also much uncertainty about the magnitude of the effect of changes in government asset policy on changes in product demand. If the policy takes the form of controls on the terms of private assets, the effect will depend upon the importance of lending in total purchases and the effect of the change in the willingness to lend and borrow. If policy moves take the form of a change in the money stock, the ultimate effect will depend upon the response of interest rates to changes in money and the response of product demand to changes in interest rates. In general, it is the indirect nature of asset control that renders it uncertain as a means of influencing aggregate demand.

These uncertainties have led some observers to the belief that short-term fluctuations in government financial policy are undesirable. In this view changes in policy can be, contrary to their intent, destabilizing, and the possibility of changes in policy adds to uncertainty in the economy. With respect to money, advocates of this view generally propose a policy which allows for a constant, predetermined rate of growth in money. They suggest a growth rate which corresponds to the long-term potential growth rate of real output in the economy. The timing problem would then no longer be of consequence. Whatever the lag, monetary policy would always be the right policy, in that it is providing a money supply which permits the economy's achievable output growth. Discretionary monetary policy attempts to do more than this—to curb money growth in times of inflation and to provide a stimulus through increased money growth during economic recession.

Though it would lessen interest-rate fluctuations, stable money growth would not remove such fluctuations because the demand for money and other liquid assets would continue to change with fluctuations in income. If the economy were sluggish, money demand would grow at a slower rate than the money stock, and interest rates would tend to fall. This effect would occur automatically as income grew at more or less than the target rate, and thus the constantly growing money stock would operate as a kind of automatic stabilizer. It would not be subject to the lags of discretionary policy. Interest-rate fluctuations would probably be lessened under the plan because it removes two of the sources of such fluctuations—unexpected changes in the money stock and uncertainty about the future course of monetary policy.

Those who oppose stable monetary growth believe that discretionary policy can successfully reduce fluctuations in economic activity. They hold that interest rates should be influenced directly to counter destabilizing influences in the economy. They feel that it is impossible to set the course of monetary policy for the indefinite future. One obstacle to so doing is the possibility of shifts in the public's concept of liquid assets. If the concept of money chosen for the target growth rate becomes the wrong concept in terms of the institutional practices of the economy, then its growth may be inappropriate for the growth in demand for it. Stable money growth also means that monetary policy is set toward achieving domestic output goals and cannot be used for other purposes. For example, higher interest rates may be needed to solve a problem in the nation's international balance of payments, but an automatic monetary policy could not accommodate such a need.

An alternative form of setting long-term monetary policy is to establish an interest-rate goal that is compatible with long-term investment needs. Fluctuations in money demand would be offset by compensating variations in supply. Business investment decisions need not fluctuate in accord with changing interest-rate expectations, but can be set on the basis of long-term expectations regarding the expected return on capital. The maintenance of economic stability would then be the responsibility of fiscal policy, and if investment were contributing to inflationary pressures, tax policy would be used to reduce excess demand. Since the interest rate chosen will affect the level of investment, the interest-rate target involves a somewhat greater involvement in government determination of the allocation of consumption and investment than does the money-stock target.

SUMMARY

The public's stock of money claims on the government depends upon the government's decision with respect to the money component of its total debt. Governments finance some of their outlays, such as gold purchases and loans to banks, automatically through money creation. The public can take its government money claims in the form of currency or as deposits held through the private banking system. The government money held by banks serves as reserves which allow the banks to create deposit liabilities, the maximum creation being determined by the reserve requirement. Some countries also require the banks to hold a portion of assets in the form of government securities, called a *liquidity ratio*.

Governments also impose selective financial controls in the form of regulation of the terms of private assets. An important form of such control is setting maximum interest that financial institutions may pay on deposits. The tighter this control the less effective are the institutions in intermediating between borrowers and lenders. Minimum down payments and maximum length of maturities are other means of influencing consumer credit, mortgages, and other assets on a selective basis. There is no single measure of all government financial policy, but among the indicators are the government's discount rate on its loans to banks, changes in the money stock, changes in government money (bank reserves and currency), and the ratio of money to national output.

Allowing bank creation of demand deposits shifts some of money determination from the government to private banks. Proponents of stronger government control advocate a reserve requirement of 100 percent against demand deposits. An argument against such control is that other assets have near-money characteristics, and control would not be sufficiently effective to offset the disruption to existing institutions. A similar argument applies against proposals to control the money stock at a stable, predetermined rate. Those who propose this measure argue that discretionary monetary policy is not stabilizing because of the long lag between changes in money and the effect of the change on national output.

SELECTED REFERENCES

Commission on Money and Credit, *Money and Credit*. Englewood Cliffs, N.J.: Prentice-Hall, 1961.

Committee on the Working of the Monetary System, *Report*. London: H. M. Stationary Office, 1959.

Duesenberry, James, *Money and Credit: Impact and Control*, 2d ed. Englewood Cliffs, N.J.: Prentice-Hall, 1967.

Fousek, Peter, *Foreign Central Banking: The Instruments of Monetary Policy*. Federal Reserve Bank of New York, 1957.

Jacoby, Neil (ed.), *United States Monetary Policy*, rev. ed. New York: Praeger, 1964.

Report of the Royal Commission on Banking and Finance. Ottawa, Ont.: The Queen's Printer, 1964.

Ward, Richard (ed.), *Monetary Theory and Policy*. Scranton, Pa.: International Textbook, 1966.

DISCUSSION QUESTIONS

1. Explain the mechanism by which the government can provide the economy with additional money, even if it is not running a deficit in its budget position.

2. Show balance sheet changes for the central bank when it: (a) buys securities on the open market, (b) loans to commercial banks, and (c) provides currency to banks in exchange for deposit liabilities to banks.

3. Show the balance sheet changes for a commercial bank which: (a) loses deposits to another bank, (b) makes a loan to a customer, and (c) receives currency in deposit.

4. Show the balance sheet changes for the banking system as a whole when it: (a) loses reserves, with reserve requirements unchanged; (b) must adjust to increased reserve requirements, with reserves unchanged; and (c) sells government securities to the central bank.

5. What are some ways in which discount operations are used as an instrument of central bank policy, aside from providing reserves to the banking system?

6. Contrast selective and general financial policy.

7. What are the arguments for the 100 percent reserve plan?

8. What are the arguments for a stable money growth rate?

17

Fiscal Policy

As government demand has taken a larger share of national output, partly as a result of World War II and its residual effects, the role of government in economic stability has mounted. Government increases total demand for output by its own purchases and by transfers of purchasing power to elements in the private economy who use it to acquire current output. Government reduces private demand through taxation. The extent of government influence on the economy is measured by the ratio of the total of expenditures and transfers to output or the ratio of taxation to output. In advanced industrial countries government accounts for a rather uniform one-fourth to one-third of national product.

Although there is uniformity in the size of government activity, uniformity disappears when examining its composition. (See Table 17-1.) Transfers to alleviate inadequate private incomes are one-fifth of total government outlays in the United States and over 30 percent in West Germany and Italy. Military-type expenditures account for one-third of all expenditures (including transfers) of government units in the United States. In some European countries these expenditures are 11 percent or less.

This wide divergence is one explanation for the uniformity in the public share of output between such diverse countries as the United States and countries with Socialist governments—military procurement tending to offset the greater involvement of Socialist governments in domestic programs. Another explanation for the consistency is the size of national income itself. A country with small national income has less discretion in the allocation of its product even if it desires a high level of social product.

The tax structure differs among countries, but in general the classifications are taxes on sales (indirect) and taxes on income and wealth (direct), including mandatory contributions to social insurance funds. The United States places a relatively high reliance on direct taxes on income, with a large share paid at the corporate

TABLE 17-1
Current and Capital Expenditure (Combined) of the General Government by Main Purposes, in Selected Western European Countries
(Percentages)

	Belgium	France	Western Germany	Italy	Netherlands	Austria	Denmark	Norway	United Kingdom
	1959	1959	1959	1959	1959	1962	1965-1966	1965	1965
Administration, etc.	10.2	9.1	8.9	12.0	9.7	8.5	..‡	8.6	5.9
Defence	10.5	16.8	10.5	7.7	10.2	2.4	10.0	10.3	15.1
Transport and communications	9.8	7.6	7.5	6.8	8.8	8.5	6.0	7.7	7.2
Agriculture and foodstuffs	1.5	2.1	3.8	3.9	4.4	3.3	2.5 }	16.0 }	2.4
Industry and services	1.6	6.4	2.6	2.0	3.5	2.5	..‡		7.2
Education research	12.6	9.9	9.4	9.0	13.1	6.9	16.0	14.2	12.6
Health and welfare	34.9 }	5.8	6.8	6.7	4.8	8.9	15.9	12.9	10.7
Pensions and allied items*		27.0	31.0	31.0	24.6	31.5	23.7	17.9	17.4
Housing	1.3	5.2	5.2	1.1	8.5	4.5	..‡	..‡	6.6
Others†	17.6	10.2	14.3	19.8	12.4	23.0	25.8	12.4	15.0
Total	100.0	100.0	100.0	100.0	100.0	100.0	100.0	100.0	100.0

*Sickness, invalidity and old-age pensions; family and children's allowances, unemployment benefits, public assistance (excluding medical care).

†Includes interest on internal debt and internal debt amortization.

‡This item cannot be identified and is therefore included with "Others."

Source: United Nations, *Incomes in Postwar Europe: A Study of Policies, Growth and Distribution*, Part 2 of Economic Survey of Europe in 1966 (Geneva, 1967), Chap. 6, p. 9.

TABLE 17-2
Taxation in Selected Countries

Country	Percent of Total Taxes in 1965				
	Indirect Taxes	Direct Taxes*		Central Government	Total Taxes as a % of Gross National Product (GNP)
		Corporation	Private		
Australia	48.5	16.2	35.2	84.6	23.1
Canada	53.6	15.9	30.3	58.5	26.8
France	47.0	5.4	47.5	53.9	37.6
Germany (West) . .	40.7	7.8	51.4	69.3	34.9
Norway	42.0	4.2	53.9	73.9	25.6
Switzerland.	33.7	10.5	55.6	55.3	21.5
United Kingdom .	47.2	8.4	44.2	88.3	28.7
United States . . .	34.6	15.4	49.9	66.3	27.0

*Includes Social Security contributions.
Source: *Yearbook of National Accounts Statistics 1965* (New York: United Nations, 1966). Compiled from separate tables.

rather than individual level. The tax is progressive, meaning that higher-income recipients pay a relatively larger share of income in taxes. (A tax is regressive if lower-income recipients pay a larger share of their income in taxes than do those in higher-income strata.) Employers withhold taxes from wage payments, which renders the tax quickly sensitive to changes in income. Corporations pay income taxes quarterly in the United States, and monthly in Canada, where corporate taxes are relatively more important.

An example of selectively applied indirect taxes is the purchase tax of the United Kingdom, levied at the wholesale level at rates depending upon the type of product. The high degree of selectivity of United Kingdom taxes is indicated by the fact that tobacco levies account for over one-fifth of indirect taxes. The purchase tax applies only to consumer, not producer goods, and about one-half of consumer purchases, by value, are exempt from the tax, which firms remit to the government quarterly.

The French employ a system of general sales taxation called the *value-added tax*, which contributes one-third of national tax receipts. Producers, except at the retail level, pay a base rate of one-fourth of the value of sales (measured at prices excluding tax), although there is some differentiation according to type of good. The taxpayer credits against his taxes due the taxes paid on purchases of both current and capital items, and makes monthly remittances. In this way the tax for each producer is on his value-added only, and is noncumulative as goods move through various producers in the production process. The tax is aimed at consumption, since companies credit taxes paid on capital goods. Sales subject to the tax include commodities, services, and building construction. The tax is somewhat progressive in that luxury goods, such as photographic equipment, require premium rates (up to one-third), and widely consumed products, such as flour and fuel, bear reduced rates. The tax does not apply to exports, and imports bear the same rate as domestic products. The French value-added tax has become a model toward which other European countries are moving.

A declining number of countries employs general sales taxation on a "turnover basis," which has been the principal indirect tax of Germany, Belgium, Italy, and the Netherlands. The turnover tax applies to sales of firms without regard to their purchases. Though they impose the tax on producers, countries assume that the purchaser of the product bears the ultimate burden. There are two main problems with the tax, causing it to interfere with the allocation of resources. One is that its burden varies with the number of transactions through which a product passes before its final sale, with resulting favorable treatment for a firm which maximizes its share of a product's total value-added (vertical integration). Another objection to the tax is that by including capital purchases it alters the economy's desired ratio between capital and the other factors of production, favoring the use of capital-saving methods of production.

Social security taxes are mandatory contributions which entitle the taxpayer to certain specific benefits, such as retirement income, health services, unemployment compensation, and sickness benefits. In addition to payments by the insured taxpayer, the system also requires payments by employers based upon their payrolls. Benefits tend to be higher in those countries placing greater reliance on employer contributions. The employer contribution means that the tax is based on a factor of production—labor—and possibly influences factor allocation. This is one way in which the tax differs from a straight income tax. Another difference is that the employee contribution tends to be regressive, in that a few countries have flat-rate payments and in others payments are required out of income only up to an income ceiling. Between countries income taxes and social security contributions tend to be offsetting—the greater the importance of social security payments in total collections, the less the importance of income taxes. Social security has shown the greatest relative increase in recent years.

AUTOMATIC STABILIZATION

Fiscal policy has an automatically stabilizing effect on demand through a combination of government spending which is insensitive to income changes and tax payments which vary with income. Automatic stabilization takes place without changes in government spending for the specific purpose of influencing demand and without changes in tax rates.

Figure 17-1 shows the automatic stabilizing effect of taxes responding to autonomous changes in investment expenditures. As a result of the combination of propensity to save and propensity to tax, the multiplying effect of a given change in investment is less than it would be without the tax function. A fall in investment, say, brings forth a smaller fall in total income than would otherwise occur. By the same token, a rise in investment exercises a smaller influence than would otherwise be the case. As the U.S. Council of Economic Advisers has pointed out, when the economy is operating below full employment,

> . . . automatic stabilization becomes an ambiguous blessing. The protection it gives against cumulative downward movements of output and employment is all the more welcome. But its symmetrical "protection" against upward movements becomes an obstacle on the path to full employment, throttling expansion well before full employment is reached.[1]

The effects of automatic fiscal policy are perhaps most pronounced in the United States, which relies more heavily on income taxes. The combination of these taxes—which are more sensitive to changes in income than are indirect taxes or social security contributions—and transfer payments (which are relatively fixed except for unemployment compensation) tends to maintain the public's after-tax income in the face of economic contraction, and moderate rises when output is rising. One study, on the basis of tax rates prevailing in the 1950's, estimated that the combination of changes in taxes and transfers equals about one-half the change in national output.[2] If output fell by 100, transfers would rise by 10 and taxes would fall by 40, assuming the fall is spread over at least a quarter of a year. Much of the tax change is in corporate tax liabilities. One factor which has tended to reduce the sensitivity of taxes to income changes, in the United States and in other countries, has been the drift toward social security taxes. In many countries the general tendency in the 1960's was for the social security component of total taxes to rise.

A proposal which would tend to increase the automatic stabilization effect of fiscal policy, though not necessarily designed for the purpose, is the *negative income tax*. This proposal would have tax

[1] *Annual Report of the Council of Economic Advisers* (January 1963), p. 68.
[2] Albert Ando and E. Cary Brown, "Lags in Fiscal Policy," *Stabilization Policies*, Commission on Money and Credit (Englewood Cliffs, N.J.: Prentice-Hall, 1963).

rates gradually diminish to zero as an individual's income falls. At some level a small negative rate would emerge, meaning that the government was obligated to make a transfer payment to the income recipient. At smaller levels of income the rate of transfer payment rises. Such a scheme means that as income levels for the nation fall below full employment, an increasing number of persons receive transfer payments by an increasing amount, tending to bolster income. As income tends to rise above the full-employment level, the rapid reduction in transfer payments increases tax collections. In terms of Fig. 17-1, the negative income tax would increase the steepness of the saving-and-tax line.

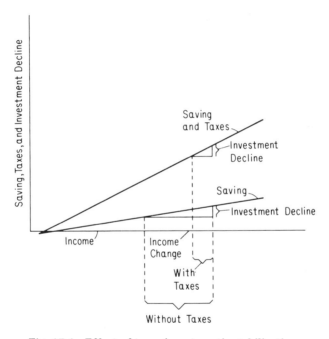

Fig. 17-1. Effect of taxes in automatic stabilization.

Changes proposed in capital-gains taxation would also have the effect of increasing automatic stabilization effects. The tax on such gains now applies when the asset is sold at its appreciated value. This allows the taxpayer to determine the time of payment, within limits, by postponing gains when income is high, and perhaps taking losses at this time. The effect of such actions tends to reduce fluctuations in tax revenue along with fluctuations in income. A proposed change to levying the tax as the asset accrues in value, rather than when realized, would increase its stabilization value.

DISCRETIONARY POLICY

Discretionary fiscal policy involves changes in tax rates or in government demand for the specific purpose of influencing economic activity, where the change would not otherwise be made. Discretionary fiscal policy may be described as planned or as compensatory. Planned fiscal policy takes place in countries which wish to influence the allocation of private product for social purposes. They construct national economic budgets for future output goals and product distribution, with fiscal policy used as one means of implementing the goals. Compensatory policy applies to those countries which leave more of the determination of output distribution to the private economy, but prefer to maintain aggregate demand by a fiscal policy which offsets imbalances in the private economy. Planned fiscal policy is characteristic of, but not limited to, Socialist governments which have eschewed public ownership of the means of production. Compensatory fiscal policy is operated in capitalist governments which stop short of full-scale economic planning but nevertheless feel a government responsibility for the maintenance of aggregate demand.

Among countries engaging in extensive planning are the Scandinavian countries and France, and to a lesser extent the United Kingdom. A United Nations study observed that in Europe since the Great Depression:

> It was more and more widely admitted that, useful as it may be in other respects, the price mechanism was inadequate both to ensure a high level of activity and to provide an appropriate basis for long-term investment decisions. Interference with the free market has therefore become a normal feature of government policies.[3]

The first step in plan formulation is to project potential output on the basis of assumed population trends and productivity ratios. The plan estimates government consumption needs and desired capital formation in the public and private sectors, and the residual is consumption. After an initial projection the overall plan is then adjusted for balance. The plans are made internally consistent so that, for example, residential construction matches expected family formation. The commitment to planning assumes that this type of social allocation will achieve a more optimal product mix than would emerge from the unfettered market mechanism.

Along with the national economic budget the government projects its own current and capital budget. The current budget shows expenditures of a consumption nature and current transfers. The

---

[3] *Economic Planning in Europe*, Part 2 of Economic Survey of Europe 1962 (Geneva, 1965), Chap. 1, p. 1.

difference between these disbursements and current receipts—essentially tax revenues—is government saving. The capital account shows government capital formation and capital-type transfers to others. If capital expenditures exceed government saving, the difference will be made up by borrowing—a component of saving in the private sector. Government saving is one-fourth of the total in Norway, and 30 percent in Australia.

Government saving through current surpluses is an important means by which underdeveloped countries attempt to increase capital formation. This route has the advantage that private wealth does not rise with the capital formation, which might contribute to socially undesirable income distribution. If the people have a high propensity to consume, characteristic of underdeveloped countries, public saving may be the only means of significantly increasing capital formation. India has increased its taxation to 12 percent of GNP from the 7 percent that prevailed at the start of its development program at mid-century. One development economist has warned that countries are often frustrated in their attempt at government saving because of a tendency of current expenditures to increase with the increased revenue.[4]

Fiscal policy is one of the more important means by which plan-oriented economies attempt to implement the national economic budget. The government's own spending must be within limits imposed by the plan, and the bigger the proportion of spending controlled by government the greater the government's ability to achieve its target. This is one of the reasons for the success of French planning, which has been operating for two decades. The government controls its own spending, that of the public monopolies (such as railroads and power), and much of the financing of residential construction. Investment of the autonomous public authorities was somewhat of a problem in United Kingdom plan fulfillment, and steps were taken in the 1960's to integrate it more fully into the public sector. The jurisdiction of local authorities over public housing construction has also been a problem in United Kingdom planning.

Because of their preference for private-market allocation, countries employing compensatory fiscal policy place greater reliance on general, as opposed to selective taxation, for the maintenance of aggregate demand. The United States and Canada are examples of such systems. Some degree of economic projection is necessarily involved in these systems at least at the time of annual government budgeting, but its purpose is more to anticipate than to guide the

[4] Stanley Please, "Saving through Taxation—Reality or Mirage?" *Finance and Development*, Vol. 4 (March 1967), pp. 24-32.

private sector. Because such policy responds to changes originating elsewhere, it requires a good deal of flexibility to be successful. The difficulties involved in such policy have led to considerable reliance upon automatic fiscal effects for economic stabilization in these countries.

Most countries employ a number of tax devices to influence private-spending behavior, and those emphasizing planning do so extensively. General taxes on income or sales reduce consumer expenditures to accommodate government needs and planned capital formation. Selective excise taxes reduce the consumption of some goods more than others as a means of reducing the tax burden on low-income groups. Taxes on business income are varied by industry, through variable depreciation allowances or variable rates, to influence investment in the direction most consistent with the economy's needs. In a broad sense, subsidies to particular industries such as national airlines are a part of the tax system. Some governments, such as Norway and United Kingdom, have placed limits on the dividends of corporations or taxed them so as to discourage distributions and promote saving at the corporate level.

A tax plan which assists Swedish economic planning is the investment reserve. Under this plan businesses may put up to 40 percent of pretax profit into a tax-free, noninterest-bearing account with the government. Acting through a board with private and government representation, the government then may authorize later use of the investment reserve on a general or selective basis in accord with the economy's needs. Failure to comply with the board's request to use the reserve results in imposition of the tax liability plus a 10 percent penalty. After the funds have remained on deposit for five years, a firm may begin using them without specific government approval. Norway initiated a similar investment reserve in 1962.

A special problem in national planning which the United Kingdom has attempted to attack through taxation is land usage. The Labour government feared that speculative land price rises were pushing up the general price level. The price of land, which is in fixed supply, inevitably tends to rise as the other factors of production increase. This was a particularly troublesome problem in the small island of Great Britain, and has been a subject of economic inquiry since the days of David Ricardo (1782-1823). The British Socialist government attempted during its administration of 1945-51 to implement a tax on land sales which would insure that any further gains in land prices would accrue to the state rather than the landholder. The Conservative government repealed the tax, and when the Labour government returned to power in 1964 it undertook new measures for land reform. The aim of the government is to nationalize land and lease it out for private use. In addition to price control the program is aimed at the maldistribution of wealth that occurs from speculative land sales and at more effective social planning of land use.

Some of the same considerations were involved in a number of other countries—Israel, Argentina, Brazil—which enacted special tax rates on capital gains from the sale of land. The tax rate in Israel is from 20 to 40 percent, increasing with the proportion of capital gain in the transaction price.

The theoretical justification for control of land speculation in a market economy is the inability of the market mechanism to stimulate supply, which natural endowment determines. Returns to capital and to labor are rewards which increase the supply of the factor. But payments to landowners cannot affect the supply of land, and its owner is being rewarded for no sacrifice in bringing it into existence. Unlike the other factors of production land would be available to society even if it carried no return.

As long as land is privately held the owner may withhold it from production. The motivation may be speculation on future sales of the land or, in the case of wealthy owners, the mere psychic reward of "ownership," or an inflation hedge qualifying as an adequate return. The withdrawal of land from its most productive social (as opposed to private) use involves a social loss of output. Some tax systems and proposals are designed to discourage the holding of unimproved land. A progressive tax on landholdings would encourage the breakup of large estates. Another use of the tax for reform purposes is assessment at site value, or development value. This is the value of the land in its potential as opposed to its actual use. Such an assessment becomes a penalty for holding land for speculation, encouraging its sale for use. These taxes offer most promise in underdeveloped countries, where productive use of agricultural land can provide increased food supplies and release manpower for industrial pursuits. On the other hand, the political power of the landed interests in such countries is a potent obstacle to such reform.[5]

A few countries—India, Japan, Scandinavian countries, Italy—have imposed systems of taxation on net wealth. This differs from the property tax which is imposed on selected assets. The base of the net wealth tax is the total of the taxpayers assets minus liabilities. The reason for the net wealth tax is the belief that, as a supplement

[5] For an interesting account of such problems see Albert O. Hirshman, *Journeys Toward Progress: Studies of Economic Policy Making in Latin America.* (New York: Twentieth Century Fund, 1963).

to the income tax, the two are a better measure of taxable capacity than income tax alone. The income tax does not respond to capital gain until realized, whereas the wealth tax would cover annual increments to asset values. The income tax favors assets with low yield and good prospects for price increases, where the wealth tax would not. The principal difficulties with the tax are the difficulties of detecting and valuing the individual's assets.

LAGS IN FISCAL POLICY

Perhaps the greatest difficulty in the administration of fiscal policy is timing. The government must be able to make changes quickly, and these must have a fast impact on economic activity if they are to achieve a stabilizing effect. There are inevitable lags in the process which greatly complicate the execution of compensatory policy.

First there is the recognition lag, which refers to the time between the need for a change to influence the economy and the time the authorities can recognize this need. One aspect of this lag is the collection of economic data. National product data are never available more frequently than quarterly, and then several weeks or months after the end of the quarter. Analysts must therefore rely on more frequently available data, such as unemployment statistics, available monthly, but after a few weeks' lag. A clear-cut decision on a policy change will generally require observation of a turn in several sets of data, and a turn of more than one period's observation to eliminate the possibility of statistical abberations. All of these problems mean that two or three months may elapse before there is an obvious need for change, depending upon the statistical facilities and the economic environment of the country concerned.

The implementation lag, the time required to put a policy in force, is a function of the particular governmental organization of a country. In the United States this lag is quite long and unpredictable because of the separation of the executive branch, which proposes economic measures, and the legislative branch, which must approve them. Enactment of tax rate changes are especially prolonged, even when the same political parties control the two branches of government. The United States Congress considered the tax reduction of 1964 for more than a year after the President formally proposed it.

The implementation lag is somewhat less in parliamentary governments, as in Canada, where parliamentary approval of the government's programs is almost automatic. To increase flexibility the Swedish government uses a base-rate system which requires parliamentary enactment of tax rates annually. Each year it sets taxes as a percentage of the base rate, and in this way tax-rate changes do not get entangled with tax-reform proposals.

Other governments have sought this objective by the imposition of "surcharges" on existing taxes. The surcharge is a means of expressing the temporary nature of a proposed change. A device which has been used in the United States and United Kingdom is the "investment credit," under which the government allows companies to reduce income taxes in some relation to their investment expenditures. In this way the tax reduction takes place only if the desired expenditure comes about. Investment credit is also more easily reversed than a straight income tax reduction.

A number of countries have used changes in depreciation allowances to achieve tax flexibility. Alteration in depreciation allowances is similar in effect to rate changes, but governments find them politically easier to maneuver. A similar device used in Canada is mandatory loans to the government as an alternative to taxation. In 1966-67 Canadian firms paid a 5 percent profits tax, which the government was obliged to refund over a period of three years beginning in mid-1967, with 5 percent annual interest. The refunding took place on schedule, even though tax rates rose in late 1967.

Once a tax change is enacted, its effect on incomes is not immediate, but with payroll withholding this lag can be made very short. The tax withdrawal will not have its full impact on spending immediately, considering that any initial impact will then have a multiplying effect through the economy.

Public expectations of a tax-rate change may influence expenditures prior to the actual change. In the case of income taxes the change will alter remaining income, and the expectation reaction will be in the desired direction—an expected rate increase tending to reduce demand. In the case of indirect taxes the expectation effect is perverse. An expected rate increase will accelerate anticipated consumption expenditures to beat the new tax. For this reason indirect taxes are a less frequent means of stabilization moves than are income taxes.

In the United Kingdom, corporations pay income taxes annually, with a lag after the end of the tax year. This considerably reduces the sensitivity of the tax to changes in rates or in economic conditions, and there is some evidence that tax payments have fluctuated in a manner not wholly consistent with economic stabilization.

If fiscal policy changes take the form of government expenditures specifically designed to affect demand, the recognition and implementation lags apply as with taxation, although it might be possible to shorten the implementation lag by maintaining authorizations for projects which the government would only initiate in the case of an economic downturn. The lag in effect on demand is rather prolonged for this type of policy. There are lags in the letting of contracts, and once a construction project gets underway, its effect on demand continues for a long period of time regardless of what may be happening elsewhere in the economy.

MULTIPLE GOVERNMENT AUTHORITIES

The effectiveness of fiscal policy depends upon the size of the government's spending and taxing. To maximize the share of total demand subject to fiscal direction, the agency conducting policy needs to encompass the largest possible governmental unit. Execution of fiscal policy is more difficult in countries in which states, municipalities, and other governmental bodies exercise autonomous spending and taxing powers. Even in the presence of such diffusion of authority fiscal policy can still exercise its automatic stabilizing effect. All that is required is that the governmental units be insensitive in their spending to fluctuations in tax revenue, and that taxes are imposed so that revenue fluctuates with changes in income. This seems to have been the effect of state and local government expenditures in the United States since mid-century. These governmental units have often accounted for about half of total governmental spending, and their expenditures have shown a steady rise, both in absolute amounts and as a percent of national output.

Part of the stability of state and local government demand arises from grants from the federal government, which have comprised one-fifth of the total income of these governmental units in recent years. The central government lets these grants for specific purposes, and the recipient state can plan expenditures with assured revenue. One effect of grants-in-aid is to extend the reach of federal government fiscal policy. A proposal which might further work in this direction is a plan for federal "revenue sharing" with the states, with state governments exercising discretion over use of the funds received. Though not necessarily designed for this purpose, the plan might be a politically acceptable way by which the federal government could further take over the nation's taxing decisions to strengthen use of the tax as a stabilizing tool. Another effect of the plan would be some degree of income redistribution. Income tax is the federal government's principal tax, while it would make distributions to the states on a population basis (or some more refined concept of need).

INTERNATIONAL INTEGRATION

To some extent nations have limited their autonomy in fiscal policy by international agreement. Import taxes have long been subject to multilateral negotiations, and a rapidly growing restriction on autonomy in Europe is the European Economic Community (EEC), a sweeping agreement in principle for the economic integration of six nations.

The purpose of the EEC is the elimination of national boundaries within the area covered for a freer flow of goods and factors of production. The intended result is the elimination of uneconomic duplication of production facilities in different countries and the reorganization of production along its most rational lines. Production can achieve its optimum size and geographic location. The member countries have largely removed tariffs with each other, and are committed to a common tariff schedule with the rest of the world. The agreement also affects other elements of fiscal policy in that wide differences in taxation and government benefits to industry could create uneconomic relocations of industry, where factor movements are not prohibited. Since wide divergences in tax burdens are inconsistent with the plan, governments face some restriction in their ability to use fiscal policy, lest they stray too far from their neighbors.[6] The tax structure among members must also be similar, and much work is now in progress to achieve tax harmonization.

Nearly fifty countries throughout the world have restricted their ability to change import levies, through the General Agreement on Tariffs and Trade (GATT). It is through GATT that countries periodically agree on their tariff schedules, and only in exceptional cases can a country depart from the agreed schedule. In general a country's tariffs must be nondiscriminatory, i.e., applied uniformly to imports from all countries. The purpose of GATT is to provide a forum for gradual tariff reduction and the prevention of tariff wars among nations. Since its beginning in 1947, significant tariff reductions have resulted from several "rounds" of tariff negotiations, the last of which terminated in 1967.

---

[6] ". . . if economic integration is to achieve its objective a certain harmonization of national revenue systems is called for. Once this principle is admitted, however, it is evident that each member country must relinquish part of its power to use fiscal policy exclusively for domestic stabilization goals. Thus the goals of optimum allocation, considered in terms of static welfare criteria, and those of stabilization policy are conflicting and contradictory objectives." G. K. Shaw, "European Economic Integration and Stabilization Policy," in Carl S. Shoup (ed.), *Fiscal Harmonization in Common Markets* (New York: Columbia U.P., 1967), Vol. 2, pp. 345-346.

SUMMARY

Industrial countries impose taxes ranging from one-fourth to one-third of national output. Taxes are imposed on income, property, and sales. A value-added tax is based on a producer's contribution to the market value of a product. A turnover tax uses the whole value of a product as its base each time the product is sold as an intermediary or final good.

Stable government demand and tax rates exert an automatic stabilization effect on aggregate demand. Discretionary fiscal policy involves changes in tax rates or government spending to influence demand. Countries using economic planning to govern the size and allocation of product use discretionary fiscal policy as a tool for implementation of planning, with considerable use of selective taxation. Fiscal policy is "compensatory" in countries which use it to maintain demand without attempting extensive determination of the allocation of product.

Lags in the implemenatation of fiscal policy and its effects on the economy vary considerably among countries, but they are sufficiently long in all countries to make fiscal policy an imprecise tool. Various devices have been used to make fiscal policy more flexible, including mandatory loans to government and tax-free investment reserves released to their owners at the discretion of government. Multiple governmental units also reduce the effectiveness of fiscal policy. United States federal grants to states have helped spread the economic influence of the central government.

Countries have limited their autonomy in fiscal policy by international agreements on tariffs and by regional agreements for freer movement of goods and factors across national boundaries.

SELECTED REFERENCES

Chamberlain, Neil, *Private and Public Planning.* New York: McGraw-Hill, 1965.
Commission on Money and Credit, *Fiscal and Debt Management Policies.* Englewood Cliffs, N.J.: Prentice-Hall, 1962.
Dow, J. C. R., *The Management of the British Economy, 1945-60.* New York: Cambridge U.P., 1964.
Gruchy, Allen, *Comparative Economic Systems.* Boston: Houghton Mifflin, 1966.
Kirschen, E. S. (ed.), *Economic Policy in Our Time,* 3 vols. Chicago: Rand McNally, 1968.
Lewis, Wilfred, Jr., *Federal Fiscal Policy in the Postwar Recessions.* Washington, D.C.: The Brookings Institution, 1962.
Lutz, Vera, *French Planning.* Washington, D.C.: American Enterprise Institute, 1965.
Tinbergen, Jan, *Central Planning.* New Haven, Conn.: Yale U.P., 1967.

DISCUSSION QUESTIONS

1. What are the principal differences between a value-added tax and a sales tax imposed at the retail level?

2. Should social security contributions be considered a tax? Should voluntary private insurance payments be considered a tax?

3. Name some automatic stabilizers in the private economy similar to those operating from government policy.

4. What problems are involved in the use of discretionary fiscal policy for stabilization purposes?

5. What are the advantages of the investment reserve (Sweden) over frequent tax rate changes designed to accomplish the same purpose?

6. Contrast the lags that might be expected in the use of government spending and government taxation as stabilization devices.

7. Cite some problems that might arise from differing tax structures among members of the EEC.

18

The Social Distribution of Income

Because the purpose of the economic system is to provide goods which satisfy human wants, it is as important to know how widely the goods are distributed as to know their aggregate value. An economy of nobles and slaves may appear very efficient from the standpoint of the nobility yet be considered a failure by the slaves.

There are various ways of measuring the social distribution of income, and perhaps the most widely used is a tabular presentation of the distribution of income according to equal percentage groups of the population. This is the measure used in Tables 18-1, 18-2, 18-5, and 18-6. These tables show the extent to which the distribution of income before taxes differs from a uniform distribution according to population, which would require that 10 percent of income go to each 10 percent of population. After-tax data would be superior, but these are not available except as the result of special studies. (Note that the taxes in Tables 18-5 and 18-6 are income taxes only.)

The distribution of income is not the same thing as the distribution of goods to income recipients, though the two are closely related. This is because some individuals may consume in excess of income and others may consume less. Those who consume more either receive the difference in the form of gifts, sell previously acquired assets, or incur liabilities. Those who consume less than income reduce liabilities, acquire claims on capital goods, or make donations. As shown in Table 18-2 and Fig. 18-2, consumption is more evenly distributed than income, with those in the lower income classes being net dissavers.

Although data are sparse, it is probable that the distribution of wealth is more unequal than the distribution of income. In 1953 the top 1 percent of the adult population held almost one-fourth of

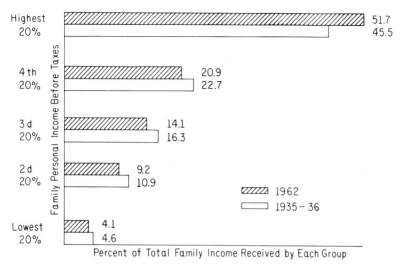

Fig. 18-1. Changes in income distribution in the United States, 1935 to 1962. (*Source:* Herman Miller, *Income Distribution in the United States*, Washington, D.C.: U.S. Bureau of the Census, 1966, p. 21.)

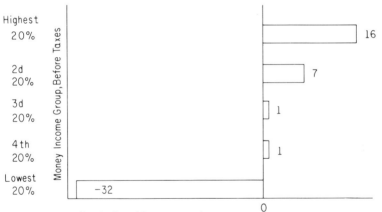

Fig. 18-2. Saving behavior among income classes. (*Source: Federal Reserve Bulletin*, Vol. 37, September 1951, p. 1072.)

privately held wealth in the United States. In England and Wales 1 percent owned one-half of the wealth in 1946.[1]

There are many reasons an individual's relative position with respect to assets may differ from his relative income position. An

[1] All data in this paragraph are from R. J. Lampman, *Changes in the Share of Wealth Held by Top Wealth-Holders, 1922-1956* (New York: National Bureau of Economic Research, 1960).

TABLE 18-1
Income Distribution by Decile Groups*

Groups	Percent of Total Before-Tax Income		
	United States, 1965	France, 1962	Poland, 1962
1 (lowest)	1	1	} 9
2	3	1	
3	5	3	} 14
4	6	5	
5	8	6	} 18
6	9	8	
7	11	10	} 23
8	13	13	
9	16	17	15
10	28	37	21
Inequality coefficient†	.40	.52	NA‡

*A decile group is 10 percent of households by number of households.
†See Appendix for explanation.
‡Not available.
Sources: 1966 Survey of Consumer Finances (Ann Arbor: University of Michigan),
p. 17; United Nations, Incomes in Postwar Europe: A Study of Policies, Growth and Distri-
bution, Part 2 of Economic Survey of Europe in 1965 (Geneva, 1967), Chap. 6, p. 15.

important example is farmers, whose assets tend to be high relative
to income. In any one year businessmen may have a poor income
experience, with assets remaining relatively high. Persons on retirement income may have accumulated assets which they regularly
deplete, but their income position might be quite low.

The possibility of capital gains and losses—changes in the value of
assets—is one way by which changes in a person's potential purchas-

TABLE 18-2
Distribution of Total Saving Among Income Classes
United States, 1950

Income Before Taxes	Percent of Total Accounted for by Each Income Class	
	Money Income	Net Saving*
Highest decile	29	73
2d decile	15	20
3d decile	13	11
4th decile	11	10
5th decile	9	4
6th decile	8	-1
7th decile	6	1
8th decile	5	Negligible
9th decile	3	-2
10th decile (lowest)	1	-16

*Negative saving (–) means the group had expenditures in excess of income. This is
taken as a percent of net positive saving.
Source: Federal Reserve Bulletin, Vol. 37 (September 1951), p. 1067.

TABLE 18-3
Distribution of Wealth—United States, 1953

Net Worth	Percent of Spending Units in Each Net Worth Class	Percent of Net Worth Held by Spending Units in Each Class
Negative —→ $1,000	31	1
$1,000 —→ $5,000	23	5
$5,000 —→ $25,000	35	34
$25,000 and over	11	60
	100	100

—→ Means "up to but not including."
Source: From "1953 Survey of Consumer Finances," reprinted in *Federal Reserve Bulletin,* 1953.

ing power may differ from changes in income. When a person sells his asset for current purchases, there is an unrecorded transfer of income from the buyer of the asset to the seller. The larger a person's assets, the more important are capital gains. It is therefore reasonable to assume that capital gains tend to make more unequal the distribution of purchasing power.

TABLE 18-4
Relationship of Wealth to Income—United States, 1962

Income Classes Before-Tax Annual Income (dollars)	Average Net Worth of Each Income Class (dollars)
0 —→ 3,000	8,875
3,000 —→ 5,000	10,914
5,000 —→ 7,500	15,112
7,500 —→ 10,000	21,213
10,000 —→ 15,000	30,389
15,000 —→ 25,000	74,329
25,000 —→ 50,000	267,996
50,000 —→ 100,000	789,582
100,000 and over	1,554,150

—→ Means "up to but not including."
Source: U.S. Bureau of the Census, *Statistical Abstract of the United States: 1966* (Washington, D.C., 1966), p. 345.

Although data are not available, it is probable that the distribution of wealth becomes more unequal over time even if income becomes less concentrated. As long as there is any inequality in income, some will be able to save—add to their assets—more than others. As the British economist Nicholas Kaldor has stated,

> Owing to the fact that the savings of the community are more unevenly distributed than income, there is an inevitable tendency, unless effectively counteracted by the tax system or other instruments of public policy, for the wealth of the largest property owners to grow at a

faster rate than wealth in general. The more income and wealth grow, therefore, the more the inequality of wealth between individuals increases.[2]

INCOME DISTRIBUTION AND ECONOMIC DEVELOPMENT

Economic theory has lagged in explaining the determinants of income distribution, but empirically it has been observed that income inequality tends to diminish with economic development. The higher the average income level, the more widely is income distributed. Observations between regions and countries with different income levels tend to bear this out. Data for historical observations are quite limited, and in some cases contradictory, but there is some evidence that in this century reduction in distributional inequality accompanied economic development in United States, United Kingdom, and Germany.[3]

One explanation for the reduction in inequality holds that it may arise from the tendency of rising income to allow higher average education levels, which in turn increases the productivity and income of those receiving the education. Or it may be that the causal connection is in the other direction—social and political forces which redistribute income may be a stimulant to economic development. In a way, the observation of a wider distribution is counter to what one might expect *a priori*. The wide disparity in saving—wider even than in income—leads to increased inequality in asset distribution, and assets are a source of income. Whatever the forces leading to reduced inequality, they must be strong to counteract this effect.

The social distribution is undoubtedly related in some way to the "functional" or "factoral" distribution, referring to the allocation of total product between property and labor (no measurable distinction being possible between the return to land and to capital). There has been observed in the aggregate a rather constant allocation of product between these factors in the history of capitalist development. This constancy in relative shares is the result of offsetting changes in underlying variables.

(a) The ratio of the price of capital (essentially interest) to the price of labor has tended to fall. Interest has tended to remain more stable than wages, which have risen to reflect the

[2] Nicholas Kaldor, "The Expenditure Tax in a System of Personal Taxation," in Richard Bird and Oliver Oldman (eds.), *Readings on Taxation in Developing Countries* (Baltimore: Johns Hopkins Press, 1967), p. 254.
[3] For evidence bearing on observations of this paragraph see *American Economic Review*, Vol. 57 (March 1967), pp. 59-72, 175-184. Simon Kuznets discusses the historical trend in *Economic Growth and Structure* (New York: Norton, 1965), pp. 257-287.

increased productivity of labor. The rise in the price of labor is undoubtedly closely associated with the decreasing inequality of income, since wage income is more likely to be evenly distributed than is property income.

(b) The ratio of the capital stock to the labor supply has tended to rise. This rise in the capital stock has tended to compensate for the relatively smaller return to capital in the maintainance of relative shares.

The relation between the variables (a) and (b) and the shares of total product going to labor and capital are shown graphically in Fig. 18-3. The curve shows points at which the relative shares of

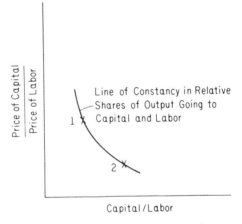

Fig. 18-3. Relative returns to labor and capital. (*Source:* Maurice Wilkinson, "Factor Supply and the Direction of Technological Change," *American Economic Review*, Vol. 57, March 1968, p. 121.)

product going to capital and labor will be constant. As the ratio of per unit returns to capital (the price of capital) and labor falls, the amount of capital relative to labor must rise if constancy of product shares is to be maintained. (This curve is a rectangular hyperbola. Along it a fall of 1 percent in the units of the vertical axis is just equal to a rise of 1 percent along the horizontal axis.) Over time the economy has moved along this curve, say from point 1 to point 2.

There is no generally accepted explanation for the stability in the shares of product going to labor and capital. One possible approach to the problem is to view the constancy curve as a demand curve for capital. As the price of capital falls relative to wages, the demand for capital rises. Thus the demand for capital relative to labor moves along the curve. There is also the possibility that changes in the nature of capital may play a stabilizing role. The greater is the wage rate, the greater is the incentive of entrepreneurs to shift the nature of capital to labor-saving technology. In this way technology tends to maintain constancy of relative shares.

CORPORATE ALLOCATION

Another feature of capitalistic development is the growth of the corporation, and it is probable that the corporation has an influence on income distribution. Robert Solo has expressed this influence as follows:

> There is, within the limits of operational necessity, a considerable proportion of corporate income which can be shared among equity holders, workers, salaried officials, and executives as a matter of company (and trade union) policy without jeopardizing the effective organization of economic activities.[4]

By retaining income (i.e., income not distributed in dividends) the corporation plays an active role in the determination of national saving. The saving decisions made by the corporation and the state are in fact the major determinants of saving. Even in the United States, where income received by individuals is relatively high, they save only 7 percent of the income left to them after the drain through taxes and corporate retention. Corporate saving is about three-fifths of total gross saving in the United States and Canada, and about two-fifths in Japan.

If corporate income were added to the total of income in statistics on income distribution, there would be a greater degree of inequality, since the ownership of corporate shares resides in the higher-income classes. In some respects the shareholder effectively receives the income, because the shareholder can normally sell his shares at a higher price as a result of the increased value of the corporation's assets.

The decision with respect to dividend distribution does not rest with the shareholder in most corporations, but with the corporate managers. Shareholders routinely sign over their voting powers to management, including the power to select the board of directors, which is the *pro forma* instrument for choosing management. In most corporations the more highly placed executives sit on the board of directors which chooses them, and in some, "outside" board members—chosen by management but not among its ranks—are a

[4]*Economic Organizations and Social Systems* (Indianapolis, Ind.: Bobbs-Merrill, 1967), p. 229.

minority. Studies of the largest U.S. corporations in 1929 and again in 1963 showed that ". . . 44 percent of the 200 largest nonfinancial corporations in 1929 and 58 percent of their assets were management controlled. In 1963, however, 84.5 percent of the '200 largest' of that year and 85 percent of their assets were so controlled."[5]

Countries sometimes use policy measures to encourage corporate retention of income. Though this is a means of increasing national saving, it has the disadvantage that reliance on internal sources of funds for investment encourages the large established firm, which has earnings to retain, and discourages the emergence of competition. Firms are also more subject to the effects of monetary policy when they must rely on external sources of funds. When firms distribute their income as dividends, the shareholders then have the option of taking their saving as claims on other firms, and the smaller firms have a greater opportunity to acquire external financing.

GOVERNMENT DISTRIBUTION POLICY

An important function of fiscal policy in all countries is to effect a distribution of current output which differs from that which would prevail in its absence. This redistribution occurs through reduction of purchasing power by taxation and the government's selective provision of goods to the private sector. Virtually all expenditures of government involve some income redistribution, but those with the most direct influence are social security type payments and the provision of services not under social security, such as education. The United Nations has estimated that 40-50 percent of government expenditures of European countries are for redistribution purposes.[6] The lowest proportion among European countries is the United Kingdom, partly because of its heavy defense spending.

Measurement of the net income distributive effect of government activity depends upon the combination of taxation and redistributive expenditure among different strata of income recipients. Social security contributions are progressive taxes up to a point, but not throughout the entire income structure because of the ceiling on taxable income. Income taxes tend to be progressive. (See Tables 18-5 and 18-6.) Income tax rate schedules generally overstate the progression because of wealth transfers through gains on the sale of assets, often untaxed or taxes at lower rates, and allowable exclusions for tax purposes. In the United States increments to income in

[5] Robert J. Larner, "Ownership and Control in the 200 Largest Nonfinancial Corporations, 1929 and 1963," *American Economic Review*, Vol. 51 (September 1966), p. 780.
[6] United Nations, *Incomes in Postwar Europe*, Chap. 6, p. 11.

TABLE 18-5

Income Distribution and Taxes Percentage Distribution of Personal
Income and of Income Taxes Among Decile Groups

Decile Groups*	United Kingdom 1964		Norway 1963		Netherlands 1962	
	Personal Income	Income Tax	Personal Income	Income Tax	Personal Income	Income Tax
1,2	5.1	0	4.5	2.9	4.0	0.5
3	4.2,	0.5	5.3	3.6	4.2	1.2
4	6.0	2.1	6.8	5.4	5.8	3.0
5	7.5	3.6	8.5	7.2	7.4	4.1
6	9.1	5.5	10.0	8.7	8.6	4.8
7	11.0	6.7	11.3	10.4	10.0	5.6
8	12.9	9.4	13.1	12.0	11.6	7.1
9	14.9	12.7	15.6	14.6	14.6	10.7
10	29.3	59.5	24.9	35.2	33.8	63.0

*A decile group is 10 percent of the number of taxpayers or income recipients, starting with the 10 percent in the lowest category of each.
Source: United Nations, Incomes in Postwar Europe, Chap. 6, pp. 15, 24.

TABLE 18-6

Distribution Effects of Income Taxes—United States, 1962

Quintile Group*	Percent Distribution of		
	Family Income Before Taxes	Federal Income-Tax Liabilities	After-Tax Income
1	4.6	1.7	4.9
2	10.2	6.3	11.5
3	16.3	12.3	16.8
4	22.7	18.8	23.1
5	45.5	60.9	43.7
Total	100.0	100.0	100.0
Top 5 percent of income receivers	19.1	36.1	17.7

*A quintile group is 20 percent of the population, starting with the quintile receiving the lowest income as quintile. 1.
Source: U.S. Department of Commerce, Survey of Current Business, Vol. 44 (April 1964).

the highest income categories are taxed at 70 percent, and yet the U.S. Internal Revenue Service reports cases of millionaire income recipients who pay no tax, largely as a result of deductions for contributions to private organizations. Such contributions may involve income redistribution, but they shift the decision on the nature of the redistribution from public to private criteria.

The redistributive effect of corporate income taxes and indirect taxes is more difficult to assess because of obscure incidence. Indirect taxes are likely to be regressive, in that higher income earners consume a lower proportion of income, and taxes based on sales will thereby take a bigger portion of incomes in the lower strata. The same observation holds for corporate income taxes on the assumption the corporation shifts the incidence forward to purchasers of its output. Taken as a whole the tax structure is likely to be regressive, as Table 18-7 exemplifies for West Germany. For the United States a study concluded that the combination of regressive indirect taxes and progressive direct taxes resulted in a pattern that "... is U-shaped, being somewhat regressive at the lower end of the income scale, more or less proportional as a middle range, and progressive at the upper end of the scale."[7]

For Europe the United Nations staff suggests:

> Thus, when all taxes (direct *stricto sensu*, social security contributions and indirect taxes) are taken into account, progressiveness tends to disappear, except, in some countries, at the top of the income pyramid; indeed, for the great majority of households, the total tax system tends to become regressive.[8]

Opposing this regressive tendency, social security transfers and redistributive expenditures are strongly progressive (again exemplified in the West Germany table), as they are specifically intended to be.

> On the whole, therefore, it seems legitimate to conclude that for the bulk of the population the pattern of primary income distribution is only slightly modified by government action ... One reason for this may be that the reduction of inequality (except at the extremes) has not recently been a significant objective of policy. Another reason may be that the combined effects on income distribution of the various forms of government action are rarely regarded as integrated parts of a single policy.[9]

A government payment which may tend to have a regressive effect is interest on the public debt. The regression would result if those who pay taxes for the payment of interest are in lower-income categories than those who receive interest from the holding of government debt, either directly or indirectly. Such payments are not in compensation for current production and therefore are in the nature of transfer payments. The redistributive effect is one argument against a fiscal policy which results in public borrowing—it increases the problems of income distribution in later periods.

A proposal which would tend to integrate programs of taxation and transfers is the negative income tax, a means of automatic in-

---

[7] R. A. Musgrave, "Estimating the Distribution of the Tax Burden," in Colin Clark and Geer Stuvel (eds.), *Income and Wealth: Series X* (London: Bowes and Bowes, 1964), p. 192.

[8] United Nations, *Incomes in Postwar Europe*, Chap. 6, p. 41.

[9] *Ibid.*

TABLE 18-7
Western Germany: Taxes and Benefits as a Percentage of Household Income from Employment and Property, 1960
(Percentages)

Taxes and Benefits	Ranges of Income from Employment and Property, Deutschemarks per Year													Total
	0 up to less than 1,200	1,200–2,400	2,400–3,600	3,600–4,800	4,800–6,000	6,000–7,200	7,200–8,400	8,400–9,600	9,600–12,000	12,000–15,000	15,000–18,000	18,000–24,000	24,000 and above	
Taxes														
1. Direct taxes . . . . · · · · · · ·	4.6	4.7	4.8	4.5	4.4	3.5	4.0	4.5	5.1	6.2	7.6	9.5	17.2	9.0
2. Social insurance contributions	7.2	13.7	15.4	16.4	16.7	20.2	20.0	19.9	18.7	18.4	14.5	12.6	6.6	14.3
3. = 1 + 2 . . . . · · · · · · · · · ·	11.8	18.4	20.2	20.9	21.1	23.7	24.0	24.4	23.8	24.6	22.1	22.1	23.8	23.3
4. Indirect taxes less subsidies . . . . . . ·	160.9	71.8	50.3	36.6	27.9	17.5	17.3	17.4	16.9	16.7	16.3	15.4	10.7	16.9
5. = 3 + 4 (all taxes less subsidies) . . . . ·	172.7	90.2	70.5	57.5	49.0	41.2	41.3	41.8	40.7	41.3	38.4	37.5	34.5	40.2
Benefits														
6. Transfer incomes (cash) . . - · · · · · · · · · · ·	748.4	286.9	177.9	108.4	64.3	13.5	12.6	12.3	10.7	10.4	7.1	6.1	4.0	17.1
7. Transfer incomes (cash) minus taxes (6 – 5) .	575.5	196.7	107.4	50.9	15.3	–27.7	–28.7	–29.5	–30.0	–30.9	–31.3	–31.4	–30.5	–23.1
Number of households (percentage distribution)	16.5	3.7	2.4	2.4	2.6	6.7	7.3	8.2	12.9	13.2	9.0	8.4	6.7	100.0

Source: United Nations, *Incomes in Postwar Europe*, Chap. 6, p. 31.

come redistribution. Individuals in lower-income classes would receive payment from the government, rather than make payments to it, and the lower their income, the greater would be their receipts. This method would be a way of guaranteeing a certain level of income to all, but still providing an incentive to self-earnings. As a person increases his own income, his payment from the government diminishes, but not by the full amount of the increased income. The plan would reduce some of the administrative problems of public welfare payments, where an individual's entitlement depends upon which of a number of possible programs (veterans, handicapped, dependent children, etc.) he may come under.

Going beyond direct fiscal policy, in recent years a number of industrial countries has undertaken the execution of "incomes" policy with respect to the distribution of output among the factors of production. Incomes policy is an attempt to establish some social determination of factor gains—social referring not only to government but to public groups such as trade unions and employer councils.

The principal problem leading to the establishment of incomes policy was the shortage of labor in postwar Europe and the resulting pressure on wages and prices. A national wages policy necessarily leads to a price policy. If the policy limits wage gains in money terms, rising prices could result in falling real wages. Then, too, controlled wages and uncontrolled prices leave the obvious possibility of profit gains resulting from wage control. Ultimately, then, incomes policy must embrace wages, prices, and profits. In so doing it enters an area traditionally considered reserved for the market and is thus a significant extension of government influence.

An incomes policy implies some acceptance of cost-push explanations of price increases. If price rises were only demand determined, then only a policy limiting demand would be effective. If price rises can originate on the cost side, a policy limiting increments in remuneration to increments in real supplies treats the problem at its source.

Wages are somewhat more amenable to social guidance than prices. Wages are the result of direct bargaining between two sides, employer and employee representatives, and the contract in many cases may run for one or more years. Prices arise in many different markets, and a price has no fixed time period.

The prevailing practice is for the government to set a kind of "guideline" for increments to wages. The guideline may originate with a board containing government, industrial, and labor interests to enhance its public acceptance. This guideline results from an assess-

Productivity, Profits, and Wages

Assumption:

$$\text{Capital stock} = 100$$
$$\text{Wages} \quad = \;\; 90$$
$$\text{Sales} \quad\;\; = 100$$

Profit rate:

$$\frac{100 - 90}{100} = 10\%$$

Productivity increases 5% through changing technology without enlarging the size of capital stock, and wage rates rise 5%:

$$\text{Sales} \; = 105$$
$$\text{Wages} = \;\; 94.5$$

Profit rate:

$$\frac{105 - 94.5}{100} = \frac{10.5}{100} = 10.5\%$$

Conclusion: Wage rate increases equal to productivity increases will share the fruits of productivity between capital and labor.

ment of future product available for distribution, and its basic source is expected productivity in terms of output per man-hour. The assumption is that if wage rates rise no more than productivity, wage increases need not result in pressure on prices. If applied rigidly the guideline would tend to freeze occupational and industrial groups in their same relative positions. For this and other reasons application of a guideline requires some flexibility, and the flexibility allowed depends upon the administrative machinery provided for its enforcement.

The guideline principle assumes price movements will take place, but that they will largely net out to zero. If some degree of net price increase is assumed, then the guideline must make allowance for this in determining allowable wage increases, or else real wage increases will be smaller than productivity allows, with resultant increases in profits. If average prices are to remain stable, then industries which have higher than average productivity, such as airlines and utilities, will have to lower prices. They are able to do so because wage increases, based on national average productivity rises, are less than productivity increases for the industry. Industries which have lower than average productivity, as in service industries, will be allowed to raise prices.

Incomes policy is undergoing continual change. In the United States there is no provision for enforcing guidelines, with compliance dependent upon the sensitivity of the groups involved to public pressure. In the Netherlands the authorities must approve all wage settlements, and actual wages must be within the terms of approved contracts. All sellers of goods must give advance notification of all price increases to the government and attempt to justify them. The government seeks voluntary compliance through negotiation where possible, but it has powers of compulsion. The United Kingdom has established incomes policy within its planning machinery, but the system is newer than in the Netherlands and is less formal. The government establishes a pay increase norm based on productivity through the National Board for Prices and Increases, which has only persuasive, not compulsory, powers. The government has sought voluntary notification of proposed price and wage increases. Pay increases are cleared through a national labor organization, which examines them for consistency with the guideline.

SUMMARY

Income distribution refers to the degree of inequality between each person's income and the per capita national average. For statistical purposes the population is divided into equal groups and the proportion of income going to each group is shown. The distribution of assets, of changes in purchasing power through asset revaluation, and of consumption differ from the distribution of income.

Distributional inequality tends to decrease as the average income rises. The distribution of total income between labor and property income tends to remain fairly stable. Corporations affect income distribution in their policy with respect to dividend distribution.

Fiscal policy influences income distribution through taxes and transfers. Taxes on income tend to be progressive, but indirect taxes and social security contributions tend to be regressive, at least within certain income ranges. Overall, the tax structure tends to be regressive. Direct transfers, and provision of services in kind, more than compensate for this regressivity, with a net result of some progression. Governments also employ incomes policy, designed to impose social objectives in the determination of wages, prices, and profits. Guidelines are set for allowable increases in wages and profits, but in most countries the chief reliance is on voluntary compliance.

268   Descriptive Economics

APPENDIX

There is no simple way of expressing income distribution. There are an infinite variety of possible distributional patterns, and it is a matter of judgment as to which one displays a more or less "equitable" distribution than the other.

A means of graphing income distribution is the Lorenz curve, Fig. 18-4. On the horizontal axis is the cumulative percentage of

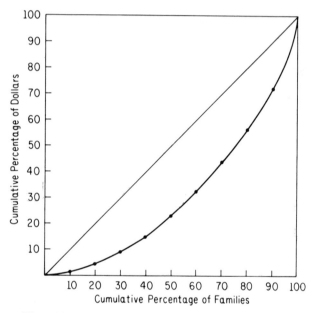

Fig. 18-4. Total family income, 1965—Lorenz curve. *(Source: 1966 Survey of Consumer Finances,* Ann Arbor: University of Michigan, p. 6.)

income receivers, ranging from lower to higher income groups. The 10 percent mark is the 10 percent receiving the lowest incomes the 20 percent is the lowest 20 percent of income recipients, and so on to 100 percent. On the vertical axis is cumulative percentage of total income received. A 45° line from the origin would graph complete equality in income distribution. As the percent of income recipients rose from 10 to 20, so would their percent of income received. The further the actual curve lies from this diagonal, the greater is inequality, or concentration, in income distribution.

A numerical expression of distributional inequality derives from the area lying between the diagonal and the Lorenz curve. This "Gini coefficient" is the proportion of the total triangle which the area between the two curves covers. If the coefficient is zero, the Lorenz curve lies on the diagonal and there is complete equality. The larger the coefficient (with 1 as a theoretical maximum), the greater the inequality. The coefficient is of some use for comparative purposes between countries (or areas) at any one time and between time periods in the same country. The Gini coefficients for two countries are shown in Table 18-1 on page 256.

The coefficient has changed little in the United States since World War II. It was .378 in 1947 and .369 in 1960.[10]

The top one-fifth of income recipients accounted for 43 percent of income in 1947 and 42 percent in 1960.

The data chosen for inclusion in the Lorenz calculation can greatly influence the result, and the relevant data are by no means unambiguous. For one thing, whose income should be considered? A plotting of individual income will differ greatly from the plotting of household income. A household plotting will show a 10-member household as having the same income as a single person living alone; an individual plotting would have to count children as having zero income, or divide total family income among the members. If household is chosen, what is its definition? Are all relatives living under the same roof a household? And there is the question of groups living together, as in the military or college dormitories.

Income is subject to many interpretations. If capital gains are included, total income tends to be overstated for the nation; if they are excluded, important distributional influences are overlooked. The distinction between capital gains and other income is often fuzzy. If undistributed income is included, how is it to be allocated? If attempts are made to state income on an after-tax basis, there are significant problems in deciding who actually pays taxes. True income should include more than money income. The rental value of owner-occupied housing is one obvious case, but there are others. The benefits of government goods need in some way to be allocated. Public education benefits all, but those with children in school receive the larger return. Even the total of income, if all could be computed, is not the sole determinant of inequality. Some families maintain their income because the wife works and the husband maintains two jobs. They are clearly not sharing in the nation's output equally with someone else who has the same income from rents off inherited property, or dividends off inherited shares. The one has lesiure time and the other does not, and clearly this must be considered in evaluating distributional equality. That there is great eco-

[10] Herman Miller, *Income Distribution in the United States* (Washington, D.C.: U.S. Bureau of the Census, 1966), p. 21.

nomic inequality is obvious; all one must do is look about him. Measuring that inequality is quite another thing.

SELECTED REFERENCES

Budd, Edward (ed.), *Inequality and Poverty*. New York: Norton, 1964.
Clark, Colin, and Geer Stuvel (eds.), *Income and Wealth: Series X*. London: Bowes and Bowes, 1964.
Marchal, J., and B. Ducros (eds.), *The Distribution of National Income*. New York: St. Martin's, 1968.
Miller, Herman, *Income Distribution in the United States*. Washington, D.C.: U.S. Bureau of the Census, 1966.
United Nations, *Incomes in Postwar Europe: A Study of Policies, Growth and Distribution*, Part 2 of Economic Survey of Europe in 1965. Geneva, 1967.

DISCUSSION QUESTIONS

1. What explanations might be offered for the tendency to greater income equality with economic growth?

2. What explanations might be offered for the relative constancy in the allocation of total returns between capital and labor?

3. Does corporate income distribution policy tend to contribute to total income equality or inequality?

4. Cite some examples of the redistributive effects of government expenditures. Of transfer payments.

5. Which of the following taxes do you think are regressive and which progressive: (a) individual income taxes, (b) corporate income taxes, (c) residential property taxes, (d) business property taxes, (c) luxury taxes, (d) import duties, and (e) general excise taxes.

6. What are the advantages of the net wealth tax over the income tax as a redistributive device?

19

International Monetary Policy

Economic transactions between countries, as within a nation, take place through the medium of a financial asset fulfilling a money function. A person making payment to a foreigner wishes to transfer his own domestic money claim. If the foreigner accepts such a claim, and if he can pass it on to others when he wishes to relinquish it, then international monetary transactions bear no special problems. Problems do arise because residents of a country are often unwilling to hold money claims on foreign countries, and monetary claims in different countries are expressed in different units. International monetary policy, as the term is used here, refers to the whole mechanism which governments follow, individually and through international organizations, to handle these special problems.

If a country has no policy for regulating the international acceptability of its money issue, the country is on a system of *free-exchange rates*. This means that the value of its monetary issue, in terms of other national moneys, is left for the market to determine. To illustrate, we start from a situation in which all transactions are valued at a 1:1 ratio between the monetary unit of a country and some foreign money unit. If at this ratio the desire of the country to import and lend exceeds the desire of foreigners for the country's exports and borrowing, the markets do not clear. There is an excess of demand for foreign money in terms of domestic money. Alternatively, this could be expressed as an excess supply of domestic money for foreign money. A depreciation of domestic money—say 1.1 domestic units for 1 foreign unit—will clear the market and bring equality between a country's foreign purchases and lending and its foreign sales and borrowing. The situation is similar to the determination of commodity prices in terms of money in a market system. If desired buying exceeds desired selling at one price level, then more

money will be offered relative to goods until equality between desired purchases and sales is achieved.

Various countries have employed free-exchange rates at times,
the most recent example for a relatively large country being Canada,
from 1950 to 1962. The Canadian dollar fluctuated with reference to
all other monetary units, though its relationship to the U.S. dollar is
the usual means of measuring this fluctuation. Obviously this means
that other countries' money was fluctuating with reference to the
Canadian dollar, though not necessarily with each other.

EXCHANGE-RATE STABILIZATION

Most countries of the world have undertaken measures to stabilize their rates of exchange. The principal reason for preferring
exchange rates fixed over long periods of time is the belief that
market-determined exchange rates create an unacceptable degree of
uncertainty for those who would engage in international trade and
lending. Proceeds from trade, and the principal and interest payments from lending, have an uncertain value in terms of the money
used by the seller and lender. The lender might avoid this uncertainty
by specifying repayment in terms of his own monetary unit, but then
the deterring effects of uncertainty are merely transferred to the
borrower. Since international trade and financial flows can raise the
total economic satisfaction of all participating countries, the assumption is that measures to assure satisfactory conditions for such flows
are desirable even if these measures involve some cost.

The international organization for the coordination of exchange-
rate stabilization is the International Monetary Fund, founded in
1944. It counts among its membership most nations outside the
Communist world. The major monetary unit used in international
transactions is the U.S. dollar, and the form of such international
money is, for the most part, claims on U.S. banks, held either directly, or indirectly through foreign banks.

Each country stabilizes its own monetary unit at "par" value
with the U.S. dollar and thereby to all others which are tied to the
dollar. To do so it is necessary for the country to maintain a stabilizing stockpile of dollar claims or any asset which it can readily convert to dollar claims. If a country's receipts (borrowing and exports
to the rest of the world) equal its expenditures (imports and lending
to the rest of the world), no stabilization measures are necessary. If
at given rates of exchange desired expenditures exceed receipts, there
is an excess demand for dollars in exchange for the country's monetary claims. To avoid the depreciation that would occur the govern-

ment may use its stabilization fund to supply the excess dollars demanded. A country's total receipts and expenditures are still in balance, but a part of the receipts was the government's reduction in foreign claims. The government would consider this reduction in foreign claims a measure of deficit in its external balance of payments (receipts and expenditures). If a country's receipts tend to exceed its desired use of dollars (including increases in private holdings) the government must be ready to buy surplus dollars, and this is how the government acquires dollar holdings for stabilization. As long as the government provides the residual demand and supply of dollar holdings, there is no alteration in the exchange rate.

Initially the government acquires claims as dollar claims on U.S. banks, but it may convert its claims to other forms, such as holdings of U.S. government securities. Some countries conduct their trade largely in major money units other than the dollar, such as British sterling, and they hold sterling assets and stabilize their own money in terms of sterling.

Outside these special areas a country will usually receive dollars from its international transactions, even though receipts are from countries other than the United States. A holder of dollar claims in one country uses them for transactions in another country, and for the United States there is merely a shift in the ownership of its liabilities. If residents of two countries conduct transactions in one of their own monetary units, the dollar may still become involved as national reserves flow from one country to another. If residents of, say Import Country, want Export Country's money to make purchases, Import Country's government may sell dollars to Export Country in exchange for its money. The money is then sold to importers. Alternatively gold, or some other asset may be traded, in which case the dollar does not become involved.

In the IMF system of fixed exchange, although the United States does not have to support actively the dollar in terms of foreign money, it does so in terms of a physical asset, gold, at $35 per ounce. A country acquiring dollar claims may then convert them to gold with the United States, and a country holding gold can always convert to dollars at the stated ratio. In addition to direct dollar assets, then, countries also hold gold in their stabilization funds, and can exchange the gold for dollar assets. A country's receipt of gold and losses of gold are additional transactions classified as elements of "surplus" or "deficit," respectively, in the balance-of-payments accounts. Gold flows are by choice the major form in which countries take balance of payments surpluses, even though initially the receipt of the stabilization fund is in the form of a monetary type claim on the United States.

In addition to dollar claims, claims denominated in other money units have increased in acceptability as payments through official declaration of *convertibility*. In present usage, complete convertibility of claims on a country means that there are no restrictions on holders' of the claim selling it for claims denominated in other monetary units. This freedom, combined with the commitment of countries to support the exchange rate of their monetary unit, tends to assure the interchange of moneys at fixed rates. For several reasons the foreign acceptability of claims on all countries is not complete. For one thing, convertibility is not complete for all possible kinds of transactions. The other obstacle is that no country can guarantee its exchange rate in the indefinite future, and the possibility of an alteration in the par value, as discussed below, is a discouragement to the holding of foreign assets.

The accumulated assets which countries have for defense of their exchange rates are called *international reserves*. When a country is losing reserves for any prolonged period it must begin to take policy measures to correct its balance-of-payments problem. Generally these are the same types of policy measures used for internal purposes. Increases in tax rates or decreases in government expenditures decrease domestic demand, and thereby imports, since some portion of demand is for foreign, as opposed to domestic, goods. A restrictive government financial policy will tend to raise domestic interest rates, with the resultant effect on demand. An additional balance-of-payments effect of higher interest rates is an attraction to lending in the country from foreigners. This rather immediate effect of financial policy leads to a tendency for countries to prefer it over fiscal policy to defend their external payments positions.

The balance of payments imposes a constraint on a country's internal expansion. A balance-of-payments deficit may cause a country to take restrictive measures when on purely domestic grounds it would prefer not to. If a country has unemployed resources, but is faced with a loss of reserves, it may be unable to take the expansive measures it would prefer to raise domestic employment. The problem of a balance-of-payments drain may prevent a country from undertaking domestic programs of a social nature, such as school or hospital construction which it otherwise would prefer.

Countries can take some measures aimed directly at international flows with a minimum of domestic spillover, but these are limited. The classic policy of this type is the tariff on imported goods. Other such measures include restrictions on lending outside the country, government lending and direct subsidies to export industries, and reduction of government spending with a high import content. The basic limitation on most of these measures is that they are direct

restrictions on foreign trade and lending. As such they impose limitations on the very thing that fixed-exchange rates are designed to encourage. Because of this, countries have voluntarily agreed to some
limitations of these measures, especially tariffs, through the General
Agreement on Tariffs and Trade (GATT) and other international
commitments.

DETERMINATION OF PAR VALUES

When countries established their par values with the IMF they
largely adopted those which had developed from other systems prior
to World War II. In the absence of any scientific basis for establishing
a rate of exchange that would clear receipts and expenditures, they
appealed to historical experience. If a particular rate of exchange
develops a loss of reserves over a long period of time, there is a
presumption that the exchange rate is fundamentally a wrong one,
and there are provisions for IMF approval of alterations. In practice,
alterations have been infrequent but apparently have been largely
unilateral determinations of the countries concerned.

The equilibrium rate of exchange for a country is the rate that
will bring equality between external receipts and expenditures. This
generalized statement takes into account not only a country's import
propensities, and the propensities of the rest of the world to buy its
products, but also its desires for foreign lending (a function of relative rates of return). There is a strong presumption that movements
in the country's price level, relative to price movements elsewhere,
will be an important determinant of the equilibrium exchange rate.
This is known as the *purchasing-power parity theorem*. If prices rise
in one country more than others, there is a growing incentive to
purchase abroad, assuming no change in the rate of conversion from
domestic to foreign money. At the same time there is a reduction in
the incentive of foreigners to purchase in the country whose prices
are rising. Consequently a discrepancy in aggregate price movements
is a cause for eventual alteration in the rate of exchange, working to
compensate for the price discrepancy.

This rough guide is subject to many qualifications, and is not a
workable means for calculating any exact change in the equilibrium
rate. For any one country the "rest of the world" encompasses more
than 100 other countries, so that calculating a country's relative
position vis-à-vis the rest of the world would be a frustrating task.
Even if discrepancies in price changes do appear, this is no prima
facie case for revaluation, because desired capital flows may have
changed in such a way as to offset any emerging trade gap. Perhaps
the most difficult problem is deciding what prices to include in the

theory. Surely not all of a country's prices are relevant, because some things such as haircuts and medical treatment are largely unobtainable abroad regardless of price differentials. It might seem that a more relevant comparison is a country's export and import prices, but this will not do because the composition of exports and imports is determined by relative price changes. Perhaps a more meaningful concept is comparison of the prices of "potential" foreign-traded products, but these would be extraordinarily difficult to isolate in practice.

If a country devalues as a means of correcting reserves losses, the effectiveness of any given change in par values in restoring the reserve position will depend upon a number of responses. In the short run an important factor is the confidence of the rest of the world in the stability of the rate. Foreigners do not wish to hold assets denominated in a monetary unit which may be devalued, i.e., worth less in terms of the foreigners' own monetary unit. If they feel the new exchange rate is stable, they increase their willingness to hold assets in the devaluing country.

In the long run the effectiveness of a given devaluation depends upon the response of foreign trade. This in turn depends upon what happens to prices expressed in domestic money units and the response of trade—called *elasticities*—to changes in relative prices. In the case of imports, foreign producers may continue to sell to the country at unchanged prices in terms of the producer's monetary unit. Under these conditions, prices of imports, in terms of the devaluing country's monetary unit, will rise, discouraging imports and improving the reserve position. Alternatively foreign producers might lower prices, in terms of their own monetary unit, so that import prices in the devaluing country rise less than the amount of the devaluation. In any event it is probable that prices of imports will rise some in terms of domestic money and this will cause some reduction in imports, with a consequent improvement in the reserve position.

In the case of exports, the devaluing country's producers may continue to charge the same prices in terms of their own monetary unit. This lowers the price in terms of foreign money. If foreigners continue to buy the same amount of exports, there is a loss of reserves because the amount of foreign money received, per unit of export, is less. If foreigners increase their purchases because of the lower price, the net result will depend upon the extent of this increase.

Domestic producers might raise export prices in terms of their own money, tending to maintain the foreign money price of their exports. At the extreme, though it is unlikely for all goods, they might maintain the foreign money price, with no impact on export demand. The full effect of trade responses on reserves will depend upon the combined effect of export and import response. The more elastic the responses, the smaller the devaluation needed for a given improvement in reserves. It is possible that a devaluation could actually worsen the situation, where producers sell their goods cheaper and foreigners do not increase their purchases. If devaluation has this effect, then a change in the opposite direction—an upward revaluation—would necessarily have the desired effect. The point is that there is always some exchange rate that will bring equality between external receipts and expenditures, but the right rate may be hard to find. For this reason some economists advocate a period of free-exchange rates if a country is to change its par value, so that the exchange rate may find its own level. The difficulty with this proposal is that under such conditions changes in international claims are likely to be very erratic, due to exchange-rate uncertainty, and no long-run equilibrium exchange rate may emerge.

COSTS UNDER ALTERNATIVE SYSTEMS

The necessity of governments' holding reserves implants a kind of cost in the system of fixed-exchange rates. Every country, no matter how poor, must employ resources to acquire and hold internationally acceptable claims. There is a net cost for the world as a whole where this claim is a physical asset, gold, requiring real resources for its production. This cost must be considered in computing the net benefits of exchange-rate stabilization. There are other contrasts with systems of flexible exchange rates, but a precise comparison of relative costs under the two systems is not possible.

Flexible exchange rates involve more automatic adjustment to changes in external transactions than do fixed rates. As a country's external receipts tend to fall, the result would be a loss of reserves under fixed rates. Under flexible rates there is a depreciation of the rate of exchange, increasing the cost of imported goods in terms of the monetary unit which is depreciating. This increase in cost reduces real income, and thus automatically some of the same effects occur which policy action might bring about under a system of fixed rates. Under flexible rates the brunt of real income reduction falls first on those sectors of the economy which purchase imports, though the secondary effects spread to other sectors as reductions in real income cause reductions in domestic purchases. Under fixed rates the brunt of the restraints on income, when the government finds them necessary, will depend upon the incidence of government policy. Under fixed rates the government may delay income reductions while reserves last; under flexible rates the reductions occur automatically. When government aims its actions specifically at external expenditures, such as controls on foreign lending, it may achieve very much the same effects that would come about as a result of a depreciating exchange rate under the flexible rate system. An argument is sometimes made that flexible rates are superior to fixed rates because they free a country from balance of payments constraints in setting its domestic policy. Obviously this is not entirely true, since the effects of exchange-rate changes are similar to the effects of government policy action. There are differences in timing, in the degree of discretion, and in the incidence of policy, but no system frees a country from the effects of external flows on the domestic economy.

There may be a significant difference in the two systems in the reactions of speculative foreign lending, defined as purchases of foreign claims in the expectation of a change in the rate of exchange. Under fixed-exchange rates a serious loss of reserves by a country signals the possibility of a devaluation. This sometimes leads to a desire to avoid holding claims in that country's monetary unit, for fear that the claims will be worth less in terms of other monetary units. As foreigners withdraw claims from the country, converting them to other monetary units, and residents acquire claims in other countries, the reserve position further weakens. In such circumstances capital flows are destabilizing, meaning that they tend to widen balance-of-payments deficits rather than correct them.

Advocates of flexible exchange rates contend that under such a system capital flows will tend to be stabilizing. As a country's external position tends to an excess of foreign expenditures over receipts, its exchange rate depreciates. This makes it less costly to purchase claims in the country, encouraging inflows of foreign lending. Under fixed rates this cheapening of the monetary unit does not occur. The incentive to inflows of lending, and the discouragement to outflows, through the higher costs of foreign money, is blocked by government intervention in the foreign exchange market.

The possibility of destabilizing capital flows has led to considerable restrictions on international lending, although they are almost impossible to eliminate completely by controls. The IMF sanctions such restrictions, and may even request their implementation if speculative flows appear troublesome. But the reader should not get the impression that all lending under fixed-exchange rates is destabilizing. It is only when there is expectation of a devaluation that the problem tends to arise. Otherwise, international lending in response to interest rates can be a stabilizing element minimizing the need for employment of reserves.

Whether international lending would be more or less stabilizing under flexible exchange rates is a much debated matter. It was stabilizing in the Canadian experiment, but other cases of flexible exchange rates have been less successful. If exchange depreciation leads to the belief there will be still further depreciation, international lending becomes destabilizing.

INTERNATIONAL RESERVES

Under fixed-exchange rates, the greater a country's international reserves, the less its need for restrictive measures to protect its external position. From the standpoint of the world as a whole, a plentiful supply of reserves will tend to have a buoyant effect on economic activity. Reserves can be excessive if they tend to lead countries to inflationary policies, but there is no necessary reason for reserves to have this effect as long as each country is concerned about its own price level.

One of the functions of the IMF is to provide for sufficient reserves, and the efficient utilization of existing reserves, so that the balance of payments does not place an undue restraint on countries' economic expansion. One means by which the IMF does this is to require each country to place a relatively small amount of its own gold reserves with the Fund, and the Fund in turn can lend the reserves to countries in need. In this way there is some reduction in the overall need for reserves by centralization of a portion. Secondly, the Fund can lend a specified amount of monetary claims on one country to other countries which may wish to borrow them. There are limits on the amount of monetary claims on each country which the Fund can lend, and limits on the total borrowings of any one country. Such a loan increases the borrowing country's claims on the country whose money was lent, and for the time the loan is outstanding, world reserves are thereby increased. The effect of this procedure is a type of mandatory lending of surplus countries to deficit countries by amounts previously agreed on through the Fund. Loans under this program are short-term, and countries must repay their indebtedness, so that reserves so acquired are not regarded as a permanent addition to reserves of the borrowing country. The amounts of any one country's currency which can be lent to other countries is a part of the lending country's "quota" in the Fund, and is determined roughly on the basis of the economic size of a country. In practice only the monetary units of relatively strong countries are actually borrowed from the Fund.

In 1967 the IMF approved a new type of program by which it can use its lending facilities to create permanent additions to world reserves. Under this program, at five-year intervals the Fund sets up "Special Drawing Rights" (SDR) for those countries wishing to participate, with the allocation of drawing rights roughly proportional to countries' quotas. A drawing right entitles a country which is losing reserves to draw, or borrow, foreign money from other countries participating in the program. At the same time, participating countries must also agree to provide their own currencies to other countries when called upon by the Fund, but generally a country would not be called unless it were running a surplus.

The distinguishing feature of this program is that drawing rights can be looked upon as a long-term addition to world reserves. The assured availability of drawing rights can allow countries to consider their allocation as the equivalent of an addition to stocks of gold or foreign money. It is assumed that countries will maintain some proportion of drawing rights to other reserves. But a country with a balance-of-payments deficit can, on the average over a period of time, use 70 percent of its allocation. A country who is called upon to furnish its currency receives an equivalent amount of drawing rights for the currency it relinquishes. Thus a drawing is essentially a redistribution of drawing rights from the deficit to the surplus country. The effect is the same as though the deficit country held gold and sold it to the surplus country, and the new system is sometimes called *paper gold*. Gold is a net addition to all reserves because all countries will accept gold. Claims on the IMF, or any other asset, can become net additions to world reserves if all countries agree to accept them.

There are two principal advantages in this kind of reserve creation. One is that it does not involve a resource cost, as does gold, which requires men and machines to dig it out of the ground and store it. The other is that the amount of reserves created is subject to determination on the basis of economic need. With gold, the vagaries of nature play a role in determining availability, and these are not necessarily in accord with economic need.

The new system was established when it appeared that increments to monetary holdings of gold would no longer be adequate to provide reserves necessary to maintain fixed-exchange rates and still allow the economic expansion which real resources would permit. Private citizens rather than governments were purchasing most of the newly mined gold, apparently on the belief that it would someday be necessary for the United States to raise the price of gold in order to provide for increases in the monetary value of world reserves.

Countries were no longer adding to the dollar holdings on the United States, many preferring to hold gold instead, apparently for the same reason private gold holdings were rising.

Member countries of the IMF determine periodically the number of SDR's to be issued. If gold flows out of monetary reserves, then the Fund can step up the issuance of SDR's, and if monetary gold increases, there is a lesser need for SDR's. The total of gold and SDR's can be kept stable. The unit in which the SDR is expressed may be in any national monetary unit, though the customary unit is the U.S. dollar. Any SDR sale by a deficit country will bring the dollar equivalent in other monetary units at the official rate of exchange. A devaluation of the dollar would not affect the amount of

---

Special Drawing Rights (SDR) as Reserves

Assumption:

Two countries A and B each receive 10 SDR units in a distribution from the International Monetary Fund. Each country's money is on a 1 = to = 1 parity with the SDR unit. Country A purchases country B's money with 5 of its SDR's.

Changes in international assets and liabilities.

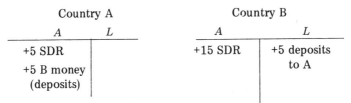

Country A			Country B	
A	*L*		*A*	*L*
+5 SDR			+15 SDR	+5 deposits
+5 B money				to A
(deposits)				

Country A has excess imports over exports of 5:

Country A		Country B	
A	*L*	*A*	*L*
+5 SDR		+15 SDR	

B's liabilities have changed from international to domestic holders. Its reserves have increased by 5 as a result of the balance of payments surplus.

---

other moneys which an SDR sale would yield, but it would increase the number of dollars which each SDR is worth. The same holds true in the case of devaluation of any other monetary unit.

Although the dollar is often used in international calculation, it is not necessary that any one national money be the anchor for all others. It is probable that the use of the dollar is playing a decreasing role in effecting international transactions. There is some convenience in using one money for international comparison, but it is important to realize that the system does not depend upon any single national money. All national moneys can be linked to the SDR, for example, and they are thereby linked to each other. Around the turn of the century national moneys were linked to gold.

GOLD POLICY

The present system of fixed exchange rates evolved from the international gold standard, which operated well into the twentieth century. Under a gold standard, or any other commodity standard, all monetary issues of the governments are either a commodity stamped as money or some form of substitute for the commodity. The rules of the gold standard require that the government be willing to convert all substitutes for gold into gold at a fixed rate of conversion, whether the holder is a domestic or foreign resident. Each monetary unit therefore is the equivalent of a specified portion of gold. If any two monetary systems are on the gold standard, it follows that there is a fixed relationship between the two monetary units. Shipments of gold between the countries will maintain this relationship. The mechanisms work in this way: if a resident of one country wants to purchase the money of another, and is unable to obtain it on the private market at the parity rate, he may obtain the foreign money through gold. He purchases gold from his own government with its money, ships the gold to the foreign country, and sells the gold to the foreign government for its money. In practice individual shipments are not necessary, as banks maintain supplies of foreign money, through gold shipments where necessary.

Although countries maintain gold reserves, no country is on the gold standard in the rigorous sense of the word. No country maintains the gold convertibility of its monetary issues for all holders. Most countries hold gold which they sell at their discretion to obtain foreign money for exchange rate stabilization. The country closest to the gold standard is the United States, but it departs from it in significant ways. Only foreign governments may demand gold in exchange for dollars; neither U.S. nor foreign private citizens have that right. U.S. citizens can neither buy gold domestically nor from foreign sources except under license. The purpose of these restrictions is to conserve the U.S. gold supply for its international uses. Gold is not an integral part of any country's domestic monetary system.

The single-country gold system has developed some strains. The increase in total world official gold holdings through new mining at the official price of $35 per ounce has not kept pace with the increase in the money value of international transactions. For many years the value of international reserves grew sufficiently to accommodate payments flows through increases in dollar claims on the United States. This situation created something of a gold-reserve shortage for the United States as its liabilities grew and its gold stock shrank through foreign purchases.

The new IMF program of SDR will provide a supplementary source of international reserves which will tend to fill in the gap from the shrinkage in the use of dollars as reserves. Countries became unwilling to acquire additional dollars as the ability of the United States to make gold conversions became increasingly restricted. By obligating themselves to accept SDR's member countries of the IMF were able to create a new form of asset with many of the monetary characteristics of gold.

SUMMARY

A country's money issue will tend to have a fluctuating value relative to the issues of other countries unless governments take measures to stabilize relative money values. Under the IMF system, countries hold assets with international value which they may use to supply to the market to maintain the value of their monetary issues. The assets, called *reserves*, can provide the residual supply if a country's demand for foreign money tends to exceed the supply at given rates of exchange.

The equilibrium rate of exchange is that which over time will bring equality in foreign receipts and expenditures. One factor which may cause movements in the equilibrium rate of exchange of a country is relative movements in domestic prices. If a country's prices rise at a greater rate than foreign prices, this will, over time, tend to call for a depreciation in a country's money relative to other monetary units. The effects of a revaluation on restoring equality in foreign receipts and expenditures—restoring equilibrium—will depend on the sensitivity of exports and imports to the new relationships, and the response of international lending.

To maintain fixed-exchange rates, countries must protect their reserves against serious losses. Monetary and fiscal policy are used for this purpose to restrain domestic demand and thereby the demand for imports. Under a system of free-exchange rates, foreign purchases are held in check by alterations in the exchange rate. If foreign expenditures tend to exceed receipts, the country's exchange rate depreciates on the market, and incomes in domestic money are thereby worth less in terms of foreign money.

The United States maintains the dollar value of gold held by governments. Decreases in U.S. gold holdings relative to its foreign liabilities to governments reduced foreign countries' willingness to hold dollar assets as reserves. The IMF has provided another supplement to gold through the issuance of claims on the IMF. These claims become usable in the same way gold is used because balance-of-payments surplus countries, by agreement, are obligated to exchange the IMF claims for their monetary liabilities. The issuance of this new type of reserve allows the IMF to offset fluctuations in official gold holdings and maintain international reserves at levels considered economically desirable.

SELECTED REFERENCES

Clement, M. O., et al. (eds.), *Theoretical Issues in International Economics.* Boston: Houghton Mifflin, 1967.

Grubel, H. (ed.), *World Monetary Reform.* Stanford, Calif.: Stanford U.P., 1963.

Hinshaw, Randall (ed.), *Monetary Reform and the Price of Gold.* Baltimore, Md.: Johns Hopkins Press, 1967.

Sohmen, Egon, *Flexible Exchange Rates.* Chicago: U. of Chicago Press, 1961.

Ward, Richard, *International Finance.* Englewood Cliffs, N.J.: Prentice-Hall, 1965.

DISCUSSION QUESTIONS

1. Contrast the means by which a country's foreign receipts equal its expenditures under (a) the gold standard, (b) the IMF system, and (c) free-exchange rates.

2. What are international reserves and what is their purpose?

3. Define balance-of-payments "surplus" and "deficit" under the IMF system.

4. What are the criteria for determining the equilibrium rate of exchange?

5. Under what circumstances will a devaluation improve a balance-of-payments deficit?

6. Which groups in the economy tend to benefit from fixed-exchange rates? Which benefit from free-exchange rates?

7. What were the reasons for the establishment of SDR by the IMF?

20

Underdeveloped Economies

Compared to the United States standard of living, the great mass of the world lives in poverty. Precise measurement of differences in economic welfare is not possible, but for the skeptical there is some rather persuasive evidence that the fruits of economic progress are very unevenly distributed over the earth. The most pervasive measure used is output per capita, which consists of national output valued at market prices, divided by the population. For comparison purposes a common monetary unit is employed, usually the U.S. dollar.

There are many statistical difficulties in output comparisons. In addition to the difficulties of accepting market values as true values to society (as discussed in Chapter 13), in many countries the market is not the distributor of all goods. Food is grown and eaten on the farm, laundry is washed in streams, sandals are made from straw. When a population lives off the land, the market is dethroned, and it is statistically difficult to impute values to self-sufficiency.

Differing valuations of the same product in separate countries and valuations in different monetary units further complicate international comparisons. Each monetary unit can be converted to the dollar at prevailing exchange rates, but exchange rates do not necessarily measure equivalent purchasing power except in goods which are traded internationally. A Mexican peso is worth 8 cents, but that does not mean that everything which costs a peso in Mexico would cost 8 cents in the United States. There is a tendency for exchange rates to represent equivalent purchasing power for internationally traded goods, but for services and domestically traded goods, there can be wide divergences from purchasing power parity.

The United Nations and other research groups have attempted by special techniques to overcome the exchange-rate problem. One method is to take a country's products and reevaluate them in terms of the prices they would carry in the comparison country, say the United States. This technique means that the market of the United States is used to evaluate the output of another country. The statisti-

TABLE 20-1
Per Capita National Product, 1965*
Selected Countries and Areas

	U. S. Dollars
United States.	3,210
Mexico	443
Latin America	380
Iran.	240
Brazil.	232
Jordan.	198 (yr 1964)
Asia, excluding Japan	150 (yr 1963)
Cambodia.	120
Africa	110 (yr 1958)
Korea	93
India.	92
Haiti.	86
Nigeria.	68
Ethiopia.	47

*Gross Domestic Product converted to dollars at the prevailing exchange rate, divided by Population.
Source: United Nations, Yearbook of National Account Statistics, 1966.

cal difficulties are so great that only a limited number of such comparisons is now available.

For the purposes of establishing the existence of wide disparities, crude techniques are adequate. The disparities in living standards are so very wide that it does not matter if the margin of error is large. The crude data show that about half of the world lives in areas, especially Asia and Africa, where per capita income is only 3 percent of what it is in the United States. Even if one arbitrarily doubled or tripled the income of the lower-income areas, a startling disparity still remains. And these income measures are corroborated by other comparisons: Infant mortaility is four times higher in the poor than in the richer countries. In the United States there is one physician for every 670 persons; in the poor nations there is one per 14,390 persons. Literacy rates are three times higher in the rich than in the poor countries.

Some growth is taking place in the underdeveloped areas, but it is slow. Help is coming to the poorer lands both from individual countries and from multilateral institutions, such as the World Bank Group[1] and the United Nations. The World Bank estimates that in the fifteen years ending in 1967 the underdeveloped areas, represent-

[1] The International Bank for Reconstruction and Development, International Finance Corporation, and International Development Association.

ing half the world's population, nearly doubled their national output. Population increased, leaving a per capita output increase of 40 percent. This was about the same rate of per capita growth as the United States, which started with a much larger base. Output increased a little over 4 percent per annum in the first half of the 1960's but per capita rises were small, as shown by Table 20-2.

TABLE 20-2
Annual Growth Rates in Underdeveloped Regions, 1960–65

Region	Population, 1960 (Millions)	Compound Percentage Growth Rates		
		Real Product	Population Growth	Per Capita Product
Southern Europe	86	7.5	1.5	6
Middle East	76	6.6	2.3	4
Far East	125	6.1	3.0	3
Central Africa	175	3.7	2.1	2
Mexico and Central America . . .	58	5.3	3.0	2
South America	144	4.2	2.7	1
South Asia	592	3.3	2.2	less than 1
North Africa	28	0.8	2.2	-1 to -2
Indonesia	100	. . .	. . .	Probably negative
Congo, Democratic Rep. of	16	. . .	. . .	

Source: International Monetary Fund, *Annual Report 1967*, p. 101.

Even if the underdeveloped areas could grow at a faster rate than the richer lands, they could not realistically hope to close the income gap. Alchian and Allen have pointed this out with a comparison of U.S. per capita income of $4,000 and country "Alpha" with $200.

> . . . even if Alpha maintains the very impressive growth rate of 4.95% for a century, while the U.S. grows at 2%, the absolute gap [$3,800] at the end of 100 years will be as large as it was initially; and during most of that period, the gap will be much larger.[2]

DEVELOPMENT THEORIES

Why has the pace of economic development been so uneven? This is a question which many have pondered, but no general theory has yet evolved to explain economic development. Most generalizations offered have too many exceptions to serve as adequate explanations of the failure of some societies to advance economically. Differing natural resource endowments is an explanation which readily comes to mind, but there are many underdeveloped areas, particularly in South America and Africa, with vast natural resources. Cli-

[2] Armen Alchian and William R. Allen, *University Economics*, 2d ed. (Belmont, Calif.: Wadsworth, 1967), p. 772.

mate has been ruled out as an explanation, for there are wide divergencies in climate within both the developed and the underdeveloped areas.

An official of international organizations active in economic development has rejected attempts to devise theories of differential economic development, stating it is

> . . . due to differences in people—in their attitudes, customs, traditions and the consequent differences in their political, social and religious institutions.[3]

A leading student of development, Simon Kuznets, does not believe that economics is yet able to explain long-run economic growth.

> It is clear, however, that the empirical findings that we now have, being based largely on data for a few developed countries for insufficiently long periods, cover too narrow a range; that the functional relations established from them cannot be extrapolated too far in time and in space; that the very conceptual structure of economic analysis, having been geared to the Western economies and to the short-run problems, may need substantial revision before it can effectively explain the past economic growth of the presently developed countries—let alone be applied to the growth problems of underdeveloped countries today.[4]

In viewing their prospects for eventually following the course of the now-developed countries, Kuznets has compared the situation in the poorer lands now with that in the richer countries in the period before their industrialization. Land scarcity emerges as a general feature of the underdeveloped areas, which have fewer acres per capita now than did the rich countries in their preindustrial phase. The income per capita in the underdeveloped areas is lower now than was the income of the developed countries in their preindustrial period. Other differences which Kuznets sees are

> Social and political concomitants of the low-income structure of the underdeveloped countries today appear to constitute more formidable obstacles to economic growth than they did in the pre-industrialization phase of presently developed countries . . . .
>
> Most underdeveloped countries have attained political independence only recently, after decades of colonial status or political inferiority to the advanced countries that limited their independence . . . .
>
> The population in underdeveloped countries today are inheritors of civilizations quite distinctive from and independent of European civilization. Yet it is European civilization that through centuries of geographical, political, and intellectual expansion has provided the matrix of modern economic growth.[5]

In some respects the underdeveloped countries have advantages over areas which developed in earlier centuries. They can draw on

[3] Robert R. Garner, president of the International Finance Corporation quoted in *University Economics*, p. 765.
[4] *Economic Growth and Structure* (New York: Norton, 1965), p. 192.
[5] *Ibid.*, pp. 180-183.

technology already developed in the industrial countries, and the developed nations of the world are taking explicit measures to assist economic development in other areas. But it is easy to overrate these advantages. For one thing, foreign technology is not easily adapted to underdeveloped areas. Technology is designed to maximize output with the resources available in developed economies. One problem is that technology in the advanced countries has a labor-saving orientation, while in underdeveloped areas labor is plentiful and land and capital are scarce.

Not only is equipment designed for advanced countries, but technicians themselves find it difficult to adapt to conditions in the underdeveloped economies, as the following illustrates:

> For instance, the design of a water supply system for a large Far Eastern city included the use of an advanced electronic control system for checking water levels. It was found that the job performed by the control system could be done adequately by a man with a pencil and paper and a bicycle to carry him from one check point to another. The engineers had obviously allowed their desire for technical perfection to run away with them and in fact recommended a solution to the water supply problem that was not the least costly.[6]

Some of the external assistance which underdeveloped countries receive has the long-term effect of tending not to raise but to lower per capita income by increasing the size of the population. Emergency food shipments in time of famine remove a check to population growth. Programs of public health have increased the population by reducing death rates by 75 percent in the last fifty years. Public health is not entirely negative in its effects on output, since improved health increases work ability and reduces the utilization of manpower to care for the sick, but it does prolong the life of the aged and the newborn, who are not members of the work force. Programs of population control have been less successful. The birth rate in India has dropped 20 percent since 1950, but the death rate has dropped 75 percent, with the result that population rises by more than a million a month.

Another problem of attempting development in an already developed world is the lack of trade outlets, a subject we turn to in the following section.

TRADE POLICY

Countries now attempting development face a formidable problem not faced by the early starters, and that is competition from

---

[6] Robert Sadove, "Economists, Engineers, and Development," *Finance and Development*, Vol. 4 (June 1967), p. 128.

industrial countries abroad. It is hard for them to develop products for which there is a world demand, since the industrial countries are already in production. It is hard for them even to produce for home markets and provide a product which is not inferior or more costly than those supplied from abroad.

Some spokesmen for underdeveloped areas believe their problems call for a special trade policy. They believe that tariffs or other import controls are justified as means of stimulating the development of local industry. It is contended that without such protection the country can never develop industrially, and the advanced countries should allow them to impose trade restriction without retaliation.

Traditional theory would hold that underdeveloped countries should increase their total product by producing more for export and trading for the products they want. But if they concentrate in those things where they have already demonstrated comparative advantage, it means producing more primary (unmanufactured) products for export. Dependence upon such exports offers a precarious economic existence. The industrialized nations of the world are tending to use proportionately less of such products as their incomes rise. With higher incomes, demand in these countries is increasing more in services than in goods. Also, synthetic products are reducing the dependence on some natural products. As a result underdeveloped countries find it increasingly difficult to raise exports of traditional products as a means of increasing income. It is for this reason that some feel these countries must, for a time, protect themselves from competition from the developed world and attempt to develop industrial capability.

The argument is analogous to the "infant industry" case, in which it has been recognized that tariffs may be justified where an industry needs protection only in the initial stages of its development. The argument is valid only with respect to industries for which the country does have a potential comparative advantage, but there is always danger that it will be used for inefficient industries which will never develop as least cost suppliers of the product or as exporters.

Trade restriction also may have some justification on the basis of "externalities." Development of a local industry may have benefits which go beyond those accruing to the producer and buyer of the industry's output, as when the labor skills developed by one manufacture provide a pool of labor which facilitates development of an allied manufacture. In such cases a tariff may be employed to stimulate demand for local production that otherwise would go to imports.

Certainly the case made for trade restriction for underdeveloped countries has some validity, but it must be recognized that such restriction involves costs. If a country imposes barriers to imports, it is depriving itself of the gains from trade. The total product available to the country is less than it otherwise would be. The country is diverting resources to making goods which it could acquire with lesser resources through trade. Obviously the country is not maximizing its goods over the short run if it imposes restrictions, but it might be doing so over the long run through encouragement of local industry. A similar consideration is involved in capital accumulation. To the extent that a country diverts resources to capital accumulation, it is forgoing current consumption. It is sacrificing now to increase output in the future.

One difficulty in using the tariff for protection is in determining the incidence of the burden of the reduced national product. Who has less product as a result of the tariff than he otherwise would? If the incidence falls especially heavily on the low-income sector of the population, this distribution within itself is a negative factor that must be weighed in making the decision. An alternative approach is to subsidize the local industry so that it can compete with foreign products. In this way the real cost of the program is more apparent, and the protected industry will be kept under closer scrutiny to see that it does not rely indefinitely on its favored position. The cost of the subsidy, in the form of taxes, can then be imposed on the basis of the desired effects on income distribution. Subsidy programs are politically more difficult to impose than tariffs, and apparently for this reason advocates of the special case for underdeveloped areas have framed their argument in terms of tariffs or import quotas.

CAPITAL ACCUMULATION

An essential ingredient in any development plan is provision for capital. Population, and thus labor, is in abundant supply, but land and capital are short. Capital is short because income is low, and consequently saving, the means to capital accumulation, is low. Somewhere this circle must be broken.

For a starter the attack can come in the form of a reorganization of the work force. In surveying the possibilities for improved productivity the development expert can usually find gross inefficiences in agriculture. The land is overcrowded with family plots, producing yields one-third those possible with large-scale, efficient farms. Through reorganization manpower can be released without a diminution in the total agricultural output, and the released manpower can be used for capital projects.

It is, to be sure, capital of a special and rather humble sort: capital characterized in the main by large projects which can be built by labor with very little equipment—roads, dams, railway embankments, simple types of buildings, irrigation ditches, sewers. However humble, these underpinnings of "social capital" are essential if a further structure of complex *industrial* capital—machines, materials-handling equipment, and the like—is to be securely anchored.[7]

The released workers are no longer producing food, but they must be fed, which means those who remain on the farm must give up their surplus food. The instrument for assuring this result can be taxation, a kind of forced saving for the society. Thus we see that even in this simple beginning—the reorganization of farms—development must be accompanied by a grand plan for the society. A society which has been immobile for centuries does not begin a race with a small push.

In addition to domestic saving another source of capital is external—in the form of loans and grants from foreign countries. The effect of external assistance is to allow the nation to acquire more goods and services during a period than it produces by running an excess of imports M over exports X. During a time period a country's residents and government units purchase consumer goods C and capital goods, or investment I, the total of which is called national *absorption*. These include both domestically produced and imported goods. In addition, some domestically produced goods are exported. If exports are equal to imports, then national absorption is equal to national output. Absorption can be greater than output if the country imports more than it exports. This excess of imports over exports may be made possible in many ways. We can consider that the country is receiving capital from abroad if the excess arises from a direct grant or if it is financed by a long-term liability to the foreign country. Short-term financing and the movement of reserves (gold and holdings of foreign currency) are not looked upon as a means of acquiring external capital.

A country may have an excess of imports over exports without actually increasing its capital stock. This would be the case if the excess were used to finance consumption rather than capital goods or if the excess for some reason reduced domestic capital output. For the most part external assistance in a development program has as its purpose increasing capital accumulation in a country. This purpose can be frustrated no matter what form the assistance takes. Even if it takes the form of physical shipments of capital goods, the recipient country can reduce the capital goods it otherwise would have purchased abroad and increase its consumption imports.

[7]Robert L. Heilbroner, *The Great Ascent* (New York: Harper, 1963), p. 77.

Grants and loans may be made for highly specific or for general purposes. In the earlier days of U.S. foreign aid, the "project" basis dominated, meaning that assistance was provided for specific projects, such as harbors or dams. In the 1960's there was a movement toward the "program" basis, meaning that external assistance was intended to provide the necessary imports which were part of a country's general development program. One reason for disenchantment with the project basis was the realization that designation of a specific project did not really determine a country's use of its foreign aid. The recipient country might have built the project anyway, in which case foreign assistance merely releases resources which can then be employed elsewhere.

The program approach has its own problems, however, as brought out by Hirschman and Bird.[8] It involves passing judgement on broad and far-reaching policies of the recipient country. The recipient countries may resent this intrusion into their policies and will likely feel that the country overseeing policy is dealing in matters in which it has no expertise. Groups within the country who are hurt by the policies prescribed—such as agrarian interests in cases of land reform—will oppose the measures, whereas with project aid there is no one who is patently made worse off. In short, program aid involves more surveillance by the aid-giving country, and it is this surveillance which is resented.

External capital sources can be divided into three categories: multilateral institutions, such as the World Bank; foreign governments; and foreign private sources (see Table 20-3). The bulk of the

TABLE 20-3
Capital Flows to Underdeveloped Countries, 1965
(Billions of dollars)

Inflows from official sources	
Other governments	6.1
Multilateral institutions	.9
Inflows of private capital (net of amortization)	4.1
Less outflows of private capital	2.2
Net inflows of private capital	1.9

Source: International Bank for Reconstruction and Development, *Annual Report 1966–67*.

capital flows to developing countries comes from 16 industrial nations (see Table 20-4). In the years 1961-66 flows of official capital from these countries to the underdeveloped areas have averaged $6.2

[8] Albert O. Hirschman and Richard M. Bird, *Foreign Aid—A Critique and a Proposal, Essays in International Finance*, No. 69 (Princeton, N.J.: Princeton U.P., July, 1968).

TABLE 20-4
Sources of Official Capital Flows to
Underdeveloped Countries, 1966*

Country	Millions of U.S. Dollars
Australia	129
Austria	37
Belgium	92
Canada	208
Denmark	26
Finland	2[†]
France	721
Germany	490
Italy	118
Japan	285
Kuwait	86
Netherlands	85
Norway	13
Sweden	56
United Kingdom	501
United States	3,634
Total	6,483

*Includes direct flows and flows through multilateral institutions, net of amortization.
†Preliminary.
Source: International Bank for Reconstruction and Development, *Annual Report, 1966–67*.

billion per annum. Private capital flows have averaged $3.1 billion, net of amortization but before subtracting the countries' inflows from underdeveloped countries. Total capital inflows in the period amounted to as much as 18 percent of the developing countries' gross domestic capital formation.[9]

Most estimates indicate that underdeveloped countries have the capacity to use more external capital than they have received. Estimating a country's need for capital is based on its ability to combine other factors of production with the capital made available. The technique of the World Bank is to

> ... estimate from below by a detailed study, on a project-by-project or a sector-by-sector basis, of the need for capital. An examination is then made of the possible sources of such capital locally, and a discrepancy will thus emerge between the needs for the development of all the projects under consideration and the resources which can be made available.[10]

On this basis the bank estimated in the mid 1960's that developing countries could use $3-4 billion more annually than was being provided.

[9] Poul Høst-Madsen, "Balance of Payments Problems of Developing Countries," *Finance and Development*, Vol. 4 (June 1967), p. 123.

[10] E. K. Hawkins, "Measuring Capital Requirements," *Finance and Development*, Vol. 5 (June 1968).

Another approach to estimating capital requirements is on the aggregative basis. This procedure starts with a target growth rate of output and estimates the amount of capital that will be required to achieve that target. The target can be thought of as the assumed maximum growth rate of the economy given current skills and the assumed population growth. It is somewhat arbitrarily chosen, and planners have widely employed 5 percent as the target growth rate.

To estimate capital requirements we start with the identity:[11]

$$\text{Growth rate} = \frac{\text{Saving/income ratio}}{\text{Capital/output ratio}}$$

This identity is valid for the domestic economy in the absence of foreign trade because the ratio of saving to income is the same thing as the ratio of investment (or additions to capital) to income. With the possibility of external sources of outside capital, through capital inflows, we then must formulate the growth rate as:

$$\text{Growth rate} = \frac{\text{Saving/income ratio} + \text{capital inflows/income ratio}}{\text{Capital/output ratio}}$$

The two variables in the numerator are the same thing as the investment/income ratio, since investment is always equal to saving plus the excess of imports over exports, which is is the same thing as capital inflows.

If the growth rate is assumed, and capital/output and saving ratios are estimated, then the equation can be solved for the required ratio of capital inflows to income. The absolute amount of foreign capital needed can then be estimated for any year in the future, once the growth rate has been applied to project income in that year.

Another method of estimating the needed capital inflow is by projecting exports and imports. If income does grow at, say a 5 percent rate imports will surely rise, since the demand for imports is associated with the level of income. Unless exports grow at the same rate as income, an unlikely assumption, then a rise in income will tend to create a trade gap, i.e., an excess of imports over exports. It is calculated:

Import propensity $\times$ Output - Projected exports = Trade gap

The aggregative method, then, estimates foreign capital requirements by two methods: investment needed in excess of domestic saving and the excess of imports over exports at the assumed growth rate. The two gaps which emerge are not necessarily equal. A United

[11] For the derivation of this formula see Chapter 9.

Nations study has projected the saving gap in 1975 at $20 billion (in 1960 prices) and the trade gap of $32 billion for underdeveloped countries as a whole.[12] The projections assume a growth rate of 5.5 percent between 1970 and 1975. If capital inflows of these coun-

---

Estimation of Foreign Capital Needs

Assumptions:
  Growth rate G = 5%
  Capital/output ratio K = 3
  Savings/income ratio s = .03
  Import propensity m = .3

The Savings Gap

$$G = \frac{s + \text{capital inflow/income ratio}}{K}$$

Capital inflow/income = .05 $\times$ 3 - .03 = .12

If the 5% growth rate yeilds a national output Y of $5 billion in 1975, then the required capital inflow in that year is

$5 billion $\times$ .12 = $.6 billion

The Foreign-Trade Gap

If exports are assumed to be $.75 billion in 1975, then the trade gap is

mY - exports

.3 $\times$ $5 billion - $.75 billion = $.75 billion

---

tries reached 1 percent of the national output of the developed countries, from which the capital would flow, the total inflows would still be only $17 billion.

Chenery and Strout have projected growth paths of 50 countries under 18 different sets of assumptions. They conclude:

> The most striking result of this tabulation is the predominance of the trade limit; it is more important than the saving limit in 1975 in 15 of the 18 sets of alternatives. . . . A 40 percent increase in the assumed rates of growth of exports (from the low to the high assumptions) removes the trade limit in only four to six of the 50 countries under most assumptions. Unrealistically large increases in exports would be required to reduce greatly the importance of the balance of payments limitation by 1975.[13]

[12] United Nations, *Studies in Long-Term Economic Projections for the World Economy* (New York, 1964), p. 68.

[13] Hollis B. Chenery and Alan M. Strout, "Foreign Assistance and Economic Development," *American Economic Review*, Vol. 51 (September 1966), p. 719.

SUMMARY

More than half the world lives in areas with average per capita income only 3 percent that of the United States. The growth rates of these areas in recent years has been no more than that of the developed areas. Their income per capita is less even than the advanced countries in their preindustrial phase. External assistance is helping to raise output, but it is also raising the population by dramatic decreases in death rates.

Because of the competition faced from the already developed world, underdeveloped countries find it difficult to establish local industry. Some observers believe that trade restrictions are in their long-run interest to encourage the birth of local industry, even though it would result in inefficient use of resources in the short-run.

Loans and grants from abroad allow developing countries to accumulate capital in excess of domestic saving. The need for external assistance is estimated by detailed, sector-by-sector studies, and by aggregative measures, which assess the external financing needed on the basis of an assumed growth rate. The need arises from (1) the capital required for such a growth rate in excess of anticipated saving and (2) the import demand which such a growth rate would generate in excess of anticipated exports.

SELECTED REFERENCES

Enke, Stephen, *Economics for Development*. Englewood Cliffs, N.J.: Prentice-Hall, 1963.
Gill, Richard, *Economic Development: Past and Present*. Englewood Cliffs, N.J.: Prentice-Hall, 1963.
Heilbroner, Robert L., *The Great Ascent*. New York: Harper, 1963.
Hirschman, Albert, *The Strategy of Economic Development*. New Haven, Conn.: Yale U.P., 1958.
Kindleberger, Charles P., *Economic Development*, 2d ed. New York: McGraw-Hill, 1965.
Ward, Richard J. (ed.), *The Challenge of Development*. Chicago: Aldine Publishing, 1967.

DISCUSSION QUESTIONS

1. What problems are involved in international comparisons of per capita income?

2. Does the existence of countries which have already developed assist or hinder those countries which are now attempting development?

3. What special justification is offered for tariffs for underdeveloped countries?

4. Cite some examples of the role of taxation in a development planning program.

5. What is the difference between national absorption and national income?

6. Weigh the relative merits of the "program approach" to foreign assistance.

7. What kind of data are needed, and what are the difficulties in obtaining them, in the aggregative method of projecting a country's capital requirements?

Index

Acceleration principle, 122–124
Ackley, Gardner, 104, 111
Advertising, 162, 211
Alchian, Armen, 287
Allen, William R., 287
Anderson, Paul, 88
Argentina, 247
Australia, 245

Balance of payments, 171, 197–201, 273–274
Ball, R., 97
Bank
  deposits, 19, 22, 47-48, 80, 93, 149, 215–223, 226–227
  notes, 19, 22
  reserves, 19, 218–223, 230
Barter, 8, 16, 23
Baumol, W. J., 173
Belgium, 241
Bergson, Abram, 173
Bird, Richard, 293
Brazil, 247
Brechling, F. P. R., 83
Brofenbrenner, Martin, 100, 111
Buchanan, James, 141
Budd, Edward, 270
Burk, Marguerite, 51
Business cycle, 49, 119
Butters, J. Keith, 141

Canada, 200, 222, 240, 248–249, 260, 272, 279
Capital, 5–6, 10, 29, 43, 53, 56–58, 62, 87, 106, 112–125, 127, 161, 163, 172, 180, 184, 192, 202, 205, 228, 254, 258-259, 289, 291–292, 295–297
Capitalism, 4–5, 24, 119, 202, 204, 207
Catchings, W., 118

Caves, Richard, 155
Central bank, 216, 219, 223, 226
Chamberlain, Neil, 252
Chenery, Hollis, 296
China, 207
Clark, Colin, 37, 270
Clement, M. O., 284
Coin, 17, 22, 215–216
Commission on Money and Credit (U.S.), 236, 252
Committee on the Working of the Monetary System (U.K.), 236
Communism, 202, 207
Compensation principle, 167
Competition, 157, 204, 212; see also Monopoly
Conard, Joseph, 83
Consumer credit, 49–50, 78, 229
Consumption, 6, 9, 11–12, 30, 35–51, 71, 118, 127, 136, 146–148, 180, 235, 240, 292; see also Saving
Convertibility, currency, 274

Debt management policy, 139, 218; see also Monetary policy
Deficit units; see Surplus and deficit units
Deflation, 102; see also Prices
Deflationary gap, 27; see also Unemployment
Demand and supply, 24, 35, 39–41, 50, 60, 105, 107, 117, 128, 139, 206, 238
Depreciation, capital, 8, 121, 183, 187, 208
Devaluation, 278; see also Exchange rates
Dillard, Dudley, 33
Diminishing returns; see Variable proportions, law of

Discounting, central bank, 223–225, 227, 233
Dissaving, 36, 43; see also Saving
Domar, Evsey, 112, 125
Dow, J. C. R., 252
Ducros, B, 270
Duesenberry, James, 51, 125, 236

Eckstein, Otto, 141
Economies of scale, 144
Eggers, Melville, 13
Einzig, Paul, 23
Eisenhower, Dwight, 210
Eisner, Bob, 64
Elasticity, price, 131, 276
Ellsworth, P. T., 155
England, 18, 216; see also United Kingdom
Enke, Stephen, 297
Entrepreneur, 54–55, 59, 121, 202
Equilibrium, 26, 37–38, 66, 70–71, 82, 89, 104, 111–112, 133, 151, 283
European Economic Community (EEC), 177
Exchange rates, 271–284
Exports and imports, 145, 156, 181, 185–187, 194, 272–273, 276, 292, 295
Externalities, 162–163, 290

Factors of production, 5–7, 128, 143, 149, 158, 171, 178, 183, 198; see also Capital; Labor
Fascism, 207, 209
Feiwel, George, 213
Fellner, William, 83
Feudalism, 203
Financial intermediaries, 21–22, 47, 51, 69, 86, 88, 90, 97, 193–194
Fiscal policy, 126–141, 170, 238–253; see also Taxation; Stabilization
Fisher, A. G. B., 87
Flow of funds accounts, 189–201
Foreign aid, 293
Foster, W. T., 118
Fousek, Peter, 236
France, 216, 244
Friedman, Milton, 14, 18, 51, 108, 111, 137
Full-employment output, 27–28, 50, 139, 169, 206, 243

Galbraith, John Kenneth, 105–106, 210, 212–213

Garner, Robert, 288
General Agreement on Tariffs and Trade (GATT), 251, 275
Germany, 241, 258, 263–264
Gill, Richard, 297
Gini coefficient, 269; see also Income distribution
Gold, 17–18, 198–199, 201, 203, 217, 273, 277, 280, 282–285
Goldsmith, Raymond, 51
Gordon, R. A., 125
Graaf, J. de V., 173
Gross domestic product, 8, 182
Gross national product (GNP), 8, 182–183; see also Output
Growth, economic, 113–117, 202–203, 286–287, 295–297
Grubel, H., 284
Gruchy, Allan, 207, 213, 252
Gurley, John, 86–87, 97

Haberler, Gottfried, 155
Hahn, F. H., 83
Haines, Walter, 23
Haley, Bernard, 83
Hansen, Alvin, 33
Harris, Seymour, 33
Harrod, Roy, 112, 120, 125
Hawkins, E. K., 294
Heilbroner, Robert, 13, 292, 297
Herskovitz, Melville, 4, 10, 13
Hester, Donald, 97
Hicks, J. R., 125
Hinshaw, Randall, 28
Hirshman, Albert O., 247, 293, 297
Holzman, F. D., 100, 111
Høst-Madsen, Poul, 294

Imports; see Exports and imports
Income, 8, 36, 45, 71, 87, 113–114, 147, 269, 286; see also Output; Income distribution
Income distribution, 100, 127, 130, 163, 172, 178, 245, 254–270
Income tax; see Taxation, income
Incomes policy, 265–267
Index numbers, 99, 100–102, 166–167, 186
India, 245, 247, 289
Industrial Revolution, 204
Inflation, 102, 104–105, 109, 139, 141; see also Prices
Interest and interest rates, 10, 13, 36, 46, 53–54, 60, 62–63, 65–83, 85, 90, 91, 94–95, 100, 103,

Interest and interest rates (*continued*) 118, 151, 169, 178, 215, 224, 229, 233–234, 258, 263
International Monetary Fund (IMF), 177, 197, 199, 272, 278–279, 284
International reserves, 274, 279–283, 292
Inventories, 26, 28, 33, 38, 58–62, 120–122, 181, 187
Investment, 9, 11, 30, 40, 57, 71, 76–78, 87, 112–125, 133, 146–147, 169, 179, 184, 242, 261
Israel, 247
Italy, 18, 241, 247

Jacoby, Neil, 236
Japan, 247, 260
Jean, William, 64
Johansen, Leif, 141
Johnson, H. G., 97, 155

Kaldor, Nicholas, 125, 129, 258
Katona, George, 44–45, 51
Keynes, John Maynard, 35, 90, 103, 136, 206–207, 213
Kindleberger, Charles P., 144, 155, 297
Klein, L. R., 125
Knight, Frank, 54, 62, 64
Kuh, E., 64
Kurihara, Kenneth, 33
Kuznets, Simon, 258, 288

Labor, 6, 24, 43, 60, 105, 112, 118, 161, 182, 205, 213, 241, 258–259, 289
Lampman, R. J., 255
Legal tender, 53, 215
Lerner, Abba, 141
Lewis, Wilfred, Jr., 252
Liquidity, 47–49, 74, 95–96, 222, 235
Little, I.M.D., 173
Lorenz curve, 268–269
Lutz, Vera, 252

McKean, Roland, 213
Marchal, J., 270
Marginal efficiency of capital, 56–59, 63; *see also* Interest and interest rates; Investment
Marginal propensity to consume; *see* Consumption
Markets, 4, 8–9, 13, 65; *see also* Prices
Marx, Karl, 119, 204–206, 213

Meade, James, 155, 173
Medium of exchange, 16; *see also* Money
Mercantilism, 203
Meyer, J. R., 64
Miernyk, William, 187
Military expenditures, 103, 126, 180, 210, 258
Military-industrial complex, 210
Miller, Herman, 255, 269–270
Mishan, E. J., 173
Monetary policy, 170, 215–236; *see also* Interest and interest rates
Money, 14–23, 46–48, 65–67, 78, 85, 89, 107–109, 117–118, 138, 152–153, 190, 198, 215–253, 271, 280
    hoarding, 78–79, 80, 83
    illusion, 26, 102–103
    velocity, 110
Monopoly, 126, 164, 166, 178, 203, 212; *see also* Competition; Markets
Multiplier, 37–38, 123, 134, 146; *see also* Consumption
Mun, Thomas, 203
Musgrave, R. A., 263
Myint, Hla, 173

National income; *see* Gross national product; Income; Output
Netherlands, 241
Norway, 209, 228, 245–246

Open-market operations, 216–217, 222, 233; *see also* Bank reserves; Money
Oshima, H. T., 88
Output, 8, 39, 44, 62, 107, 113, 163, 177–187, 230, 285, 287, 295–297

Papka, J. A., 141
Pareto optimum, 165, 173
Pareto, Vilfredo, 165
Permanent income, 40–42, 49
Phelps, Edmund, 125
Pigou, A. C., 23
Please, Stanley, 245
Population, 5, 112, 287, 289
Powelson, John, 201
Prices, 46, 51, 65, 74–76, 99–111, 117, 151, 157, 171, 177, 191, 208, 267, 275–276
Production; *see* Output
Productivity, 6, 9, 106, 168, 266, 291

Profit, 54, 59, 100, 105, 117, 119, 131, 157, 202, 266-267
Purchasing power parity, 275

Quiggin, A. Hingston, 16, 23

Rent, 178
Reserves; see Bank reserves; International reserves
Revel, Jack, 201
Ricardo, David, 246
Risk, 59
Royal Commission on Banking and Finance (Canada), 236
Ruggles, Richard and Nancy, 188

Sandove, Robert, 289
Samuelson, Paul, 60
Saving, 9-11, 28, 33, 35-51, 76-81, 87, 114-115, 147, 163, 169, 192, 258, 260, 291, 295-297; see also Consumption
Say, J. B., 25
Sayers, R. S., 85
Say's law, 25
Scherer, J., 141
Scitovsky, Tibor, 173
Secular stagnation, 119-120
Selective credit controls, 228-229
Shackle, G. L. S., 83
Shaw, Edward S., 86-87, 97
Shaw, G. K., 251
Shonfield, Andrew, 213
Shoup, Carl, 251
Simons, Henry, 212
Slichter, Sumner, 202-203
Smith, Adam, 126, 136, 157, 203-204, 209, 212
Smithies, Arthur, 141
Social security, 241-242, 261, 267
Social welfare function, 171
Socialism, 161, 205, 238, 244
Sohmen, Egon, 284
Solo, Robert, 213, 260
Soviet Union, 205, 207
Spain, 209
Specie payments, 18
Stabilization, 32, 136, 241-243, 218; see also Interest and interest rates; Taxation
Standard of value, 15, 18; see also Money
Strotz, R. H., 64
Strout, Alan, 296
Stuvel, Geer, 270

Subsidies, 183, 211
Suits, Dan, 51
Supply; see Demand and supply
Surplus and deficit units, 11-12, 15, 20, 25, 30-31, 63, 135, 137-140, 215
Sweden, 209, 248
Sweezy, Paul, 206-207

Tariff, 131, 143, 168, 274, 290-291
Taxation, 23, 61, 100, 126-141, 170, 182-183, 211, 217, 226, 238-253, 261, 291-292
  capital gains, 243
  consumption, 129
  excise, 128-129, 246
  income, 128-129, 208, 238, 242, 261-262
  indirect, 183, 238, 249, 262
  property, 129-130, 183
  turnover, 241
  value-added, 129, 130, 183
Terms of trade, 153-154
Tinbergen, Jan, 252
Tobin, James, 97
Trade, gains from, 143-145
Transfer payments, 180, 210, 243
Tussing, A.D., 13

Unemployment, 141, 205, 206; see also Stabilization
Unit of value, 8, 177; see also Money
United Kingdom, 20, 222, 227, 232, 240, 245-246, 249, 258, 261
United Nations, 177, 182, 184, 188, 189, 244, 260-261, 263, 270, 285-286, 296
United States, 20, 189, 200, 216-217, 222, 227, 231, 248, 249, 250, 258, 261-262, 273, 284, 286, 297
Usher, Dan, 188
Utility, 9, 56, 58, 165

Variable proportions, law of, 6-7, 12, 58
Veblen, Thorstein, 3

Wages, 100, 105, 178, 182, 258, 265-267
Warranted growth rate, 115, 119-200
Wealth, 43-44, 50, 100, 111, 149, 255, 257
Welfare, economic, 144, 157-174
Wilkinson, Maurice, 259
World Bank, 286, 293-294

Yanovsky, M., 201